The Jack

THE JACK SMITH REPORT
Final Report on Efforts to Interfere with the Lawful
Transfer of Power Following the 2020 Presidential Election
by Donald Trump and Others

First published in 2025 by Melville House
First Melville House Printing: January 2025

Melville House Publishing
46 John Street
Brooklyn, NY 11201
and
Melville House UK
Suite 2000
16/18 Woodford Road
London E7 0HA

mhpbooks.com
@melvillehouse

ISBN: 978-1-68589-217-3
ISBN: 978-1-68589-218-0 (eBook)

Printed in the United States of America
1 3 5 7 9 10 8 6 4 2

The
Jack
Smith
Report

**Final Report on Efforts to Interfere
with the Lawful Transfer of Power
Following The 2020 Presidential
Election by Donald Trump and Others**

MELVILLE HOUSE
BROOKLYN · LONDON

U.S. Department of Justice

Jack Smith
Special Counsel

January 7, 2025

DELIVERY BY HAND
The Honorable Merrick B. Garland
Attorney General of the United States
Robert F. Kennedy Department of Justice Building
950 Pennsylvania Avenue NW
Washington, D.C. 20530

Re: Final Report of the Special Counsel Under 28 C.F.R. § 600.8

Dear Mr. Attorney General:

In the fall of 2022, former President Donald J. Trump was a subject of two separate criminal investigations by the Department of Justice. The first was an investigation into whether any person violated the law in connection with efforts to interfere with the lawful transfer of power following the 2020 presidential election. The second investigation focused on the possession of highly classified documents at Mr. Trump's Mar-a-Lago social club following his presidency.

On November 15, 2022, Mr. Trump declared his candidacy to unseat President Joseph R. Biden, Jr., who had previously stated his intention to stand for reelection. Mr. Trump's announcement created a highly unusual situation, in which the Department, an agency within the Executive Branch headed by President Biden, was conducting criminal investigations regarding his newly declared challenger. Based on a longstanding recognition that "in certain extraordinary cases, it is in the public interest to appoint a special prosecutor to independently manage an investigation and prosecution," you, as the Attorney General, promptly did so here to "underscore[] the Department's commitment to both independence and accountability in particularly sensitive matters." Attorney General Merrick B. Garland, Remarks on the Appointment of a Special Counsel, Washington, D.C. (Nov. 18, 2022).

On the day that I was appointed, I pledged that I would exercise independent judgment, follow the best traditions of the Department of Justice, and conduct my work expeditiously and thoroughly to reach whatever outcome the facts and law dictated. With the aid of an outstanding team, that is what I did. Upon my appointment, I organized a staff of experienced career federal prosecutors, and together we conducted the investigations and subsequent prosecutions under our mandate, consistent with the Department's traditions of integrity and nonpartisanship that have guided all of us throughout our careers.

Attorney General Edward H. Levi, who assumed the Department's helm in the wake of Watergate, summed up those traditions best:

> [O]ne paramount concern must always guide our way. This is the keeping of the faith in the essential decency and even-handedness in the law, a faith which is the strength of the law and which must be continually renewed or else it is lost. In a society that too easily accepts the notion that everything can be manipulated, it is important to make clear that the administration of federal justice seeks to be impartial and fair . . . .

Address to the Los Angeles County Bar Association, Los Angeles, CA (Nov. 18, 1976). Attorney General Levi's remarks, shared 46 years to the day before my appointment, ring as true now as they did then.

I have been a career prosecutor in local, national, and international settings over the last three decades, working shoulder to shoulder with hundreds of prosecutors in that time. The prosecutors and staff of the Special Counsel's Office are, in my estimation, without peer in terms of accomplishment, capability, judgment, and work ethic. More importantly in my book, they are people of great decency and the highest personal integrity. The intense public scrutiny of our Office, threats to their safety, and relentless unfounded attacks on their character and integrity did not deter them from fulfilling their oaths and professional obligations. These are intensely good people who did hard things well. I will not forget the sacrifices they made and the personal resilience they and their families have shown over the last two years. Our country owes them a debt of gratitude for their unwavering service and dedication to the rule of law. Without pause they have upheld the Department's commitment to the impartial and independent pursuit of justice. For that, I am grateful—as I know you are as well.

Staffed by some of the most experienced prosecutors in the Department, my Office operated under the same Department policies and procedures that guide all federal prosecutors. The regulations under which I was appointed required that we do so, *see* 28 C.F.R. § 600.7(a), and our work benefited from those processes. The Department has long recognized that proceeding with "uniformity of policy . . . is necessary to the prestige of federal law." Robert H. Jackson, "The Federal Prosecutor" (April 1, 1940). As a result, throughout our work we regularly consulted the Justice Manual, the Department's publicly available guidebook on policies and procedures, and adhered to its requirements.

Our work rested upon the fundamental value of our democracy that we exist as "a government of laws, and not of men." John Adams, *Novanglus*, No. VII at 84 (Mar. 6, 1775). In making decisions as Special Counsel, I considered as a first principle whether our actions would contribute to upholding the rule of law, and acted accordingly. Our committed adherence to the rule of law is why we not only followed Department policies and procedures, but strictly observed legal requirements and dutifully respected the judicial decisions and precedents our prosecutions prompted. That is also why, in my decision-making, I heeded the imperative that "[n]o man in this country is so high that he is above the law," *United States v. Lee*, 106 U.S. 196, 220 (1882). Simply put: the Department of Justice's guiding mandate, which my Office strove to uphold, is that power, politics, influence, status, wealth, fear, and favor should not impede justice under the law.

When I assumed responsibility for the matters you assigned to me, I came to the work with no preconceived notion of what the just outcome of the investigations would be. I was not yet familiar with all of the relevant facts and had not yet researched the relevant law. Depending upon what the investigations revealed, I was equally comfortable closing the investigations or moving forward with prosecutions in one or both of the matters, having done both in high profile matters throughout my career.

To make prosecutorial determinations, my Office gathered relevant evidence and examined whether that evidence established violations of federal criminal law. In doing so I was guided by the Principles of Federal Prosecution, a series of considerations designed to promote the fair and evenhanded application of the law. As set forth in my Report, after conducting thorough investigations, I found that, with respect to both Mr. Trump's unprecedented efforts to unlawfully retain power after losing the 2020 election and his unlawful retention of classified documents after leaving office, the Principles compelled prosecution. Indeed, Mr. Trump's cases represented ones "in which the offense [was] the most flagrant, the public harm the greatest, and the proof the most certain." Jackson, "The Federal Prosecutor."

As directed by the Principles, I made my decision in these cases without regard to Mr. Trump's "political association, activities, or beliefs," or the possible personal or professional consequences of a prosecution for me or any member of my Office. Justice Manual § 9-27.260. "[T]he likelihood of an acquittal due to unpopularity of some aspect of the prosecution or because of the overwhelming popularity of the defendant or his cause," or the converse, were not factors in my prosecutive decisions. *Id.* § 9-27.220 (Comment). My Office also adhered at all times to the Department's policy against interfering in elections. As a former Chief of the Department's Public Integrity Section, it was important to me, as it is to you, that we adhere to both the letter and spirit of this policy. I can assure you that neither I nor the prosecutors on my team would have tolerated or taken part in any action by our Office for partisan political purposes. Throughout my service as Special Counsel, seeking to influence the election one way or the other, or seeking to interfere in its outcome, played no role in our work. My Office had one north star: to follow the facts and law wherever they led. Nothing more and nothing less.

While I relied greatly on the counsel, judgment, and advice of our team, I want it to be clear that the ultimate decision to bring charges against Mr. Trump was mine. It is a decision I stand behind fully. To have done otherwise on the facts developed during our work would have been to shirk my duties as a prosecutor and a public servant. After nearly 30 years of public service, that is a choice I could not abide.

It is equally important for me to make clear that nobody within the Department of Justice ever sought to interfere with, or improperly influence, my prosecutorial decision making. The regulations under which I was appointed provided you with the authority to countermand my decisions, 28 C.F.R. § 600.7, but you did not do so. Nor did you, the Deputy Attorney General, or members of your staff ever attempt to improperly influence my decision as to whether to bring charges against Mr. Trump. And to all who know me well, the claim from Mr. Trump that my decisions as a prosecutor were influenced or directed by the Biden administration or other political actors is, in a word, laughable.

While we were not able to bring the cases we charged to trial, I believe the fact that our team stood up for the rule of law matters. I believe the example our team set for others to fight for justice without regard for the personal costs matters. The facts, as we uncovered them in our investigation and as set forth in my Report, matter. Experienced prosecutors know that you cannot control outcomes, you can only do your job the right way for the right reasons. I conclude our work confident that we have done so, and that we have met fully our obligations to the Department and to our country.

Accompanying this letter, I am providing you "a confidential report explaining the prosecution or declination decisions reached by the Special Counsel." 28 C.F.R. § 600.8. The Report consists of two volumes: Volume One addresses the Election Case, and Volume Two addresses the Classified Documents Case. I understand that you are considering whether all or part of my Report can be made public, consistent with applicable legal restrictions. *See* 28 C.F.R. § 600.9(c). Both volumes minimize the identification of witnesses and co-conspirators, consistent with accepted Department practice, and we have provided a redacted version of Volume One that identifies certain information that remains under seal or is restricted from public disclosure by Federal Rule of Criminal Procedure 6(e). Because Volume Two discusses the conduct of Mr. Trump's alleged co-conspirators in the Classified Documents Case, Waltine Nauta and Carlos De Oliveira, consistent with Department policy, Volume Two should not be publicly released while their case remains pending.

Though not required, prior to finalizing the Report, my Office provided an opportunity for counsel for Mr. Trump to review both volumes, and for counsel for his former co-defendants in the Classified Documents Case, Mr. Nauta and Mr. De Oliveira, to review Volume Two. After their review, counsel for Mr. Trump wrote a letter to you, and we have provided a written response to you, both of which you will find as an Addendum to the Report.

With this Report, my service and the service of my staff is complete. I thank you for the trust you placed in me and my team and for affording us the independence necessary to conduct our work. Public service is a privilege, and we deeply appreciate the opportunity to serve our Nation in seeking to uphold the rule of law.

Sincerely yours,

JACK SMITH

FINAL REPORT ON THE SPECIAL COUNSEL'S
INVESTIGATIONS AND PROSECUTIONS

VOLUME ONE: THE ELECTION CASE

REPORT ON EFFORTS TO INTERFERE WITH THE LAWFUL TRANSFER
OF POWER FOLLOWING THE 2020 PRESIDENTIAL ELECTION OR
THE CERTIFICATION OF THE ELECTORAL COLLEGE VOTE
HELD ON JANUARY 6, 2021

Special Counsel Jack Smith
Submitted Pursuant to 28 C.F.R. § 600.8(c)

Washington, D.C.
January 7, 2025

TABLE OF CONTENTS

VOLUME ONE: THE ELECTION CASE.. 1

I. THE RESULTS OF THE INVESTIGATION... 2

    A.   Mr. Trump's Pressure on State Officials 8

    B.   Mr. Trump's Fraudulent Elector Plan 11

    C.   Mr. Trump's Misuse of Official Power Through the Justice Department............. 16

    D.   Mr. Trump's Pressure on the Vice President 20

    E.   Mr. Trump's Supporters Attack the United States Capitol.................................. 23

II. THE LAW 33

    A.   Conspiracy to Defraud the United States (18 U.S.C. § 371) 34

    B.   Obstruction and Conspiracy to Obstruct (18 U.S.C. § 1512(k) and (c)(2)).......... 45

    C.   Conspiracy Against Rights (18 U.S.C. § 241) 49

    D.   Defenses.. 53

    E.   Other Charges 61

    F.   Co-Conspirator Liability 67

III. THE PRINCIPLES OF FEDERAL PROSECUTION 68

    A.   Prosecuting Mr. Trump Served Multiple Substantial Federal Interests 69

        1.   The substantial federal interest in protecting the integrity of the electoral process and the peaceful transfer of power was served by Mr. Trump's prosecution. 69

        2.   The substantial federal interest in counting every citizen's vote was served by Mr. Trump's prosecution. 74

        3.   The substantial federal interest in protecting election officials and other government officials from violence was served by Mr. Trump's prosecution. 75

        4.   The substantial federal interest in the evenhanded administration of the law was served by Mr. Trump's prosecution....................................... 83

B.   Mr. Trump Was Not Subject to Effective Prosecution in Another
Jurisdiction 87

C.   There Was No Adequate Non-Criminal Alternative to Prosecution 88

D.   Mr. Trump's Conduct Had No Historical Analogue 90

IV.   INVESTIGATIVE PROCEDURE AND POLICY 92

A.   The Investigative Process 92

B.   Investigative and Prosecutive Procedures in an Election Year 95

     1.   The Department's Election Year Sensitivities Policy 96

     2.   Pre-Indictment Procedures 99

     3.   Post-Indictment Procedures 100

V.   INVESTIGATIVE CHALLENGES AND LITIGATION ISSUES 107

A.   Pre-Indictment Litigation with Third Parties 108

     1.   The Twitter/X Search Warrant 108

     2.   Legislative Privilege Under the Speech or Debate Clause 110

B.   Threats and Harassment of Witnesses 112

C.   Mr. Trump's Claims of Executive Privilege 116

D.   Presidential Immunity 122

     1.   Prosecutorial Decisions During the Charging Stage 123

     2.   Immunity Litigation 126

     3.   Unresolved Issues Regarding Presidential Immunity 132

VI.   CONCLUSION 136

APPENDIX: KEY FILINGS IN SIGNIFICANT LITIGATION 138

VOLUME ONE: THE ELECTION CASE

On November 18, 2022, the Attorney General appointed the Special Counsel to oversee an ongoing investigation into "whether any person or entity violated the law in connection with efforts to interfere with the lawful transfer of power following the 2020 presidential election or the certification of the Electoral College vote held on or about January 6, 2021." *See* Office of the Attorney General, Order No. 5559-2022, *Appointment of John L. Smith as Special Counsel* (Nov. 18, 2022). As a result of that investigation, on August 1, 2023, a federal grand jury in the District of Columbia charged Donald J. Trump with four felony offenses arising from his efforts to unlawfully retain power by using fraud and deceit to overturn the 2020 election results. After the Supreme Court held last summer that Mr. Trump was immune from prosecution for certain misuse of official power alleged in the indictment, a second grand jury found probable cause to return a superseding indictment charging the same offenses based on his non-immunized conduct. Mr. Trump was thereafter reelected as President of the United States, and as a result, on November 25, 2024, the Special Counsel moved to dismiss the case against Mr. Trump because of the Department of Justice's longstanding position that the Constitution forbids the federal indictment and prosecution of a sitting President.

This Volume focuses on the Election Case against Mr. Trump and, consistent with the applicable regulations, provides an explanation of the prosecution decisions reached by the Special Counsel. *See* 28 C.F.R. § 600.8(c). The first section of this Volume sets forth a summary of key facts gleaned from the investigation, a vast majority of which are already a matter of public record through the litigation that occurred before the district court. The second section discusses the statutes that Mr. Trump was charged with violating, applying the facts developed during the investigation to the law as the Special Counsel's Office (the Office) understood it. This section also addresses other charges that the Office considered but did not pursue, and the defenses that the Office expected Mr. Trump to raise at trial. The third section explains why the Special Counsel's decision to prosecute Mr. Trump was fully consistent with and indeed was compelled by the Principles of Federal Prosecution. The fourth section describes the Office's investigative procedures and policies. Finally, the fifth section of this Volume discusses a series of investigative and prosecutive issues that the Office confronted in the Election Case.

I.   THE RESULTS OF THE INVESTIGATION [1]

In 2020, then-President Donald J. Trump ran for reelection against Joseph R. Biden, Jr. Mr. Trump lost.[2] As alleged in the original and superseding indictments, substantial evidence demonstrates that Mr. Trump then engaged in an unprecedented criminal effort to overturn the legitimate results of the election in order to retain power.[3] Although he did so primarily in his private capacity as a candidate, and with the assistance of multiple private co-conspirators, Mr. Trump also attempted to use the power and authority of the United States Government in furtherance of his scheme.

As set forth in the original and superseding indictments, when it became clear that Mr. Trump had lost the election and that lawful means of challenging the election results had failed, he resorted to a series of criminal efforts to retain power. This included attempts to induce state

---

[1] This section of the Report summarizes the evidence uncovered by the Office's investigation, and therefore includes conduct for which the Supreme Court later held Mr. Trump to be immune from prosecution, see *Trump v. United States*, 603 U.S. 593, 597 (2024). That conduct is not included in the superseding indictment that the Office obtained after the Supreme Court's decision, see ECF No. 226, nor is that conduct included in the discussion below regarding why the evidence warranted criminal charges under the Principles of Federal Prosecution. Unless otherwise noted, all ECF citations in this Volume of the Report are to the docket in *United States v. Trump*, No. 23-cr-257 (D.D.C.).

[2] SCO-00701211 at 7 (Federal Election Commission, Election Results for 2020 Federal Elections).

[3] An indictment is an allegation, not a verdict; a person accused of a crime is presumed innocent until proven guilty beyond a reasonable doubt. The Office was prepared to present the evidence of Mr. Trump's alleged crimes in a public adversarial trial and to accept any verdicts rendered by a jury of his peers. As explained below, the Office commenced prosecution of Mr. Trump in the Election Case under both the original and superseding indictments because it concluded that the admissible evidence would be sufficient to obtain and sustain a conviction. *See* Justice Manual § 9-27.220 and *infra* at Section III.

officials to ignore true vote counts; to manufacture fraudulent slates of presidential electors in seven states that he had lost; to force Justice Department officials and his own Vice President, Michael R. Pence, to act in contravention of their oaths and to instead advance Mr. Trump's personal interests; and, on January 6, 2021, to direct an angry mob to the United States Capitol to obstruct the congressional certification of the presidential election and then leverage rioters' violence to further delay it.[4] In service of these efforts, Mr. Trump worked with other people to achieve a common plan: to overturn the election results and perpetuate himself in office. These individuals included Co-Conspirator 1, a private attorney who was willing to spread knowingly false claims and pursue strategies that Mr. Trump's Campaign attorneys would not; Co-Conspirator 2, a private attorney who devised and attempted to implement a strategy to leverage the Vice President's ministerial role in the certification proceeding to obstruct the certification; Co-Conspirator 3, a private attorney whose unfounded claims of election fraud Mr. Trump privately acknowledged were "crazy," but which he embraced and publicly amplified nonetheless; Co-Conspirator 4, a Justice Department official who worked on civil matters and who, with Mr. Trump, attempted to use the Justice Department to open sham election crime investigations and influence state legislatures with knowingly false claims of election fraud; Co-Conspirator 5, a private attorney who assisted in devising and attempting to implement a plan to submit fraudulent slates of presidential electors to obstruct the certification proceeding; and Co-Conspirator 6, a private political consultant who helped implement a plan to submit fraudulent slates of presidential electors to obstruct the certification proceeding.[5] The throughline of all of Mr. Trump's criminal efforts was deceit—knowingly false claims of election

---

[4] ECF No. 1 at ¶ 10; ECF No. 226 at ¶ 11; see ECF No. 252 at 3.

[5] ECF No. 1 at ¶ 8; ECF No. 226 at ¶ 9; see ECF No. 252 at 4.

fraud—and the evidence shows that Mr. Trump used these lies as a weapon to defeat a federal government function foundational to the United States' democratic process.[6]

Mr. Trump's false claims included dozens of specific claims regarding certain states, such as that large numbers of dead, non-resident, non-citizen, or otherwise ineligible voters had cast ballots, or that voting machines had changed votes for Mr. Trump to votes against him.[7] These claims were demonstrably and, in many cases, obviously false.[8] The Office investigated whether Mr. Trump believed the claims he made. Evidence from a variety of sources established that Mr. Trump knew that there was no outcome-determinative fraud in the 2020 election, that many of the specific claims he made were untrue, and that he had lost the election. He knew this because some of the highest-ranking officials in his own Administration, including the Vice President, told him directly that there was no evidence to support his claims.[9] Mr. Trump's private

---

[6] See ECF No. 1; ECF No. 226. Mr. Trump's conduct with Co-Conspirator 4 was charged in the original indictment, ECF No. 1, but not in the superseding indictment, ECF No. 226, because the Supreme Court held in the interim that Mr. Trump's conduct regarding the Department of Justice was immunized. Trump, 603 U.S. at 597.

[7] See, e.g., ECF No. 252 at 10; SCO-02244118 at 11-12, 14-19 (Remarks by Mr. Trump at Save America Rally 01/06/2021); SCO-04949418 at 04:15:22-04:31:46 (Video of Save America Rally 01/06/2021); SCO-04976462 at 18:34-19:12 (Video of Speech at White House 12/02/2020); SCO-00455939 (Donald J. Trump Tweet 11/19/2020); SCO-04976283 at 01:00:43-01:14:24 (Video of Dalton, GA speech 01/04/2021); SCO-04976275 at 22:00-22:40 (Video of Valdosta, GA speech 12/05/2020); SCO-00455041 (Donald J. Trump Tweet 01/02/2021); SCO-00456153 (Donald J. Trump Tweet 11/12/2020); SCO-00456144 (Donald J. Trump Tweet 11/13/2020); SCO-00456102 (Donald J. Trump Tweet 11/14/2020); SCO-00456066 (Donald J. Trump Tweet 11/15/2020); SCO-00455969 (Donald J. Trump Tweet 11/18/2020); SCO-04976266 at 20:10-37:50 (Video of Thanksgiving Call to Troops 11/26/2020).

[8] Compare SCO-02244118 at 11, 19 (Remarks by Mr. Trump at Save America Rally 01/06/2021) (Mr. Trump asserting on January 6 that there were 205,000 more votes than voters in Pennsylvania) with SCO-00709557 at 156 (SJC Tr.) (stating that Mr. Trump was told on January 3 that the allegation that there were more votes than voters in Pennsylvania was untrue); see also SCO-04976459 at 02:06:23-02:07:00 (Video of Arizona State Hearing 11/30/2020) (Co-Conspirator 1 stating that there could have been "five million illegal aliens in Arizona," and "a few hundred thousand" of those who fraudulently voted, even though the state had a total population of approximately 7.4 million).

[9] See, e.g., ECF No. 1 at ¶ 11; see ECF No. 252 at 10-14 & nn.29-53; SCO-00014655 at 37-44; SCO-00689680 (Michael Balsamo, Disputing Trump, Barr says no widespread election fraud, ASSOCIATED PRESS, Dec. 1, 2020); SCO-00764172 at 21-25 (HSC Tr.); SCO-11506911 at 96-97, 116, 125 (Int. Tr.); SCO-04957448 at 28-31 (SJC Tr.); SCO-00775937 at 57-64 (HSC Tr.); SCO-04952679 (Tweet 11/17/2020); SCO-12929351 (Tweet 11/12/2020); SCO-

4

advisors, both within and outside of his Campaign, told him the same.[10] On November 13, his

own Campaign conceded its litigation in Arizona, a state pivotal to his reelection prospects.[11]

State officials and legislators whom Mr. Trump pressured to change vote tallies or stop

certifications of results rebuffed him and informed him that his fraud claims were wrong, both

privately and through public statements.[12] Mr. Trump also monitored legal developments

---

03036930 (Joint Statement on Election Security 11/12/2020); SCO-00003294 at 37, 39-43; SCO-00015002 at 22-24; SCO-12920242 at 1-7 (Int. Rep.); SCO-00006256 at 46-47, 59, 74-76.

[10] *See, e.g.,* ECF No. 252 at 9-14 & nn.29-53, 17-18 & n.69, 21 & n.95, 25; SCO-12920242 at 1-7 (Int. Rep.).

[11] *See* ECF No. 252 at 9 & n.24; *Donald J. Trump for President, Inc. v. Hobbs,* No. CV 2020-014248, Transcript of Proceedings (Maricopa County, Az. Super. Ct. Nov. 13, 2020); *Hobbs,* No. CV 2020-014248, Docket Code 042 (Maricopa County, Az. Super. Ct. Nov. 13, 2020).

[12] *See* ECF No. 252 at 14 & nn.52-53; *see also, e.g.,* SCO-00829361 at 17 (HSC Tr.) (state legislator told Mr. Trump that "he primarily lost Michigan because of two counties that are routinely Republican counties . . . and more specifically he underperformed with educated females"); SCO-11509450 at 25 (Int. Tr.) (state legislator told Mr. Trump that state officials had not seen evidence of widespread fraud); SCO-04953053 (Joint Statement 11/20/2020) (state legislators' statement that they are unaware of "any information that would change the outcome of the election in Michigan" and noting legislative review of the state's elections process); SCO-04952823 (Statement 12/04/2020) (state legislator citing U.S. Attorney General's statement that he had not seen outcome-determinative election fraud); SCO-06730226 (Letter to Maricopa County Voters 11/17/2020) (noting "no evidence of fraud or misconduct or malfunction" in the over two million ballots cast); SCO-00614161 at 1335 (Tweets 12/01/2020) (describing Arizona election security measures, including poll ID and hand-conducted signature review); SCO-04957281 (Georgia Secretary of State News Release 10/23/2020) (refuting that electronic ballot marking is particularly vulnerable to cyberattack); SCO-04957309 (Georgia Secretary of State News Release 11/05/2020) (noting ballot count progress and listing voting security measures); SCO-12876768 (Video of Georgia Secretary of State Press Conference 11/06/2020) (giving numbers of rejected ballots from unregistered and non-citizen voters, and partially counted ballots from out-of-precinct voters); SCO-12876769 (Video of Georgia Secretary of State Press Conference 11/09/2020) (refuting allegations about ballot counting at State Farm Arena, software malfunctions, more votes than voters, and ballot harvesting, among others); SCO-12876771 (Video of Georgia Secretary of State Press Conference 11/12/2020) (addressing decision to conduct risk-limiting audit, explaining under-voting in presidential race, refuting allegations that computers and software flipped votes); SCO-04957154 (Georgia Secretary of State News Release 11/18/2020) (explaining that 2020 election absentee ballot rejection rate was equivalent to that in the 2018 general election); SCO-04957157 (Georgia Secretary of State News Release 11/19/2020) (risk-limiting audit results confirmed machine ballot count results); SCO-04957179 (Georgia Secretary of State News Release 12/07/2020) (hand recount and formal recount requested by Mr. Trump's campaign confirmed original election results; Co-Conspirator 3's lawsuit dismissed); SCO-04976277 (Video of Georgia Secretary of State Press Conference 12/07/2020) (refuting allegations about vote-switching algorithms and "secret suitcases" of ballots at State Farm Arena and noting that in-person voting always requires identification); SCO-12896570 (Video of Georgia Secretary of State Press Conference 12/16/2020) (stating that hand vote count confirmed machine count, signature matching was performed, "there were no votes flipped," and full video of vote counting at State Farm Arena confirmed no wrongdoing); SCO-04957276 (Georgia Secretary of State News Release 12/29/2020) (recounts and signature audit confirmed original Georgia election results, and signature matching in Cobb County found no fraudulent ballots); SCO-04976281 (Video of Interview 01/02/2021) (election audit and full recount confirmed that Mr. Trump lost in

regarding the election and was on notice that state and federal courts rejected every post-election

lawsuit that Mr. Trump and his allies filed claiming outcome-determinative election fraud.[13] Mr.

Trump and co-conspirators could not have believed the specific fraud claims that they were

---

Georgia election); SCO-12998394 (Tr. of Georgia Secretary of State Call 01/02/2021); SCO-04976282 (Video of Georgia Secretary of State Press Conference 01/04/2021) (among other issues, refuting specific allegations about: Dominion voting machines; State Farm Arena ballot counting; convicted felons voting—74 at most, not 2,506; underage voters—zero, not 66,248; unregistered voters—zero, not 2,423; voting past the registration deadline—zero, not 4,926); SCO-04955691 (Michigan Secretary of State web page 11/06/2020) (voting machine software did not malfunction, no ballots were backdated); SCO-12876350 (Michigan Secretary of State web page 12/08/2020) (noting that Antrim County reporting error was accidental human error and citing U.S. Attorney General, FBI, and CISA view that 2020 election was "the most secure election in our nation's history and, despite unprecedented scrutiny, there has been no evidence of widespread fraud identified whatsoever"); SCO-02243762 (Michigan Attorney General and Secretary of State News Release 12/14/2020) (affirming that the "general election in Michigan and across the country was the most secure in the nation's history"); SCO-04957382 (Michigan Secretary of State web page 12/17/2020) (hand audit confirmed Antrim County election results and showed Dominion machines accurately calculated results); SCO-12839140 (Michigan Secretary of State web page 12/18/2020) (stating that final numbers from "Antrim County hand-tallied audit yesterday continue to affirm the accuracy of the Nov. 3 general election certified results"); SCO-02963078 (Video of Statement by City Clerk in Rochester Hills, Michigan) (stating that "[t]here were no missing ballots" and "[t]he accusation that 2,000 ballots were found is categorically false"); SCO-04957413 (New Mexico Secretary of State News Release 12/14/2020) (announcing that New Mexico's electoral votes went to Mr. Biden and that the 2020 election was "the most secure in American history"); SCO-12876770 (Video of Interview of Philadelphia City Commissioner with CNN 11/11/2020) (stating that there were no dead voters and no provisional ballots cast by ineligible voters and confirming that "[w]e just had the most transparent and secure election in the history of Philadelphia"); SCO-12929345 (Tweet 11/27/2020) (Philadelphia City Commissioner responding to Mr. Trump's 11/27/2020 Tweet and confirming, "Not only is there no evidence of 'massive' voter fraud in Philadelphia, but there haven't been *any* documented instances in the many lawsuits filed in Pennsylvania"); SCO-04956023 (Pennsylvania Department of State Public Response Statement 12/29/2020) (refuting misinformation in letter from Republican lawmakers that state data was contradicted by county-level data and explaining the state's risk-limiting audit to ensure accurate vote counts); SCO-12837952 (Wisconsin Elections Commission web page 11/05/2020) (impossible to have more votes than voters, and no absentee ballots were found in the middle of the night); SCO-12848641 (Wisconsin Elections Commission web page 11/10/2020) (no credible evidence to undermine unofficial election results or support allegations of widespread election issues, only registered voters can request absentee ballots, and ballot signatures can never be added by poll workers); SCO-12838580 (Wisconsin Elections Commission web page 12/16/2020) (Dominion machines did not flip votes, 200,000 people did not illegally vote without identification, and absentee ballots were not issued without a ballot application); SCO-12845421 (Nevada Secretary of State Facts vs. Myths Release 12/18/2020) ("we have yet to see any evidence of wide-spread fraud"; "we have not been presented with evidence of non-citizens voting in the 2020 election").

[13] See, e.g., ECF No. 252 at 18, 36-37 & nn.181-183, 41 & nn.207-208, 44-45 & nn.227-230; SCO-00455873, SCO-12987569 (Donald J. Trump Tweet 11/21/2020) (about failed Pennsylvania lawsuit); SCO-00455356, SCO-12858834 (Donald J. Trump Tweet 12/12/2020) (about failed Supreme Court lawsuit); SCO-00455197, SCO-00455196, SCO-00455195, SCO-12987423, SCO-12987422, SCO-12987421 (Donald J. Trump Tweets 12/21/2020) (about failed Wisconsin lawsuit); SCO-00790949 at 170-171 (HSC Tr.) (Senior Advisor noting that, in Mr. Trump's presence, he challenged Co-Conspirator 3 about losing lawsuits across the country); SCO-00014205 at 7-8.

making because the numbers they touted—for instance, of dead voters in a particular state— frequently vacillated wildly from day to day or were objectively impossible,[14] including, for example, Co-Conspirator 3's claims about voting machines that Mr. Trump privately acknowledged sounded "crazy"[15] before he publicly amplified them.[16] Finally, at times, Mr. Trump made comments implicitly acknowledging that he knew he had lost the election. For example, in a January 3, 2021 Oval Office meeting regarding a national security matter, Mr. Trump stated in part, "[I]t's too late for us. We're going to give that to the next guy," meaning President-elect Biden.[17]

Mr. Trump aimed his deceit at the United States' process of collecting, counting, and certifying votes, which flows from the Constitution and a federal law enacted in 1887 called the Electoral Count Act (ECA). The Constitution provides that the United States President is selected through the votes of individuals called electors and that each state determines how to appoint its electors.[18] Through state laws, all fifty states and the District of Columbia have chosen to select electors based on the popular vote.[19] Therefore, after election day, pursuant to

---

[14] *See, e.g.*, ECF No. 252 at 15 & nn.55-59 (Arizona); *id.* at 21 & n.96, 30 & n.142, 122-123 & n.592 (Georgia). For Arizona, *see, e.g.*, SCO-04976384 at 20:47 (Common Sense episode 89 11/25/2020) ("36,000"); SCO-04976459 at 02:06:23-02:07:00 (Video of Arizona State Hearing 11/30/2020) ("a few hundred thousand"); SCO-06628641 at 18:52-19:42 (War Room episode 608 12/24/2020) ("about 250,000"); SCO-06628646 at 35:19-35:45 (War Room episode 625 01/02/2021) ("32,000"); SCO-02244118 at 17 (Remarks by Mr. Trump at Save America Rally 01/06/2021) ("36,000"). Additional examples are discussed below. *See, e.g., infra* at nn.155-158 (Georgia).

[15] *See* ECF No. 252 at 44 & n.224; SCO-11523477 at 94-103 (Int. Tr.).

[16] *See* ECF No. 252 at 44-45 & nn.227-229; SCO-00455825 (Donald J. Trump Retweet 11/24/2020); SCO-12858284 (Tweet 11/24/2020) (showing Donald J. Trump Retweet); SCO-00455769, SCO-12858342 (Donald J. Trump Retweet 11/26/2020); SCO-04949395 at 3 (Remarks by Mr. Trump on the Presidential Election 12/02/2020); SCO-02244118 at 18-19 (Remarks by Mr. Trump at Save America Rally 01/06/2021).

[17] *See* ECF No. 1 at ¶ 83.

[18] U.S. CONST. art. II, § 1.

[19] ECF No. 1 at ¶ 9; ECF No. 226 at ¶ 10; *see* ECF No. 252 at 4; *About the Electors*, NATIONAL ARCHIVES, https://www.archives.gov/electoral-college/electors; *see also Chiafalo v. Washington*, 591 U.S. 578, 581, 584-85 & n.1 (2020).

the ECA, each state formally determines—or "ascertains"—its electors based on the popular vote; the ascertained electors meet on a day determined by the ECA and cast their votes based on their state's popular vote; and the ascertained electors mail their electoral votes, along with a certification from the state executive that they are the state's legitimate electors, to the United States Congress to be counted and certified in an official proceeding.[20] The Constitution and ECA provide that on the sixth of January following election day, the Congress meets for that certification proceeding, which is presided over by the Vice President as President of the Senate; the legitimate electors' votes are opened and counted; and the winner is certified.[21] Until Mr. Trump obstructed it, this democratic process had operated in a peaceful and orderly manner for more than 130 years.

A.   Mr. Trump's Pressure on State Officials

One of Mr. Trump's efforts to change the results of the election involved targeting the electoral process at the state level through politically aligned state officials. Mr. Trump contacted state legislators and executives, pressured them with false claims of election fraud in their states, and urged them to take action to ignore the vote counts and change the results.[22] Significantly, he made election claims only to state legislators and executives who shared his political affiliation and were his political supporters, and only in states that he had lost.[23]

---

[20] Electoral Count Act, 3 U.S.C. §§ 5-11.

[21] U.S. CONST. amend. XII; Electoral Count Act, 3 U.S.C. § 15.

[22] *See* ECF No. 252 at 16-35; *see, e.g.*, SCO-12733339 at 3-6, 13-15 (Int. Rep.); SCO-00767550 at 10-18 (HSC Tr.); SCO-12998394 (Tr. of Georgia Secretary of State Call 01/02/2021); SCO-00829361 at 8-11, 15-24 (HSC Tr.).

[23] *See* ECF No. 252 at 16; SCO-12733339 at 3-5 (Int. Rep.); SCO-02296394 at 6 (Presidential Daily Diary 11/09/2020); SCO-00829361 at 9-10 (HSC Tr.); SCO-00767550 at 9-12, 18 (HSC Tr.); SCO-02295943 at 3 (Presidential Daily Diary 11/22/2020); SCO-02301680 at 3 (Presidential Daily Diary 12/08/2020); SCO-11509251 at 38-39, 43 (Int. Tr.); SCO-12998394 (Tr. of Georgia Secretary of State Call 01/02/2021).

For instance, Mr. Trump and Co-Conspirator 1 called the Speaker of the Arizona House of Representatives on November 22 and used false fraud claims to try to convince the Speaker to call the state legislature into session and replace Arizona's legitimate electors with Mr. Trump's illegitimate ones.[24] Co-Conspirator 1 tried to coerce the Arizona Speaker, including by telling him, "we're all kind of Republicans and we need to be working together."[25] The Arizona Speaker refused to do what he was asked and requested that Co-Conspirator 1 provide evidence to support his fraud claims.[26] Co-Conspirator 1 not only failed to ever provide such evidence, but he conceded to the Arizona Speaker at an in-person meeting a week later that "[w]e don't have the evidence, but we have lots of theories."[27] Despite this lack of fraud evidence, Mr. Trump and others continued to pressure the Arizona Speaker to overturn the election results.[28]

Mr. Trump similarly leaned on other state officials—always those of the same political party. On January 2, 2021, just days before the election results were to be certified, he called Georgia's Secretary of State and pressed him to "find 11,780 votes"—Mr. Biden's margin of victory in the state.[29] When the Secretary of State refuted Mr. Trump's false fraud claims, Mr. Trump issued a threat, stating that because the Secretary of State knew "what they did and you're

---

[24] See ECF No. 252 at 19 & nn.77-79; SCO-02295943 at 3 (Presidential Daily Diary 11/22/2020); SCO-00767550 at 9-12, 18 (HSC Tr.).

[25] See ECF No. 252 at 19 & n.80; SCO-00767550 at 15-16 (HSC Tr.).

[26] See ECF No. 252 at 19 & n.81; SCO-00767550 at 10-12, 15-16 (HSC Tr.); SCO-00715584 (Arizona House Speaker News Release 12/04/2020) ("I and my fellow legislators swore an oath to support the U.S. Constitution and the constitution and laws of the state of Arizona. It would violate that oath, the basic principles of republican government, and the rule of law if we attempted to nullify the people's vote based on unsupported theories of fraud.").

[27] See ECF No. 252 at 19 & nn.82, 84; SCO-00767550 at 12-13, 35-36 (HSC Tr.).

[28] See ECF No. 252 at 20-21 & nn 88-91; SCO-00455536, SCO-12987478 (Donald J. Trump Retweet 12/06/2020), SCO-00455538, SCO-12858634 (Donald J. Trump Tweet 12/06/2020); SCO-00767550 at 43-49 (HSC Tr.); SCO-11540788 at 51-53 (Int. Tr.).

[29] See ECF No. 252 at 29 & nn.134, 137; SCO-00825967 at 105-107, 123-124 (HSC Tr.); SCO-12998394 at 12 (Tr. of Georgia Secretary of State Call 01/02/2021).

not reporting it . . . that's a criminal offense. And you know, you can't let that happen. That's a big risk to you . . . ."[30] Mr. Trump also pressed state legislators in Michigan by inviting them to the White House on November 20, raising false claims of election fraud, and bringing Co-Conspirator 1 into the meeting by phone.[31] Michigan's Senate Majority Leader told Mr. Trump that he had lost the election not because of fraud, but because he had underperformed with educated females—an assessment that displeased Mr. Trump.[32]

Mr. Trump engaged in these efforts even though trusted state and party officials had told him from the outset that there was no evidence of fraud in the election. In Arizona, Mr. Trump called the Governor on November 9—a week after election day, and after both Fox News and the Associated Press had projected that Mr. Trump had lost the state.[33] Using a baseball metaphor, the Governor told Mr. Trump that "it was the ninth inning, two outs and he was several runs down."[34] During the call, Mr. Trump raised false claims of election fraud; the Governor asked Mr. Trump to send evidence of the alleged fraud, and Mr. Trump suggested he would do so.[35] He never did.[36] In Pennsylvania, just two days after the election, the Chairman of the state's Republican Party, who had represented Mr. Trump in previous election litigation, refuted Mr.

---

[30] *See* ECF No. 252 at 30 & n.144; SCO-12998394 at 12 (Tr. of Georgia Secretary of State Call 01/02/2021).

[31] *See* ECF No. 252 at 32 & nn.157-159; SCO-11532925 at 53-56 (Int. Tr.); SCO-00829361 at 15-24 (HSC Tr.).

[32] *See* ECF No. 252 at 32-33 & nn.160-161; SCO-00829361 at 16-18 (HSC Tr.).

[33] *See* ECF No. 252 at 17 & n.63; SCO-12733339 at 3-5 (Int. Rep.); SCO-02296394 at 6 (Presidential Daily Diary 11/09/2020); *see also Democrats flip Arizona as Biden, Kelly score key election wins*, FOX NEWS (Nov. 3, 2020), https://www.foxnews.com/video/6206934979001; Jonathan J. Cooper and Anita Snow, *Biden wins Arizona, flips longtime Republican stronghold*, APNEWS.COM (Nov. 4, 2020), https://apnews.com/article/election-2020-joe-biden-donald-trump-race-and-ethnicity-legislature-218ad4d596e87c6b1a223f19f817776e.

[34] *See* ECF No. 252 at 17 & n.66; SCO-12733339 at 14 (Int. Rep.).

[35] *See* ECF No. 252 at 17 & nn.67-68; SCO-12733339 at 4 (Int. Rep.).

[36] *See* ECF No. 252 at 17 & n.68; SCO-12733339 at 4 (Int. Rep.).

Trump's claim that it was suspicious that his early lead was slipping away.[37] The Chairman explained that there were still roughly 1,750,000 mail-in ballots being counted, which were expected to weigh heavily in Mr. Biden's favor.[38] In the course of conversations like these, state officials—better positioned than Mr. Trump to know the facts in their states—repeatedly told Mr. Trump that his fraud claims were unfounded and that there was no evidence of substantial election fraud in their states. And apart from Georgia's Secretary of State, Mr. Trump never contacted other election officials to determine whether there was merit to any specific allegation of election fraud in their states—even though they would have been the best sources to confirm or refute such claims.

B.   Mr. Trump's Fraudulent Elector Plan

As December 14—the date the ECA required each state's electors to vote and send their certificates of vote to Congress—approached, Mr. Trump and co-conspirators launched another plan. Under this plan, they would organize the people who would have served as Mr. Trump's electors, had he won the popular vote, in seven states that Mr. Trump had lost—Arizona, Georgia, Michigan, Nevada, New Mexico, Pennsylvania, and Wisconsin—and cause them to sign and send to Washington false certifications claiming to be the legitimate electors.[39] Ultimately, as explained below, Mr. Trump and co-conspirators used the fraudulent certificates to

---

[37] *See* ECF No. 252 at 37-38 & nn.187-190; SCO-00016926 at 10-11, 19-23; SCO-02300357 at 3-4 (Presidential Daily Diary 11/06/2020).

[38] *See* ECF No. 252 at 38 & n.190; SCO-00016926 at 21.

[39] *See* ECF No. 252 at 48, 56 & n.301; SCO-02341381 (Fraudulent "Arizona's Electoral Votes for President and Vice President"); SCO-02341386 (Fraudulent "Georgia's Electoral Votes for President and Vice President"); SCO-02341398 (Fraudulent "Michigan's Electoral Votes for President and Vice President"); SCO-02341415 (Fraudulent "Nevada's Electoral Votes for President and Vice President"); SCO-02341409 (Fraudulent "New Mexico's Electoral Votes for President and Vice President"); SCO-02341435 (Fraudulent "Pennsylvania's Electoral Votes for President and Vice President"); SCO-02341449 (Fraudulent "Wisconsin's Electoral Votes for President and Vice President").

try to obstruct the congressional certification proceeding. The fraudulent elector plan's arc is reflected in a series of memoranda drafted in late November and early December by Co-Conspirator 5, who initially portrayed it as a contingency to preserve the possibility that Mr. Trump's electors' votes would be counted on January 6 if he prevailed in ongoing election litigation.[40] But as described below, the plan quickly transformed into a corrupt strategy to obstruct the certification proceeding and overturn the valid election results.[41]

Mr. Trump set the fraudulent elector plan into motion in early December, ensured that it was carried out by co-conspirators and Campaign agents in the targeted states, and monitored its progress. On December 6, for instance, Mr. Trump and Co-Conspirator 2 called the Chairwoman of the Republican National Committee and told her that it was important for the RNC to help organize Mr. Trump's elector nominees in the targeted states.[42] During the call, Co-Conspirator 2 told a lie that the co-conspirators would use to induce the cooperation of many of the fraudulent electors: that Mr. Trump's electors' votes would be used only if ongoing litigation in their state proved successful for Mr. Trump.[43] From that point on, Mr. Trump communicated with Co-Conspirators 1 and 2 about the plan, and they in turn communicated with Co-Conspirators 5 and 6.[44] At Co-Conspirator 1's direction, Co-Conspirator 5 generated and

---

[40] *See* ECF No. 252 at 48-49 & nn.250-253; SCO-00310619 (Co-Conspirator 5 memo 11/18/2020); SCO-00310626 (Co-Conspirator 5 memo 12/06/2020); SCO-00039311 (Co-Conspirator 5 memo 12/09/2020).

[41] *See* ECF No. 252 at 48-49 & nn.250-253; SCO-00310626 (Co-Conspirator 5 memo 12/06/2020); SCO-00039311 (Co-Conspirator 5 memo 12/09/2020); SCO-00039408 (Email from Co-Conspirator 5 12/08/2020).

[42] *See* ECF No. 252 at 50 & nn.258-260; SCO-00009955 at 8-10; SCO-00806514 at 7-10 (HSC Tr.).

[43] *See* ECF No. 252 at 50 & nn.258-260; SCO-00009955 at 10; SCO-00806514 at 9-10 (HSC Tr.).

[44] *See* ECF No. 252 at 50-51 & nn.266-267, 64 & nn.344-345, 65 & n.353; SCO-00245354 (Email among Campaign staff 12/14/2020); SCO-11572270 (Email from Co-Conspirator 6 12/09/2020); SCO-04858082 (Text messages between Campaign staff and Senior Advisor 12/13/2020); SCO-03661463 (Email from Co-Conspirator 5 12/11/2020); SCO-00039102 (Email from Co-Conspirator 6 to Co-Conspirator 5 12/10/2020); SCO-00039461 (Email from Co-Conspirator 5 to Co-Conspirator 6 and others 12/11/2020); SCO-00309939 (Email from

sent directions to the Trump electors in each targeted state on how best to mimic the manner in which the state required valid electors to gather and vote,[45] and Campaign staff and agents helped carry out Co-Conspirator 5's plans.[46]

For the most part, the co-conspirators deceived Mr. Trump's elector nominees in the targeted states by falsely claiming that their electoral votes would be used only if ongoing litigation were resolved in Mr. Trump's favor.[47] Indeed, the co-conspirators deliberately

---

Co-Conspirator 5 to Co-Conspirator 1 12/13/2020); SCO-02296764 (Presidential Daily Diary 12/23/2020); SCO-02296763 at 7 (Presidential Daily Diary, Flight Manifest 12/23/2020); SCO-11618747 at 115, 156-158, 166-169 (Text messages including Co-Conspirator 6); SCO-02301015 at 4 (Presidential Daily Diary 01/04/2021).

[45] See ECF No. 252 at 51-52 & n.274; SCO-00039311 (Co-Conspirator 5 memo 12/09/2020); SCO-03660671 (Email from Co-Conspirator 6 to Co-Conspirator 5 12/11/2020); SCO-03661463 (Email from Co-Conspirator 5 12/11/2020); SCO-00039412 (Email from Co-Conspirator 5 to others, including Co-Conspirator 1 and Co-Conspirator 6 12/10/2020); SCO-00310094 (Email from Co-Conspirator 5 to Co-Conspirator 1 12/10/2020); SCO-00039381 (Email from Co-Conspirator 5 12/10/2020); SCO-03660648 (Email from Co-Conspirator 5 12/10/2020); SCO-03660731 (Email from Co-Conspirator 5 12/10/2020); SCO-00039442 (Email from Co-Conspirator 5 12/10/2020); SCO-05396682 (Text message from Co-Conspirator 6 12/13/2020); SCO-05389962-SCO-05389971 (Text messages between Campaign staffer and Co-Conspirator 5 12/13/2020).

[46] See ECF No. 252 at 51 & n.268; SCO-00310140 (Email from Co-Conspirator 6 12/09/2020); SCO-03660557 (Email from Co-Conspirator 6 to others, including Co-Conspirator 1 and Co-Conspirator 5 12/10/2020); SCO-00039412 (Email from Co-Conspirator 5 to others, including Co-Conspirator 1 and Co-Conspirator 6 12/10/2020); SCO-05390131-SCO-05390136 (Text messages between Co-Conspirator 6, Co-Conspirator 5, and Campaign staffer 12/11/2020); SCO-00430180 (Text messages between Co-Conspirator 6 and Campaign staffer 12/11/2020); SCO-00309359 (Email to Co-Conspirator 1 and Co-Conspirator 6 12/14/2020); SCO-00405057 (Email among Campaign staff 12/15/2020); SCO-06452193 (Email among Campaign staff 12/12/2020); SCO-00312444 (Text messages among Co-Conspirator 1, Co-Conspirator 6, and others 12/12/2020); SCO-12185268 (Email from Co-Conspirator 6 to Co-Conspirator 1 and others 12/13/2020); SCO-03656456 (Email from Co-Conspirator 5 to Campaign staffer 01/05/2021); SCO-00039215 (Email to Co-Conspirator 5 01/05/2021); SCO-04022107 (Email to Co-Conspirator 5 01/05/2021); SCO-04022176 (Text messages from Co-Conspirator 5 01/05/2021); SCO-12804411 (Text messages from Co-Conspirator 5 01/06/2021); SCO-12804414 (Text messages between Co-Conspirator 5 and Campaign staffer 01/05/2021); SCO-03666178 (Email from Co-Conspirator 5 01/05/2021); SCO-00038522, SCO-00038523, SCO-00038527 (Email with attachments 01/07/2021).

[47] See, e.g., ECF No. 252 at 53 & n.282; see, e.g., SCO-12949797 at 82-83 (Int Tr.); SCO-11547433 at 4, 6 (Int. Rep.); SCO-00009540 at 15-16; SCO-00017495 at 42-45; SCO-11551879 at 51-55 (Int. Tr.); SCO-00017100 at 53-55; SCO-11548772 at 75-85 (Int. Tr.); SCO-11568208 at 107-109; SCO-11514688 at 6-7 (Int. Tr.); SCO-12832045 at 75-78 (Int. Tr.); SCO-12808771 at 24-30, 40-41 (Int. Tr.); SCO-11523905 at 153-154 (Int. Tr.); SCO-12741405 (Email from Co-Conspirator 5 12/14/2020); see also SCO-00310647 (Email to Co-Conspirator 1, Co-Conspirator 5, Co-Conspirator 6, and others 12/11/2020).

withheld from the elector nominees information showing otherwise.[48] This deception was crucial to the conspiracy, as many who participated as fraudulent electors would not have done so had they known the true extent of the co-conspirators' plans.[49] Not all of Mr. Trump's elector nominees were persuaded, forcing the co-conspirators to recruit substitutes in some of the targeted states.[50] For example, one Trump elector nominee in Pennsylvania recognized the plan as "illegal" and an attempt "to overthrow the Government," and he declined to participate.[51] Conversely, a select few of Mr. Trump's agents and elector nominees had insight into the

[48] See ECF No. 252 at 53 & n.282; SCO-03660393 (Email from Co-Conspirator 5 to Campaign staff 12/10/2020); SCO-03660734 (Co-Conspirator 5 streamlined memo 12/10/2020); SCO-11509937 at 257-260 (Int. Tr.).

[49] See, e.g., SCO-12949797 at 121 (Int. Tr.) (Trump Elector: "Nobody—nobody suggested, hey, you know what, let's just get this signed because we're gonna put pressure on . . . Pence on the 6th. Cause if I had known that was the plan, I wouldn't have signed a contingent on it."); SCO-00017495 at 57-58; SCO-11551879 at 89-90 (Int. Tr.) ("Q: [W]ould you have agreed to this plan if you knew that the forms you were signing might be used to delay or prevent the certification of the election on January 6, [2021]? Trump Elector: Nobody told me, and I don't remember anything, so no. And I would not agree for—if somebody else use this . . . for some other reasons. Q: And . . . did anyone ever inform you that the documents you were signing on December 14, 2020 might be used as a reason not to count Georgia's electoral votes during the certification of the election on January 6, 2021? A: No, nobody told me. Q: Would you have agreed to that? Trump Elector: No."); SCO-00017100 at 54-55; SCO-11548772 at 79 (Int. Tr.) (Trump Elector: "[M]y expectation was that the electoral votes that were cast were, were in the event that President Trump won New Mexico . . . and not to be used for any other purpose."); SCO-11568208 at 108; SCO-12832045 at 75 (Int. Tr.) ("Q: [W]ould you have wanted to know, before you cast that vote, if somebody else intended to use your vote to delay the certification, regardless of the outcome of the certification? Trump Elector: I never thought about that. Q: Is that something that would've mattered to you when you were deciding whether or not to cast the vote if, if they were gonna use it that way? Trump Elector: Yes, it would've mattered. . . . Because that's unethical. Q: Okay. And would it have mattered to you if somebody was going to try to convince Vice President Pence that he could just pick between these things, regardless of litigation? Would you have wanted to know that before you cast your vote? Trump Elector: . . . I hadn't thought of something that high up, quite frankly. But my vote was not cast to be used for anything that was unethical, illegal, immoral, or not justified."); SCO-12808771 at 29, 40 (Int. Tr.) (Q: "[The certificates] were only to be used in the case that . . . something actually changed the outcome of the election in New Mexico? Trump Elector: That's correct. Q: And that was important to you? Trump Elector: Yes. . . . Q: And were you surprised by [how the certificates were used on January 6th]? Trump Elector: Extremely surprised.").

[50] See, e.g., SCO-00016926 at 61-69; SCO-11531008 at 9-10 (Int. Tr.); SCO-11524990 at 14 (Int. Tr.); SCO-00312444 (Text messages among Co-Conspirator 1, Co-Conspirator 6, and others 12/12/2020); see also SCO-02341386 at 6-9 (Fraudulent "Georgia's Electoral Votes for President and Vice President") (noting substitute "electors"); SCO-02341398 at 4-5 (Fraudulent "Michigan's Electoral Votes for President and Vice President") (same); SCO-02341435 at 4-10 (Fraudulent "Pennsylvania's Electoral Votes for President and Vice President") (same).

[51] SCO-11531008 at 10, 79 (Int. Tr.).

ultimate plan to use the fraudulent elector certificates to disrupt the congressional certification on January 6 and willingly assisted. [52] On December 9, after a phone call with Co-Conspirator 5, one of the Campaign's agents wrote in an email that Co-Conspirator 5's plan for the electors to "send[] in 'fake' electoral votes to Pence" was "[k]ind of wild/creative." [53] Two and a half hours later, he replied to his own email and, as cover, wrote that "'alternative' votes is probably a better term than 'fake' votes" and that he agreed with a suggestion "to keep [the plan] under wraps until Congress counts the vote on Jan. 6th." [54] In each of the targeted states, Mr. Trump and his co-conspirators successfully organized enough elector nominees and substitutes to gather on December 14, cast fraudulent electoral votes on his behalf, and send them to Washington, D.C., for the congressional certification [55]—a fact that the RNC Chairwoman relayed to Mr. Trump on the evening of December 14. [56]

At the same time that Mr. Trump's elector nominees in the targeted states were preparing to gather and cast fraudulent votes, his co-conspirators were planning to use them to overturn the election results at the January 6 certification. On December 13, Co-Conspirator 5 sent Co-Conspirator 1 a memorandum that envisioned a scenario in which the Vice President would use the fraudulent slates to claim that there were dueling slates of electors from the targeted

[52] See ECF No. 252 at 53 & n.283; SCO-12876963 at 03:15-05:09 (Audio of Interview 12/16/2020); SCO-11572270 (Email from Co-Conspirator 6 12/09/2020).

[53] SCO-11572270 at 2 (Email to Co-Conspirator 6 12/08/2020).

[54] Id. at 1.

[55] See ECF No. 252 at 56 & n.301; SCO-02341381 (Fraudulent "Arizona's Electoral Votes for President and Vice President"); SCO-02341386 (Fraudulent "Georgia's Electoral Votes for President and Vice President"); SCO-02341398 (Fraudulent "Michigan's Electoral Votes for President and Vice President"); SCO-02341415 (Fraudulent "Nevada's Electoral Votes for President and Vice President"); SCO-02341409 (Fraudulent "New Mexico's Electoral Votes for President and Vice President"); SCO-02341435 (Fraudulent "Pennsylvania's Electoral Votes for President and Vice President"); SCO-02341449 (Fraudulent "Wisconsin's Electoral Votes for President and Vice President"); SCO-00405057 (Email to Campaign staff 12/15/2020).

[56] See ECF No. 252 at 57-58 & nn.308-310; SCO-00009955 at 64-66; SCO-00806514 at 18 (HSC Tr.); SCO-02270392 (Emails between RNC Chairwoman and Trump Executive Assistant 12/14/2020).

states and negotiate a solution for Mr. Trump to seize power.[57] And on December 16, Co-Conspirator 5 traveled to Washington with a group of private attorneys who had done work for Mr. Trump's Campaign in Wisconsin for a meet-and-greet with Mr. Trump in the Oval Office;[58] as the group left, Co-Conspirator 5 had a direct, private conversation with Mr. Trump.[59]

Days later, on December 19, Mr. Trump publicly posted a Tweet demonstrating his own focus on the certification proceeding and directing his supporters to gather in Washington, D.C., to oppose it. At 1:42 a.m., he posted a copy of a report falsely alleging outcome-determinative election fraud and wrote, "Statistically impossible to have lost the 2020 Election. Big protest in D.C. on January 6th. Be there, will be wild!"[60] That same day, Co-Conspirator 5 notified another attendee of the December 16 Oval Office meeting of Mr. Trump's Tweet, and he indicated that Mr. Trump had privately foreshadowed his plans for January 6, writing, "Wow. Based on 3 days ago, I think we have unique understanding of this."[61]

C.   Mr. Trump's Misuse of Official Power Through the Justice Department

As his efforts to directly pressure state officials to discount legitimate votes failed and the fraudulent elector plan unfolded, Mr. Trump also tried another tack: he attempted to wield federal power to perpetuate his fraud claims and retain office. Mr. Trump was frustrated with the Justice

---

[57] See ECF No. 252 at 58 & n.312; SCO-05390160 (Text message from Co-Conspirator 6 to Co-Conspirator 5 and Campaign staffer 12/12/2020); SCO-00309946 (Email from Co-Conspirator 5 to Co-Conspirator 1 12/13/2020).

[58] See ECF No. 252 at 58 & n.315; SCO-00039255 (Email to Co-Conspirator 5 and others 12/15/2020); SCO-02337874, SCO-02337893, SCO-02337993 (Photographs of Oval Office Meeting 12/16/2020); SCO-02297155 at 2 (Presidential Daily Diary 12/16/2020); SCO-02297163 at 12-13 (Presidential Daily Diary 12/16/2020); SCO-11510314 at 86-90 (Int. Tr.).

[59] See ECF No. 252 at 59 & n.317; SCO-11621981 at 48-52 (Int. Tr.).

[60] See ECF No. 252 at 60 & n.319, 136 & n.632; SCO-00455253, SCO-12987427 (Donald J. Trump Tweet 12/19/2020).

[61] See ECF No. 252 at 60 & n.320; SCO-12982941 at 2 (Text messages from Co-Conspirator 5 12/19/2020).

Department because its criminal investigations had identified no evidence of substantial fraud[62] and the Attorney General had publicly acknowledged this fact in an interview on December 1 by saying, among other things, "to date, we have not seen fraud on a scale that could have effected a different outcome in the election."[63] As a result, Mr. Trump considered appointing Co-Conspirator 4—a Justice Department attorney who worked on civil matters—to be the Acting Attorney General, because as described below, Co-Conspirator 4 was willing to use the Justice Department to spread Mr. Trump's lies and pressure targeted states to overturn election results.[64]

Throughout the post-election period, Justice Department officials reviewed Mr. Trump's claims of election fraud, found no support for any of them, and informed him of such.[65] In one such discussion, when the Acting Attorney General advised Mr. Trump that the Justice Department could not just "snap its fingers" and change the election outcome,[66] Mr. Trump told the Acting Attorney General and Acting Deputy Attorney General that they should "just say that the election was corrupt and leave the rest to me and the Republican congressmen."[67] In the same call, alluding to replacing Justice Department leadership if they did not do as he directed, Mr. Trump also said, "people tell me [Co-Conspirator 4] is great. I should put him in."[68] Mr. Trump knew about Co-Conspirator 4 because he had been introduced to Co-Conspirator 4 by a

---

[62] *See, e.g.*, ECF No. 252 at 158-159; SCO-04957448 at 139-140 (SJC Tr.); SCO-00775937 at 59-63, 106-108 (HSC Tr.); SCO-12263324 at 5-12 (Handwritten notes 12/27/2020); SCO-00764172 at 18-19 (HSC Tr.).

[63] *See* ECF No. 252 at 158-159 & n.705; SCO-00689680 at 2 (Michael Balsamo, *Disputing Trump, Barr says no widespread election fraud*, ASSOCIATED PRESS, Dec. 1, 2020).

[64] SCO-00775937 at 62, 107 (HSC Tr.); SCO-04957448 at 46-51 (SJC Tr.); SCO-11522446 at 23-24 (Int. Rep.); SCO-11511407 at 177-183 (Int. Tr.); SCO-11542142 at 90-98 (Int. Tr.); SCO-11517380 at 96-99 (Int. Tr.).

[65] *See, e.g.*, SCO-00775937 at 47-58 (HSC Tr.); SCO-00764172 at 18-19 (HSC Tr.).

[66] SCO-00775937 at 58 (HSC Tr.); SCO-12263324 at 8 (Handwritten notes 12/27/2020).

[67] SCO-00775937 at 58 (HSC Tr.); SCO-12263324 at 9 (Handwritten notes 12/27/2020).

[68] SCO-12264603 at 88 (SJC Tr.); *see also* SCO-00775937 at 62 (HSC Tr.).

Member of Congress and had been secretly engaging with Co-Conspirator 4, who was communicating with Mr. Trump in contravention of policies designed to protect the independence of the Justice Department.[69]

On December 28, as his secret communications with Mr. Trump continued, Co-Conspirator 4 emailed the Acting Attorney General and Acting Deputy Attorney General a proposed letter that falsely claimed that the Justice Department had "identified significant concerns that may have impacted the outcome of the election in multiple States" and recommended that those state legislatures convene in special session to reconsider certification of their electoral votes.[70] Co-Conspirator 4 proposed to "send it to the Governor, Speaker, and President pro temp of each relevant state to indicate that in light of time urgency and sworn evidence of election irregularities presented to courts and to legislative committees, the legislatures thereof should each assemble and make a decision about elector appointment in light of their deliberations."[71] Within about an hour of receiving the draft letter, the Acting Deputy Attorney General pointedly rejected Co-Conspirator 4's proposal, writing, "I know of nothing that would support the statement, 'we have identified significant concerns that may have impacted the outcome of the election in multiple states.'"[72] He also observed that the Justice Department had no role in states' administration of their own elections, writing, "I cannot imagine a scenario in which the Department would recommend that a State assemble its

---

[69] SCO-02270007 (Email from Co-Conspirator 4 12/22/2020) (coordinating arrival); SCO-04957448 at 84-86 (SJC Tr.); SCO-12420899, SCO-12420900 (Email with attachment 11/11/2020) (memo regarding White House communications); SCO-00827266 at 54-58 (HSC Tr.); SCO-12941569 (Signal messages between Co-Conspirator 4 and Member of Congress 12/21/20); SCO-12947964 (Signal messages between Co-Conspirator 4 and Member of Congress 12/22/20); SCO-12947874, SCO-12947878 (Signal messages between Co-Conspirator 4 and Member of Congress, with attachment 12/21/20).

[70] SCO-12481890, SCO-12481891 (Email from Co-Conspirator 4, with attachment 12/28/2020).

[71] Id.

[72] SCO-12392895 (Email to Co-Conspirator 4 12/28/2020).

legislature to determine whether already-certified election results should somehow be overridden by legislative action."[73]

Nonetheless, Mr. Trump continued to circumvent Justice Department leadership and engage directly with Co-Conspirator 4. With Mr. Trump's intervention, Co-Conspirator 4 obtained a highly classified briefing on foreign interference in the 2020 election on January 2, 2021—a briefing that yielded nothing to support the conspirators' allegations, as demonstrated by contemporaneous electronic messages between Co-Conspirator 4 and the same Member of Congress who had introduced Co-Conspirator 4 to Mr. Trump.[74] Yet the following day, Mr. Trump attempted to install Co-Conspirator 4 as the Acting Attorney General. On January 3, after Mr. Trump offered the position to Co-Conspirator 4 and Co-Conspirator 4 informed Justice Department senior leadership that he was accepting it,[75] Mr. Trump, Co-Conspirator 4, and senior officials from the Justice Department and White House Counsel's Office gathered for a hastily scheduled meeting in the Oval Office.[76] Mr. Trump made clear that he wanted to appoint Co-Conspirator 4 because Co-Conspirator 4 would cause the Justice Department to send to the targeted states the false letter that the Acting Attorney General and the Acting Deputy Attorney General had rejected as inaccurate and improper.[77] Mr. Trump ultimately did not do so only because he was informed that if he did, mass resignations within the Justice Department and the

---

[73] Id.

[74] SCO-12946533 at 2 (Signal messages between Co-Conspirator 4 and Member of Congress 01/02/2021) ("Bottom line is there is nothing helpful to P.").

[75] SCO-04957448 at 157-159 (SJC Tr.).

[76] SCO-12264603 at 47-48 (SJC Tr.); SCO-04957448 at 46-48 (SJC Tr.); SCO-11522446 at 23-24 (Int. Rep.); SCO-11542142 at 95 (Int. Tr.).

[77] SCO-12264603 at 49, 152-153 (SJC Tr.); SCO-04957448 at 48-52 (SJC Tr.); SCO-11542142 at 97-100 (Int. Tr.).

White House would result in Co-Conspirator 4 "leading a graveyard." [78] Near the end of the meeting, when Co-Conspirator 4 raised the idea of the Justice Department opining on the Vice President's role during the congressional certification, Mr. Trump told all those assembled that no one other than him should be talking to the Vice President. [79]

D.   Mr. Trump's Pressure on the Vice President

Mr. Trump wanted no one else speaking with Vice President Pence because he and co-conspirators were already implementing a secret plan to use Mr. Pence's ministerial role as President of the Senate to Mr. Trump's advantage.   Co-Conspirator 2, with assistance from Co-Conspirators 5 and 6, spearheaded the execution of a strategy—which Co-Conspirator 2 had recently conceded was not supported by the Constitution or federal law[80]—for Mr. Pence to decline to count the legitimate electoral certificates in the targeted states where Mr. Trump's electors had signed fraudulent ones. [81]   In the weeks before the certification, Mr. Trump began pressuring Mr. Pence to cooperate, both directly and by mobilizing Mr. Trump's supporters.

In repeated conversations, day after day, Mr. Trump pressed Mr. Pence to use his ministerial position as President of the Senate to change the election outcome, often by citing false claims of election fraud as justification; he even falsely told Mr. Pence that the "Justice Department [was] finding major infractions." [82]   When Mr. Pence repeatedly refused to act as Mr.

---

[78] SCO-00709557 at 159 (SJC Tr.); SCO-11542142 at 99 (Int. Tr.); *see also* SCO-00775937 at 125 (HSC Tr.).

[79] SCO-11517380 at 101-104 (Int. Tr.).

[80] *See* ECF No. 252 at 61 & n.324; SCO-01576281 at 2, SCO-01576283 at 2 (Email from Co-Conspirator 2, with attachment 10/16/2020); SCO-12986301.

[81] *See* ECF No. 252 at 65 & n.352; SCO-12184337, SCO-12184338 (Email and memo from Co-Conspirator 2 to Co-Conspirator 5 and Co-Conspirator 6 12/23/2020); SCO-12101300, SCO-12101301 (Email and memo from Co-Conspirator 2 to Co-Conspirator 6 01/03/2021).

[82] *See, e.g.,* ECF No. 1 at ¶ 90; *see* ECF No. 252 at 62-74; *see, e.g.,* SCO-00014655 at 157-182; SCO-00014442 at 29-43 (Pence, *So Help Me God* pp. 441-455); SCO-04982306 (Handwritten notes 12/25/2020); SCO-04982309

Trump wanted,[83] Mr. Trump told him that "hundreds of thousands" of people would "hate his guts" and think he was "stupid," and that Mr. Pence was "too honest."[84] Surrounding these communications, Mr. Trump frequently took to Twitter to exhort supporters to travel to Washington for January 6, such as when he tweeted on January 1, "The BIG Protest Rally in Washington, D.C., will take place at 11.00 A.M. on January 6th. Locational details to follow. StopTheSteal!"[85]

On January 4, two days before the certification proceeding, Mr. Trump arranged for Mr. Pence to meet with Co-Conspirator 2 in the Oval Office, in hopes that Co-Conspirator 2 could convince Mr. Pence to accede.[86] During the meeting, Co-Conspirator 2 outlined two ways that he claimed Mr. Pence could affect the election outcome using his role in the certification: he could reject the legitimate electors outright—denying Mr. Biden an electoral majority and likely sending the selection of the President to the House of Representatives, where fellow Republicans controlled the majority of state delegations—or he could send the elector slates to targeted states' legislatures for them to choose which electoral votes should be counted—affording Republican-controlled legislatures the opportunity to reject Mr. Biden's electors and replace them with Mr. Trump's.[87] In response to Mr. Pence's questioning, Co-Conspirator 2 admitted that both

---

(Handwritten notes 12/29/2020); SCO-04982313 (Handwritten notes 01/02/2021); SCO-04982315 (Handwritten notes 01/03/2021); SCO-04982330 (Handwritten notes 01/04/2021).

[83] *See, e.g.*, ECF No. 252 at 62 & nn.332-333, 63 & n.338, 65 & nn.349-350, 71 & nn.394-395; SCO-00014655 at 157-182; SCO-00014442 at 29-43 (Pence, *So Help Me God* pp. 441-455); SCO-04982330 (Handwritten notes 01/04/2021); SCO-04982320 at 2 (Handwritten notes 01/06/2021) (noting "I don't have the authority").

[84] *See* ECF No. 252 at 63 & n.338; SCO-00014442 at 34 (Pence, *So Help Me God* p. 446).

[85] *See, e.g.*, ECF No. 252 at 64 & n.340; SCO-00455068, SCO-12987393 (Donald J. Trump Tweet 01/01/2021); *see also, e.g.*, SCO-00455147, SCO-12987408 (Donald J. Trump Tweet 12/26/2020).

[86] *See* ECF No. 252 at 64 & nn.344-345, 65 & n.353; SCO-11618747 at 156-158, 166-169 (Text messages from Co-Conspirator 6 01/02/2021-01/05/2021); SCO-02301015 at 4 (Presidential Daily Diary 01/04/2021).

[87] *See* ECF No. 252 at 66 & n.362; SCO-00007167 at 50-51; SCO-11527024 at 187-189 (Int. Tr.); SCO-00016118 at 73-74; SCO-00014442 at 38-39 (Pence, *So Help Me God* pp. 450-451).

proposals violated the ECA and were untested.[88] When Mr. Pence turned to Mr. Trump and pointed out that even "[Mr. Trump's] lawyer," Co-Conspirator 2, did not think Mr. Pence had the authority to return electoral votes to the states, Mr. Trump responded that he "like[d] the other thing better," which Mr. Pence understood to mean Mr. Pence simply rejecting the electoral votes outright.[89] In the end, Mr. Pence again stated that he did not believe he could do what he was being asked.[90]

That night, Mr. Trump used a speech in Dalton, Georgia, to focus the crowd on the idea that Mr. Pence could change the results of the election, saying, "I hope Mike Pence comes through for us, I have to tell you. I hope that our great Vice President, our great Vice President comes through for us. . . . Of course, if he doesn't come through, I won't like him quite as much."[91] The next day, on January 5, when Mr. Trump again failed to make headway with Mr. Pence in a private conversation, Mr. Trump warned that he would have to publicly criticize Mr. Pence.[92] Mr. Trump then (in response to a *New York Times* report on the conversation between Mr. Trump and Mr. Pence) issued a false statement claiming, "The Vice President and I are in total agreement that the Vice President has the power to act."[93]

---

[88] *See* ECF No. 252 at 67 & n.363; SCO-00014442 at 38-39 (Pence, *So Help Me God* pp. 450-451); SCO-00007167 at 52-53; SCO-00016118 at 75-76.

[89] *See* ECF No. 252 at 67 & n.364; SCO-00014442 at 39 (Pence, *So Help Me God* p. 451); SCO-00007167 at 51; SCO-00016118 at 74-78.

[90] *See* ECF No. 252 at 67 & n.366; SCO-00014442 at 39 (Pence, *So Help Me God* p. 451); SCO-00007167 at 55-56.

[91] *See* ECF No. 252 at 68 & n.371; SCO-02235176 at 3 (Remarks by Mr. Trump at Victory Rally in Dalton, GA 01/04/2021); SCO-04976283 at 10:56-11:15 (Video of Dalton, GA speech 01/04/2021).

[92] *See* ECF No. 252 at 71 & nn.392-396; SCO-00016118 at 107-110; SCO-00014655 at 189, 193-200; SCO-00014442 at 41-42 (Pence, *So Help Me God* pp. 453-454); SCO-04982319 (Handwritten notes 01/05/2021).

[93] *See* ECF No. 252 at 72 & n.404; SCO-00444946 (Donald J. Trump Campaign Statement 01/05/2021); SCO-00016118 at 134-136; SCO-11545613 at 152-153 (Int. Tr.); SCO-00829440 at 222-225 (HSC Tr.); SCO-00810832 at 172-177 (HSC Tr.).

E.   Mr. Trump's Supporters Attack the United States Capitol

Mr. Trump's efforts to remain in power converged and culminated on January 6, the day that Mr. Biden was to be certified President. That day, Mr. Trump was scheduled to speak at the Ellipse to the crowd of supporters he had summoned to Washington with false claims of election fraud.[94] At around 1:00 a.m. on the morning of January 6, Mr. Trump tweeted: "If Vice President @Mike_Pence comes through for us, we will win the Presidency. Many States want to decertify the mistake they made in certifying incorrect & even fraudulent numbers in a process NOT approved by their State Legislatures (which it must be). Mike can send it back!"[95] Just before he left the White House to give his speech at the Ellipse, Mr. Trump phoned Mr. Pence one last time;[96] when Mr. Pence told Mr. Trump that he planned to issue a public statement making clear that he lacked the authority to do what Mr. Trump wanted, Mr. Trump expressed anger at him.[97] He then directed staffers to re-insert into his planned Ellipse speech some language that he had drafted earlier targeting Mr. Pence.[98]

---

[94] *See* ECF No. 252 at 136 & nn.631-632, 139-140 & nn.642-645; SCO-00454954, SCO-12987365 (Donald J. Trump Tweet 01/05/2021); SCO-00455147, SCO-12987408 (Donald J. Trump Tweet 12/26/2020); SCO-00455067, SCO-12987392 (Donald J. Trump Tweet 01/01/2021); SCO-00454979, SCO-12987370 (Donald J. Trump Tweet 01/04/2021).

[95] *See* ECF No. 252 at 72-73 & n.405, 137 & n.636; SCO-00454942, SCO-12987357 (Donald J. Trump Tweet 01/06/2021).

[96] *See* ECF No. 252 at 73 & n.410, 140 & n.646; SCO-00014442 at 47-48 (Pence, *So Help Me God* pp. 459-460); SCO-11532623 at 203 (Int. Tr.); SCO-11534332 at 211 (Int. Tr.).

[97] *See* ECF No. 252 at 73-74 & n.411, 140 & n.647; SCO-11522446 at 25 (Int. Rep.); SCO-00014655 at 206-207; SCO-00014442 at 47-48 (Pence, *So Help Me God* pp. 459-460); SCO-04982320 (Handwritten notes 01/06/2021).

[98] *See* ECF No. 252 at 74 & n.412, 140 & n.648; SCO-00013901 at 59-60; SCO-02241925 (Save America Rally Draft Speech 01/06/2021); SCO-00017298 at 135-139; SCO-00842413 at 163-165 (HSC Tr.); SCO-02343119 (Email among Speechwriting staff 01/06/2021); SCO-02343413 (Email from Speechwriter 01/06/2021); SCO-00006256 at 160; SCO-11522446 at 26 (Int. Rep.).

During his speech at the Ellipse,[99] Mr. Trump made one more attempt to retain power. In his remarks, Mr. Trump repeated many of the same lies he had been telling for months—regarding dead voters, non-citizen voters, and vote dumps—and he told newer ones: lies that targeted states wanted to change their electors and that Mr. Pence had the authority, and might be persuaded, to change the election results.[100] The lie regarding Mr. Pence was particularly deceptive because Mr. Trump knew what his supporters in the crowd did not: that Mr. Pence had just told him in no uncertain terms that he would not do what Mr. Trump was demanding.

Mr. Trump told the crowd—a crowd of his supporters that he had remarked to advisors the night before was "angry"[101]—that the election had been stolen and the country would no longer exist if this purported crime were not stopped; and that the discovery of "fraud" licensed them to "go by very different rules."[102] Although Mr. Trump at one point also told his supporters to "peacefully and patriotically make [their] voices heard,"[103] he used the word "fight" more than ten times in the speech before concluding by directing his supporters to march to the Capitol to give allied Members of Congress "the kind of pride and boldness they need to take back our

---

[99] Mr. Trump's speech at the Ellipse on January 6, 2021, was a Campaign event. The rally at which Mr. Trump spoke was planned and executed by private political supporters, and it was completely funded by a $2.1 million private donation. Mr. Trump promoted the event using the word "rally," a word connoting a private political effort, and Mr. Trump's White House staff recognized the event to be a private, unofficial exercise. Finally, the speech itself used campaign language and closely resembled Mr. Trump's other campaign speeches, including one he had given in Dalton, Georgia, for the Senate runoff election just two days earlier. *See* ECF No. 252 at 118-126 & nn.577-598.

[100] *See* ECF No. 252 at 75-76 & nn.423-428; SCO-02244118 at 3, 6, 11-12, 16-17 (Remarks by Mr. Trump at Save America Rally 01/06/2021).

[101] *See* ECF No. 1 at ¶ 98; SCO-00015613 at 155-156.

[102] *See* ECF No. 252 at 77 & nn.432-436; SCO-02244118 at 19-20 (Remarks by Mr. Trump at Save America Rally 01/06/2021).

[103] *See* SCO-02244118 at 6 (Remarks by Mr. Trump at Save America Rally 01/06/2021).

country."[104] He also told the angry crowd that "if you don't fight like hell, you're not going to have a country anymore."[105] Throughout the speech, Mr. Trump gave his supporters false hope that through such action, they could cause Mr. Pence to overturn the election results, even improvising new lines directed at Mr. Pence as the speech went on.[106]

At Mr. Trump's urging, thousands of his supporters marched from the Ellipse to the Capitol building.[107] There, Mr. Pence began the certification at around 1:00 p.m.[108] Outside the building, the crowd swelled and broke through barriers cordoning off the grounds.[109] The crowd that attacked the Capitol was filled with Mr. Trump's supporters, as made clear by their Trump shirts, signs, and flags.[110] As described in detail below, the crowd violently attacked the law enforcement officers attempting to secure the building.[111]

---

[104] See ECF No. 252 at 77-78 & nn.432-443; SCO-02244118 at 5, 6, 9, 22 (Remarks by Mr. Trump at Save America Rally 01/06/2021).

[105] See ECF No. 252 at 77-78 & nn.432-443; SCO-02244118 at 22 (Remarks by Mr. Trump at Save America Rally 01/06/2021).

[106] See ECF No. 252 at 76 & nn.430-431; SCO-02244118 at 3 (Remarks by Mr. Trump at Save America Rally 01/06/2021); compare SCO-02244118 at 16 (Remarks by Mr. Trump at Save America Rally 01/06/2021) with SCO-00745151 at 12 (Save America Rally teleprompter speech 01/06/2021).

[107] See ECF No. 252 at 78 & n.444; see also, e.g., SCO-11506080 at 01:09:30 (Video of Save America Rally 01/06/2021); SCO-12918852 (Video of March to Capitol 01/06/2021); SCO-12919559 at 01:30-02:52 (Video of March to Capitol 01/06/2021); SCO-06614619 at 21:13-22:07 (Video of Fox News Coverage 01/06/2021).

[108] See ECF No. 252 at 78 & n.445; SCO-12945127 at 20:47 (Video of House Floor 01/06/2021); SCO-03666330 at 2 (Congressional Record 01/06/2021).

[109] See ECF No. 252 at 78 & n.448; see also, e.g., SCO-12876233 at 02:20-03:50 (Video of Capitol Riot 01/06/2021).

[110] See ECF No. 252 at 78-79 & n.450, 82 & n.477; SCO-12806961 at 56:56, SCO-12919902 at 38:59, SCO-00029113, SCO-12738292, SCO-12806977 at 04:30 (Videos of Capitol Riot 01/06/2021); see also SCO-11506096 at 61-63 (Int. Tr.).

[111] See ECF No. 252 at 82 & nn.475-477; see also, e.g., SCO-12919902 at 38:48, SCO-12738292, SCO-12806977 at 04:30, SCO-12738332, SCO-12919680 at 54:30 (Videos of Capitol Riot 01/06/2021).

Photograph of the Capitol on January 6, 2021 (John Manchillo/AP)[112]

Photograph of the Capitol on January 6, 2021 (Ken Cedeno/UPI)[113]

---

[112] Perry Stein, Aaron C. Davis, Spencer S. Hsu, and Tom Jackman, *FBI did not have undercover agents at Jan. 6 riots, watchdog says,* WASH. POST (Dec. 12, 2024), https://www.washingtonpost.com/national-security/2024/12/12/fbi-jan-6-report/.

[113] Doug Cunningham, *Jan. 6 rioters face criminal penalties as sentences, convictions mount,* UNITED PRESS INTERNATIONAL, INC. (June 2, 2023), https://www.upi.com/Top_News/US/2023/06/02/Jan-6-rioters-sentences-convictions/1151685561006/.

Photograph of the Capitol on January 6, 2021 (Shannon Stapleton/Reuters)[114]

Photograph of the Capitol on January 6, 2021 (Lev Radin/Pacific
Press/LightRocket/Getty Images)[115]

---

[114] *Harrowing scenes from the Jan 6 U.S. Capitol attack,* REUTERS (Oct. 13, 2022),
https://www.reuters.com/news/picture/harrowing-scenes-from-the-jan-6-us-capit-idUSRTSC60V8/.

[115] Aaron Blake, *More Republicans now call Jan. 6 a 'legitimate protest' than a 'riot,'* WASH. POST (July 7, 2022),
https://www.washingtonpost.com/politics/2022/07/07/many-republicans-no-longer-call-jan-6-an-insurrection-or-
even-riot/.

Photograph of the Capitol on January 6, 2021 (David Butow/Redux)[116]

Photograph of the Capitol on January 6, 2021 (Roberto Schmidt/AFP via Getty Images)[117]

---

[116] Statement from Leaders, Updated: 'Our Children Are Watching': Nonprofit and Foundation Leaders Respond to Capitol Hill Violence, THE CHRONICLE OF PHILANTHROPY (Jan. 7, 2021), https://www.philanthropy.com/article/how-nonprofit-and-foundation-leaders-are-responding-to-capitol-hill-violence.

[117] Eric Westervelt, *Off-Duty Police Officers Investigated, Charged With Participating In Capitol Riot*, NPR (Jan. 15, 2021), https://www.npr.org/2021/01/15/956896923/police-officers-across-nation-face-federal-charges-for-involvement-in-capitol-ri.

After his speech, Mr. Trump returned to the White House and, at around 1:30 p.m.,
settled in the dining room off of the Oval Office.[118] There, he watched television news coverage
of events at the Capitol and reviewed Twitter on his phone.[119] When the angry crowd advanced
on the Capitol building and breached it at around 2:13 p.m., forcing the Senate to recess,[120]
several of Mr. Trump's advisors rushed to the dining room and told him that a riot had started at
the Capitol and that rioters were in the building.[121] Over the course of the afternoon, they
forcefully urged Mr. Trump to issue calming messages to his supporters.[122] Mr. Trump resisted,
repeatedly remarking that the people at the Capitol were angry because the election had been
stolen.[123]

Just before 2:24 p.m., the news channel playing on the television in the dining room
where Mr. Trump was sitting aired an interview with an individual marching from the Ellipse to
the Capitol, who expressed his anger at Mr. Pence and stated, "But I still believe President

---

[118] See ECF No. 252 at 79 & n.452; SCO-00783547 at 36-39 (HSC Tr.); SCO-00015613 at 180.

[119] See ECF No. 252 at 79 & nn.451-452; SCO-00783547 at 38-39 (HSC Tr.); SCO-11528445 at 52-53 (Int. Tr.); SCO-00015613 at 183-185; SCO-00006256 at 164, 168; SCO-11522446 at 26 (Int. Rep.); SCO-00481112 (Spreadsheet of Data from Mr. Trump's White House Phone).

[120] See ECF No. 252 at 79 & n.453; SCO-12881998 at 01:04-01:25 (Video of Senate Wing Door CCTV 01/06/2021); SCO-12945145 at 44:16-44:36 (Video of Senate Floor 01/06/2021).

[121] See ECF No. 252 at 141 & n.653; SCO-00006256 at 163-166; SCO-00015002 at 37-38; SCO-00686662 at 117-119 (HSC Tr.) (recalling entering the dining room with Mr. Trump and conveying "this was a situation now out of control" while they were "all fixated on the television set"); SCO-11532623 at 222-228, 235 (Int. Tr.) (recalling Mr. Trump being told about riot at Capitol); SCO-00003294 at 114.

[122] See, e.g., ECF No. 252 at 141-142 & nn.653, 663; SCO-00015613 at 194-201; SCO-00003294 at 115-116, 121-123, 131-132; SCO-11511407 at 227-228 (Int. Tr.); SCO-00006256 at 164-166, 174; SCO-11522446 at 26 (Int. Rep.) (recalling presenting Mr. Trump with draft language for a statement that was never published); SCO-00015002 at 38; SCO-11542142 at 134-135 (Int. Tr.) ("I thought that the President had to issue a strong statement, quickly, telling everybody to leave the Capitol, and condemning what was going on there."); SCO-11532623 at 240, 262-265 (Int. Tr.) (recalling a staffer entering the dining room and telling Mr. Trump to "call for calm" and asking Mr. Trump's daughter to "come in to help advocate with the President").

[123] See ECF No. 252 at 141 & n.654; SCO-00006256 at 164-166; SCO-00015613 at 189, 202-203; SCO-00011109 at 179-182; SCO-11534332 at 193-194 (Int. Tr.) (recalling Mr. Trump commenting to House Minority Leader that "a lot of these people are upset with the election . . . they felt like it was stolen from him" and that "maybe these people are more upset about the election results than you are").

Trump has something else left."[124] Then, at 2:24 p.m., sitting alone, Mr. Trump issued a Tweet attacking Mr. Pence and fueling the riot: "Mike Pence didn't have the courage to do what should have been done to protect our Country and our Constitution, giving States a chance to certify a corrected set of facts, not the fraudulent or inaccurate ones which they were asked to previously certify. USA demands the truth!"[125] One minute later, the United States Secret Service was forced to evacuate Mr. Pence to a secure location at the Capitol.[126] When an advisor at the White House learned this, he rushed to the dining room and informed Mr. Trump, who replied "So what?"[127]

The rioters at the Capitol had been motivated and directed by Mr. Trump, and he continued to resist advisors' requests to direct them to leave. Throughout the afternoon, crowds at the Capitol hunted for Mr. Pence and other lawmakers, with some chanting, "Hang Mike Pence!"[128] At 2:38 p.m. and 3:30 p.m., Mr. Trump issued two Tweets falsely suggesting that events at the Capitol were "peaceful" and asking individuals there (whom he termed "WE") to remain that way: "Please support our Capitol Police and Law Enforcement. They are truly on the side of our Country. Stay Peaceful!" and, "I am asking for everyone at the U.S. Capitol to remain peaceful. No violence! Remember, WE are the Party of Law & Order—respect the Law

---

[124] See ECF No. 252 at 79-80 & nn.452, 460; SCO-06614619 at 21:45-22:42 (Video of Fox News Coverage 01/06/2021).

[125] See ECF No. 252 at 80 & n.462, 141 & nn.655, 657; SCO-00456476, SCO-12987690 (Donald J. Trump Tweet 01/06/2021); SCO-00015613 at 188-189, 196-198; SCO-00011109 at 160-161.

[126] See ECF No. 252 at 81 & n.465, 141 & n.658; SCO-00029459 (Video of Pence Evacuation 01/06/2021).

[127] See ECF No. 252 at 142 & n.662; SCO-00009250 at 214-220.

[128] See ECF No. 252 at 81 & n.466; SCO-12876211, SCO-12738313, SCO-12738317, SCO-12738306, SCO-12738312 at 00:59-01:40 (Videos of Capitol Riot 01/06/2021).

and our great men and women in Blue. Thank you!"[129] At 4:17 p.m., he tweeted a video message in which he for the first time asked his supporters to leave the Capitol—while at the same time falsely claiming that "[w]e had an election that was stolen from us . . . a landslide election," and embracing the people who had attacked the Capitol, telling them "we love you, you're very special."[130] And at 6:01 p.m., he tweeted, "These are the things and events that happen when a sacred landslide election victory is so unceremoniously & viciously stripped away from great patriots who have been badly & unfairly treated for so long. Go home with love & in peace. Remember this day forever!"[131]

At around the same time as he issued his 6:01 p.m. Tweet, Mr. Trump tried to reach two United States Senators, and he also directed Co-Conspirator 1 to call Members of Congress and attempt to enlist them to further delay the certification.[132] When Mr. Trump's White House Counsel called him at around 7:00 p.m. and asked him to withdraw any objections to the certification, Mr. Trump refused.[133] Nonetheless, the certification resumed late in the evening of

---

[129] See ECF No. 252 at 142 & nn.664-665; SCO-00454933, SCO-04963517, SCO-00454932, SCO-04963518 (Donald J. Trump Tweets 01/06/2021).

[130] See ECF No. 252 at 143 & n.666; SCO-00456473 (Video of Rose Garden Speech 01/06/2021); SCO-12876968 (Draft Tr. of Rose Garden Speech 01/06/2021).

[131] See ECF No. 252 at 143 & n.667; SCO-00456472, SCO-12987689 (Donald J. Trump Tweet 01/06/2021).

[132] See ECF No. 226 at ¶ 97(c) and (d); ECF No. 252 at 83-84 & nn.485-492; SCO-12706940 at row 1383 (Spreadsheet of Executive Assistant's text messages); SCO-02131850 at 2392 (Toll Records 01/06/2021); SCO-00009250 at 234-235; SCO-11616952 (Email from Executive Assistant 01/06/2021); SCO-00404535 (Text Message from Co-Conspirator 6 01/06/2021); SCO-11520423 (Co-Conspirator 1 Toll Analysis 01/06/2021); SCO-02035182 at 5396-5397 (Co-Conspirator 1 Toll Records 01/06/2021); SCO-02054919 at 71 (Co-Conspirator 1 Toll Records 01/06/2021); SCO-04134777 (Voicemail from Co-Conspirator 1 01/06/2021) (telling Senator, "We need you, our Republican friends, to try to just slow it down so we can get these legislatures to get more information to you. And I know they're reconvening at eight tonight but the only strategy we can follow is to object to numerous states and raise issues so that we get ourselves into tomorrow—ideally until the end of tomorrow."); SCO-06475675 (Voicemail from Co-Conspirator 1 01/06/2021) (asking Senator to "object to every state and kind of spread this out a little bit like a filibuster").

[133] See ECF No. 1 at ¶ 120; SCO-00003294 at 141-143; SCO-02301375 at 4 (Presidential Daily Diary 01/06/2021).

January 6 and, at 3:41 a.m. on January 7, Mr. Pence announced the certified results of the 2020 presidential election in favor of Mr. Biden. [134]

As he did in his 4:17 p.m. and 6:01 p.m. Tweets on January 6, Mr. Trump has provided additional evidence of his intent by continuing to support and ally himself with the people who attacked the Capitol. He has called them "patriots"[135] and "hostages,"[136] reminisced about January 6 as a "beautiful day,"[137] and championed the "January 6 Choir,"[138] a group of January 6 defendants who, because of their dangerousness, are detained at the District of Columbia jail. [139]

---

[134] See ECF No. 252 at 85 & n.495; SCO-04955950 at 19:14-20:34 (Video of Congress Joint Session 01/06/2021); SCO-03666330 at 41 (Congressional Record 01/06/2021).

[135] See ECF No. 252 at 83 & n.478; SCO-04976301 at 16:52-17:02 (Video of Waco Rally 03/25/2023); SCO-04976442 at 48:29-48:44 (Video of Mr. Trump at Faith and Freedom Coalition 06/17/2022); SCO-04976291 at 16:42-16:58 (Video of Trump Interview 02/01/2022).

[136] See ECF No. 252 at 83 & n.479; SCO-12982756 at 35:50-36:22 (Video of Greensboro Rally 03/02/2024).

[137] See ECF No. 252 at 83 & n.481; SCO-12851309 at 45:18-45:40 (Video of Trump Interview 08/23/2023); SCO-04958191 at 7 (CNN Town Hall Tr. 05/10/2023).

[138] See ECF No. 252 at 83 & nn.482-483; SCO-04976301 at 03:00-05:35 (Video of Waco Rally 03/25/2023); SCO-12982756 at 35:50-36:21 (Video of Greensboro Rally 03/02/2024).

[139] See United States v. Nichols, No. 21-mj-29, ECF No. 9 (E.D. Tex. Jan. 25, 2021) (ordering pretrial detention in prosecution of defendant who later became a member of the "January 6 choir"); United States v. Nichols, No. 21-cr-117, ECF No. 75 (D.D.C. Dec. 23, 2021) (denying defendant's motion for pretrial release); id., ECF No. 307 at 27 n.10, 35-36 (D.D.C. Apr. 30, 2024) (government sentencing memorandum referencing defendant's involvement in "January 6 choir"); see also United States v. Mink, No. 21-mj-105, ECF No. 19 (W.D. Pa. Jan. 29, 2021) (in prosecution of defendant who later became a member of the "January 6 choir," ordering defendant's pretrial detention); United States v. Mink, No. 21-cr-25, ECF No. 45 (D.D.C. Dec. 13, 2021) (court order denying defendant's motion to revoke pretrial detention); United States v. Sandlin, No. 21-mj-110, ECF No. 8 (D. Nev. Feb. 3, 2021) (ordering pretrial detention in prosecution of defendant who later became a member of the "January 6 choir"); United States v. Sandlin, No. 21-cr-88, ECF No. 31 (D.D.C. Apr. 13, 2021) (denying defendant's motion for release on bond); id., ECF Nos. 44, 44-1 (D.D.C. Aug. 31, 2021) (mandate return following denial of defendant's appeal of pretrial detention order); United States v. Shively, No. 21-cr-151, ECF No. 42 (D.D.C. May 9, 2022) (in prosecution of defendant who later became a member of the "January 6 choir," revoking conditions of release and ordering pretrial detention); United States v. Khater, No. 21-cr-222, ECF No. 25 (D.D.C. May 12, 2021) (in prosecution of defendant who later became a member of the "January 6 choir," denying defendant's motion for release from custody); United States v. McGrew, No. 21-cr-398, ECF No. 40 (D.D.C. Nov. 2, 2021) (order of detention pending trial in prosecution of defendant who later became a member of the "January 6 choir").

II.   THE LAW

Based on the above facts, and after analyzing the relevant criminal statutes, the Office sought, and a grand jury found probable cause for, an indictment of Mr. Trump on four federal charges: conspiring to obstruct the governmental function of selecting and certifying the President of the United States, in violation of 18 U.S.C. § 371; obstructing and attempting to obstruct the official proceeding on January 6, 2021, in violation of 18 U.S.C. § 1512(c)(2); conspiring to obstruct the official proceeding, in violation of 18 U.S.C. § 1512(k); and conspiring to violate the federal rights of citizens to vote and have their votes counted, in violation of 18 U.S.C. § 241. Because of the unprecedented facts and the variety of legal issues that would be litigated in this case, the Office was aware that the case would involve litigation risks, as would any case of this scope and complexity. However, after an exhaustive and detailed review of the law, the Office concluded that the charges were well supported and would survive any legal challenges absent a change in the law as it existed at the time of indictment.

As set forth in Section V.D below, after the original indictment was returned, the Supreme Court ruled in *Trump v. United States*, 603 U.S. 593 (2024), that Mr. Trump had absolute immunity for core presidential conduct, enjoyed a rebuttable presumption of immunity for other official presidential acts, and had no immunity for unofficial conduct. *Id.* at 606, 609, 614-615.

The Supreme Court's decision required the Office to reanalyze the evidence it had collected. The original indictment alleged that Mr. Trump, as the incumbent President, used all available tools and powers, both private and official, to overturn the legitimate results of the election despite notice, including from official advisors, that his fraud claims were false and he had lost the election. Given the Supreme Court's ruling, the Office reevaluated the evidence and assessed whether Mr. Trump's non-immune conduct—either his private conduct as a candidate or official conduct for which the Office could rebut the presumption of immunity—violated federal law. The Office concluded that it did. After doing so, the Office sought, and a new grand jury issued, a superseding indictment with identical charges but based only on conduct that was not immune because it was either unofficial or any presumptive immunity could be rebutted. This section reviews the federal laws violated by Mr. Trump's non-immunized conduct.

A.   Conspiracy to Defraud the United States (18 U.S.C. § 371)

The defraud clause of the general conspiracy statute makes it a crime "[i]f two or more persons conspire . . . to defraud the United States, or any agency thereof in any manner or for any purpose, and one or more of such persons do any act to effect the object of the conspiracy." 18 U.S.C. § 371. The defraud clause applies not just to schemes to cheat the government out of money or property, but also to schemes "to interfere with or obstruct one of its lawful governmental functions by deceit, craft or trickery, or at least by means that are dishonest." *Hammerschmidt v. United States*, 265 U.S. 182, 188 (1924). Under longstanding, established precedent, the government must prove the following elements to establish a violation of the defraud clause: (1) the defendant "entered into an agreement, (2) to obstruct a lawful function of the government or an agency of the government, (3) by deceitful or dishonest means, and (4) at least one overt act was taken in furtherance of that conspiracy." *United States v. Concord Mgmt. & Consulting LLC*, 347 F. Supp. 3d 38, 46 (D.D.C. 2018) (citation and quotations omitted); *see also Hammerschmidt*, 265 U.S. at 188; *United States v. Dean*, 55 F.3d 640, 647 (D.C. Cir. 1995). The Office concluded that Mr. Trump's conduct satisfied each of these established elements of a defraud-clause offense.

The process of selecting and certifying the President, as described above and prescribed by the Constitution and federal law, is plainly a lawful function of the federal government. *Cf. Ray v. Blair*, 343 U.S. 214, 224 (1952) (noting that "[t]he presidential electors exercise a federal function"); *Burroughs v. United States*, 290 U.S. 534, 545 (1934) (stating that electors "exercise federal functions under, and discharge duties in virtue of authority conferred by, the Constitution of the United States"); *United States v. Brock*, 94 F.4th 39, 51 (D.C. Cir. 2024) (noting the "unique congressional function of certifying electoral college votes"). Indeed, Mr. Trump never challenged the indictment on that basis, though he filed more than 100 pages in support of dismissal motions. As the court of appeals found in the context of the immunity litigation in this case, "[f]ormer President Trump's alleged efforts to remain in power despite losing the 2020 election were, if proven, an unprecedented assault on the structure of our government." *United States v. Trump*, 91 F.4th 1173, 1199 (D.C. Cir. 2024), *vacated and remanded on other grounds*, 603 U.S. 593 (2024). Mr. Trump also sought to obstruct the certification; his sole objective was to ensure that no one other than himself was certified as the President. Nor is there any doubt that Mr. Trump conspired with others to achieve his goal, and that at least one overt act was committed.

With three of the four elements of a Section 371 violation established, the Office anticipated that a central dispute at trial would be whether Mr. Trump pursued his obstructive purpose by "deceit, craft or trickery, or at least by means that are dishonest." *Hammerschmidt*, 265 U.S. at 188. The Office concluded that the evidence established beyond a reasonable doubt that he did.

The core of Mr. Trump's obstructive scheme was a false narrative of outcome-determinative voter fraud, which he and his surrogates frequently repeated and widely disseminated over the course of two months. Crucially, not only was Mr. Trump's voter-fraud narrative objectively false—he knew that it was false. Mr. Trump's false claims were repeatedly debunked, often directly to him by the very people best positioned to ascertain their truth. Campaign personnel told Mr. Trump his claims were unfounded; so did state officials, a White

35

House official who engaged with Mr. Trump in his capacity as a candidate, and even his own running mate.[140] For example, Mr. Trump's Campaign Manager informed him that a claim that had been circulating—that a substantial number of non-citizens had voted in Arizona—was false.[141] State officials issued public statements dispelling Mr. Trump's claims of widespread election fraud.[142] Georgia's Secretary of State refuted multiple false claims of election fraud directly to Mr. Trump, including the false allegation that 5,000 dead people had voted in Georgia.[143] When Mr. Trump raised various fraud allegations with Michigan's Senate Majority Leader, he was told that he had lost because he had underperformed with educated females.[144] Vice President Pence told Mr. Trump that he had seen no evidence of outcome-determinative fraud in the election.[145] And, tellingly, a Senior Advisor reiterated to Mr. Trump that Co-Conspirator 1 would be unable to prove his false fraud allegations in court, to which Mr. Trump responded, "The details don't matter."[146]

Courts in which Mr. Trump brought numerous lawsuits all rebuffed his claims, which in some instances prompted him to issue public rebukes acknowledging those decisions.[147] Still

---

[140] *See* ECF No. 252 at 11-12 & nn.34-40, 13-14 & nn.45-51, 17-18 & n.69, 24 & nn.112-113, 29-30 & nn.136-144, 32-33 & nn.159-160, 38 & nn.189-191, 39 & n.200, 46-47 & nn.241-244; *see also* SCO-00006256 at 46-50, 70-77; SCO-12920242 at 1-7 (Int. Rep.); SCO-00014655 at 38-44, 63-66, 91-96, 98-102; SCO-00016750 at 58-63; SCO-11509251 at 40-42 (Int. Tr.); SCO-12998394 at 4, 6-10 (Tr. of Georgia Secretary of State Call 01/02/2021); SCO-00829361 at 15-17 (HSC Tr.); SCO-00016926 at 20-22; SCO-00003548 at 171; SCO-00009955 at 109-112.

[141] *See* ECF No. 226 at ¶ 18; ECF No. 252 at 17-18 & n.69; SCO-00016750 at 58-63.

[142] *See* ECF No. 226 at ¶ 13; ECF No. 252 at 14 & nn.52-53; *see also supra* at n.12.

[143] *See* ECF No. 252 at 29-30 & nn.136-144; SCO-12998394 at 4, 6-10 (Tr. of Georgia Secretary of State Call 01/02/2021).

[144] *See* ECF No. 252 at 32-33 & nn.159-160; SCO-00829361 at 15-17 (HSC Tr.).

[145] *See* ECF No. 252 at 12 & n.40; SCO-00014655 at 38-44.

[146] *See* ECF No. 252 at 11-12 & nn.34-35; SCO-00006256 at 46-49; SCO-12920242 at 1, 4 (Int. Rep.).

[147] *See* ECF No. 252 at 36 & nn.181-182, 41 & nn.208-210, 44-45 & nn.225-230; *see also, e.g., Law v. Whitmer*, No. 20OC001631B, Order at 13-24, 28-34 (Nev. Dist. Ct. Dec. 4, 2020), https://electioncases.osu.edu/wp-content/uploads/2020/11/Law-v-Gloria-Order-Granting-Motion-to-Dismiss.pdf [https://perma.cc/32U2-BTA6];

other federal and state officials—some appointed by Mr. Trump, and others who publicly supported and voted for him—publicly debunked allegations of outcome-determinative voter fraud. [148] Mr. Trump did not reach out to any of these officials to ask relevant questions about the election because he was not seeking honest answers. This was a pattern revealed throughout the investigation: Mr. Trump unquestioningly accepted at face value and amplified election fraud claims that benefited his quest to retain power. Conversely, he avoided consulting informed sources, such as state election officials, who possessed evidence that could debunk his claims. The Office concluded that this consistent pattern would constitute powerful proof at trial that Mr. Trump knew the claims he was making were false.

Mr. Trump's false claims were often divergent from one day to the next and otherwise internally inconsistent. [149] For example, in Arizona, the conspirators started with the allegation that 36,000 non-citizens voted in that state; [150] five days later, it was "beyond credulity that a few hundred thousand didn't vote"; [151] three weeks later, "the bare minimum [was] 40 or 50,000. The reality is about 250,000"; [152] days after that, the assertion was 32,000; [153] and ultimately, the

---

Trump v. Biden, 394 Wis. 2d 629, 633 (Wis. 2020); SCO-00455197, SCO-00455196, SCO-00455195, SCO-12987423, SCO-12987422, SCO-12987421 (Donald J. Trump Tweets 12/21/2020).

[148] *See* ECF No. 252 at 14 & nn.52-53, 20 & nn.86-87, 23 & n.106, 33 & n.165, 38 & n.192, 42 & n.212, 42-43 & n.216, 46 & nn.238-239; *see also supra* at n.12; SCO-04976277 (Video of Georgia Secretary of State Press Conference 12/07/2020); SCO-11509450 at 103-104 (Int. Tr.); SCO-03036930 (Joint Statement on Election Security 11/12/2020); SCO-04952679 (Tweet 11/17/2020); SCO-07167983 (Email from GOP Comms Alert circulating Associated Press article titled "Barr: No evidence of fraud that'd change election outcome" 12/01/2020).

[149] *See* ECF No. 252 at 15 & nn.55-59; SCO-04976384 at 20:46-21:05 (Common Sense episode 89 11/25/2020); SCO-04976459 at 02:06:23-02:07:00 (Video of Arizona State Hearing 11/30/2020); SCO-06628641 at 18:52-19:42 (War Room episode 608 12/24/2020); SCO-06628646 at 35:19-35:45 (War Room episode 625 01/02/2021).

[150] *See* ECF No. 252 at 15 & n.55; SCO-04976384 at 20:46-21:05 (Common Sense episode 89 11/25/2020).

[151] *See* ECF No. 252 at 15 & n.56; SCO-04976459 at 02:06:23-02:07:00 (Video of Arizona State Hearing 11/30/2020).

[152] *See* ECF No. 252 at 15 & n.57; SCO-06628641 at 18:52-19:42 (War Room episode 608 12/24/2020).

[153] *See* ECF No. 252 at 15 & n.58; SCO-06628646 at 35:19-35:45 (War Room episode 625 01/02/2021).

conspirators landed back where they started, at 36,000—a false figure that they never verified or corroborated.[154] And in Georgia, the conspirators initially suggested that a large enough number of dead voters had cast ballots to overcome Mr. Trump's losing margin of about 12,000 voters;[155] one month later, the number was 10,315;[156] three days after that, the assertion was "close to 5,000 people";[157] and then two days later, the number bounced back to 10,315.[158] Mr. Trump bears legal responsibility for each of these false claims because they were made by him and his co-conspirators in furtherance of the conspiracy that he led. *See Salinas v. United States*, 522 U.S. 52, 63-64 (1997) ("The partners in the criminal plan must agree to pursue the same criminal objective and may divide up the work, yet each is responsible for the acts of each other."); *see also* Fed. R. Evid. 801(d)(2)(E) (statement by an opposing party's "conspirator during and in furtherance of the conspiracy" is admissible against that party); *United States v. Brockenborrugh*, 575 F.3d 726, 735 (D.C. Cir. 2009); *United States v. Tarantino*, 846 F.2d 1384, 1411-1412 (D.C. Cir. 1988).

The Office developed further evidence of Mr. Trump's knowledge that his claims were untrue from witnesses who reported that he planned to use fraud claims before the election had even happened. For instance, in advance of the election, advisors told Mr. Trump that the election would be close and that initial returns might be misleading, showing an early lead for Mr. Trump that would diminish as mail-in ballots were counted. In response, Mr. Trump suggested that if that prediction were true—which it ultimately was—he would simply declare

---

[154] *See* ECF No. 252 at 15 & n.59; SCO-04976283 at 01:04:04-01:04:13 (Video of Dalton, GA speech 01/04/2021); SCO-02244118 at 17 (Remarks by Mr. Trump at Save America Rally 01/06/2021).

[155] *See* ECF No. 252 at 21 & n.96; SCO-04976323 at 22:43-23:51 (Video of Trump Interview 11/29/2020).

[156] SCO-04976407 at 03:29:00-03:29:34 (Video of Georgia Senate Judiciary Subcommittee Hearing 12/30/2020).

[157] *See* ECF No. 252 at 30 & n.142; SCO-12998394 at 3 (Tr. of Georgia Secretary of State Call 01/02/2021).

[158] *See* ECF No. 252 at 122-123 & n.592; SCO-04976283 at 53:25-53:59 (Video of Dalton, GA speech 01/04/2021).

victory before all ballots were counted and a winner was projected.[159] He also made repeated public statements in the lead-up to election day in which he sowed public doubt in the election results, setting the stage for his later fraud claims.[160] And Mr. Trump made his first statement claiming fraud in the election only hours after polls closed—when no investigations had begun, much less concluded.[161]

Mr. Trump's intent in spreading knowing falsehoods was further evidenced by statements he made to those around him. In private—in contrast with his public false claims—Mr. Trump made admissions that reflected his understanding that he had lost. In a private moment, Mr. Trump confessed to his family members that "it doesn't matter if you won or lost the election. You still have to fight like hell."[162] When President-elect Biden appeared on television in November, Mr. Trump said to a staffer, "can you believe I lost to this f'ing guy?"[163] And when his own Vice President declined to join the conspiracy, Mr. Trump berated him for being "too honest."[164]

Because the evidence showed that Mr. Trump knew his claims were false, it amply satisfied the mens rea standard for a Section 371 charge, which would be satisfied by evidence that Mr. Trump either knew his fraud claims were false or that he acted with deliberate disregard for their truth or falsity. The concept of deliberate disregard—sometimes referred to as reckless

---

[159] *See* ECF No. 252 at 5 & nn.2-4; SCO-11621981 at 74-83, 92-93 (Int. Tr.); SCO-00016750 at 14-18, 27-30; SCO-00006819 at 9-12, 19-20; SCO-00003548 at 8-29; SCO-00016118 at 144-145.

[160] *See* ECF No. 252 at 6 & nn.5-10; SCO-00712149 at 37:20 (Video of Trump Interview on Fox News 07/19/2020); SCO-12998418 (Donald J. Trump Tweet 07/30/2020); SCO-12992141 at 57:33 (Video of Oshkosh, WI Rally 08/17/2020); SCO-12992142 at 22:08 (Video of Trump Speech 08/24/2020); SCO-12992143 at 03:11-03:28 (Video of Trump Statement 10/27/2020).

[161] *See* ECF No. 252 at 7 8 & n.16; SCO-04976258 (Video of White House Speech 11/04/2020).

[162] *See* ECF No. 252 at 14-15 & n.54; SCO-00009250 at 156; SCO-11529771 at 99-102 (Int. Tr.).

[163] SCO-11521307 at 88 (Int. Tr.).

[164] *See* ECF No. 252 at 63 & n.338; SCO-00014442 at 34 (Pence, *So Help Me God* p. 446).

disregard, or reckless or deliberate indifference—has deep roots in the law of fraud. *See U.S. ex rel. Schutte v. SuperValu Inc.*, 598 U.S. 739, 750-752 (2023); 1 J. Story, *Commentaries on Equity Jurisprudence* § 193 (10th ed. 1870) ("Whether the party, thus misrepresenting a material fact, knew it to be false, or made the assertion without knowing whether it were true or false, is wholly immaterial; for the affirmation of what one does not know or believe to be true is equally, in morals and law, as unjustifiable as the affirmation of what is known to be positively false."). That concept is reflected in case law and jury instructions for the District of Columbia, as well as precedent from every other circuit. *See, e.g., United States v. Philip Morris USA Inc.*, 566 F.3d 1095, 1121 (D.C. Cir. 2009); 1 Criminal Jury Instructions for the District of Columbia 5.200 (2024).[165] Here, the evidence showed that Mr. Trump decided, even before the election, that he would allege outcome-determinative fraud, whether it occurred or not, if he were not declared the winner, and he adhered to that plan—repeating false claims that he knew to be untrue.

Although Mr. Trump's conduct fell comfortably within the established elements of a defraud-clause offense, the Office noted that the Supreme Court has in several recent decisions limited the reach of other federal fraud and obstruction statutes. *See, e.g., Ciminelli v. United States*, 598 U.S. 306 (2023) (reversing conviction of construction contractor for wire fraud, 18 U.S.C. § 1343, for scheming with public official to tailor bid requirements for government contracts to favor himself because the government did not prove the defendant deprived the victim of a traditional property interest); *Kelly v. United States*, 590 U.S. 391 (2020) (reversing

---

[165] *See also, e.g., United States v. Correia*, 55 F.4th 12, 26 (1st Cir. 2022); *Knickerbocker Merchandising Co. v. United States*, 13 F.2d 544, 546 (2d Cir. 1926); *United States v. Coyle*, 63 F.3d 1239, 1243 (3d Cir. 1995); *United States v. Hester*, 880 F.2d 799, 803 (4th Cir. 1989); *United States v. Dillman*, 15 F.3d 384, 392-393 (5th Cir. 1994); *United States v. Kennedy*, 714 F.3d 951, 958 (6th Cir. 2013); *United States v. Schwartz*, 787 F.2d 257, 265 (7th Cir. 1986); *United States v. Marley*, 549 F.2d 561, 563-564 (8th Cir. 1977) ("It must also be noted that the courts have long recognized that scienter may be established where reckless disregard of truth or falsity is present."); *United States v. Dearing*, 504 F.3d 897, 903 (9th Cir. 2007); *United States v. Cochran*, 109 F.3d 660, 665 (10th Cir. 1997); *United States v. Clay*, 832 F.3d 1259, 1311 (11th Cir. 2016).

convictions for wire fraud, 18 U.S.C. § 1343, and federal program fraud, 18 U.S.C. § 666, where defendants aimed to inflict political retribution on mayor by closing lanes of a bridge that served the mayor's city because the object of the scheme was not to obtain money or property); *Skilling v. United States*, 561 U.S. 358 (2010) (paring back honest-services fraud statute, 18 U.S.C. § 1346, to reach only core bribery and kickbacks and reversing conviction of executive who was convicted of making false statements to inflate his company's value but was not alleged to have taken bribes or kickbacks for his efforts); *Arthur Andersen LLP v. United States*, 544 U.S. 696 (2005) (requiring showing of knowingly corrupt conduct under obstruction of justice statute, 18 U.S.C. § 1512(b)(2), and reversing conviction of accounting firm convicted of shredding documents in advance of an SEC investigatory demand based on failure of jury instructions to convey the requisite consciousness of wrongdoing). Given these decisions restricting the reach of other fraud and corruption statutes, the Office considered whether the Supreme Court might also adopt a new construction of the defraud clause in Section 371, such as one that would for the first time limit it to money or property fraud.

The Office concluded, however, that the creation of such a new rule would not be supported in the law given that the well-established elements of a defraud-clause offense are firmly grounded in the statute's text, history, and longstanding judicial precedent. For more than a hundred years, the Supreme Court has "stated repeatedly that the fraud covered by the statute reaches any conspiracy for the purpose of impairing, obstructing, or defeating the lawful function of any department of Government" and that this branch of liability is distinct from money-or-property limitations in other areas of fraud law. *Tanner v. United States*, 483 U.S. 107, 128 (1987) (citation and quotations omitted); *see Dennis v. United States*, 384 U.S. 855, 861 (1966) ("It has long been established that this statutory language is not confined to fraud as that term has

41

been defined in the common law. It reaches any conspiracy for the purpose of impairing, obstructing, or defeating the lawful function of any department of government.") (citation and quotations omitted); *Glasser v. United States*, 315 U.S. 60, 66 (1942) (upholding prosecution of a federal prosecutor for conspiring to receive bribes to influence his official duties; no financial fraud against the United States alleged: "The indictment charges that the United States was defrauded by depriving it of its lawful governmental functions by dishonest means; it is settled that this is a 'defrauding' within the meaning of Section 37 of the Criminal Code," the predecessor to Section 371); *Hammerschmidt*, 265 U.S. at 188 ("To conspire to defraud the United States . . . also means to interfere with or obstruct one of its lawful governmental functions by deceit, craft or trickery, or at least by means that are dishonest. It is not necessary that the government shall be subjected to property or pecuniary loss by the fraud, but only that its legitimate official action and purpose shall be defeated by misrepresentation, chicane, or the overreaching of those charged with carrying out the governmental intention."); *Haas v. Henkel*, 216 U.S. 462, 479 (1910) ("[I]t is not essential that such a conspiracy shall contemplate a financial loss or that one shall result. The statute is broad enough in its terms to include any conspiracy for the purpose of impairing, obstructing, or defeating the lawful function of any department of government.").

Against the backdrop of that Supreme Court precedent, Congress has reenacted—and indeed expanded the scope of—the defraud clause, reflecting congressional ratification of the Court's construction of it. *See, e.g., Forest Grove Sch. Dist. v. T.A.*, 557 U.S. 230, 239-240 (2009) ("Congress is presumed to be aware of an administrative or judicial interpretation of a statute and to adopt that interpretation when it re-enacts a statute without change.") (citation and quotations omitted). In 1948, for instance, when Congress codified the general conspiracy statute, 18 U.S.C. § 371, where the defraud clause currently resides, *see* Pub. L. No. 80-772, 62 Stat. 701, it was already "settled" that "defraud[ing]" the United States "by depriving it of its lawful governmental functions by dishonest means . . . is a 'defrauding' within the meaning of" the defraud clause, *Glasser*, 315 U.S. at 66, and at that time, Congress added the words "or any agency thereof" in the defraud clause after "United States." Pub. L. No. 80-772, 62 Stat. 701. The House Report from the Judiciary Committee accompanying the pertinent bill specifically stated that the amendment was designed "[t]o reflect the construction placed upon [the predecessor statute] by the courts." H.R. Rep. No. 80-304, at A28 (1947). And it has consistently been the Department's position in litigation that the defraud clause proscribes conspiracies to obstruct a lawful function of the federal government through deceit. *See, e.g.*, *Gas Pipe, Inc. v. United States*, No. 21-183, 2021 WL 5193105, Brief in Opp'n (U.S. Oct. 8, 2021) (stating petitioners' contention that defraud clause is limited to money and property schemes is "inconsistent with over a century of [Supreme Court] precedent"); *Flynn v. United States*, No. 20-1129, 2021 WL 7210413, Brief in Opp'n (U.S. May 19, 2021) (stating defraud clause is not unconstitutionally vague in part because of the Supreme Court's longstanding interpretation that interference or obstruction must be by deceit or dishonest means); *Coplan v. United States*, No. 12-1299, 2013 WL 3324197, Brief in Opp'n (U.S. July 1, 2013) (explaining that petitioner's claim that the decisions in mail- and wire-fraud cases like *McNally v. United States*, 483 U.S. 350 (1987), and *Skilling* undermine "longstanding, congressionally adopted construction of the defraud clause" is erroneous and misplaced, and "disregards important limitations inherent in the defraud clause," including the requirement that "a conspiracy under the defraud clause must be deceptive or deceitful").[166] Accordingly, the Office concluded that

---

[166] The Supreme Court denied certiorari in each of these cases. *See Gas Pipe, Inc. v. United States*, 142 S. Ct. 484

Mr. Trump's conduct fell within the scope of Section 371 given the statute's longstanding, congressionally ratified construction, and its historic use by the Justice Department.

The Office also recognized various limiting principles in the application of Section 371 that separate Mr. Trump's conduct from mere hardscrabble politics. A defraud-clause violation, as honed by years of judicial decisions, including repeated applications by the Supreme Court, requires not only an agreement among co-conspirators, but identification of a specific function of the federal government, the intent to obstruct that function through deceit, and an overt act. *See, e.g., United States v. Johnson,* 383 U.S. 169, 172, 184-185 (1966) (in exchange for undisclosed "campaign contributions" and "legal fees," congressman conspired to defeat the lawful functions of the Department of Justice by urging dismissal of pending indictments). First, a defraud clause conspiracy must be targeted at a lawful function of the United States or any agency thereof. *See, e.g., United States v. Haldeman,* 559 F.2d 31, 121 (D.C. Cir. 1976) ("The unlawful agreement to attempt to use the CIA to interfere with the investigation of the Watergate break-in was thus fairly charged in Count 1 of the indictment as one of the means by which the defendants intended to accomplish one of the principal objects of their conspiracy defrauding the United States of its right to have its officials and agencies transact their business honestly, impartially, and free from corruption or undue influence or obstruction."). In contrast, a conspiracy targeted at a private party or at a state or local government does not suffice, even if the entity receives federal funds or "serve[s] as an intermediary performing official functions on behalf of the Federal Government." *Tanner,* 483 U.S. at 130-131. Second, obstruction of the governmental function must be "a *purpose* or *object* of the conspiracy, and not merely a foreseeable consequence of the conspiratorial scheme." *United States v. Goldberg,* 105 F.3d 770, 773 (1st Cir. 1997) (emphasis

---

(2021); *Flynn v. United States,* 141 S. Ct. 2853 (2021); *Coplan v. United States,* 571 U.S. 819 (2013).

in original) (citing *Dennis*, 384 U.S. at 861). Thus, for example, financial crimes do not "automatically become federal conspiracies to defraud the IRS," simply because the crime may have foreseeable tax implications. *Id.* And this requirement means that the conspiracy must be aimed at defeating and obstructing the government function, rather than simply participating in it. Third, the defraud clause "is limited only to wrongs done 'by deceit, craft or trickery, or at least by means that are dishonest." *Hammerschmidt*, 265 U.S. at 188. Fourth, the overt-act requirement provides another limitation, the function of which is "to manifest that the conspiracy is at work, and is neither a project still resting solely in the minds of the conspirators nor a fully completed operation no longer in existence." *Yates v. United States*, 354 U.S. 298, 334 (1957) (citation and quotations omitted), *overruled on other grounds by Burks v. United States*, 437 U.S. 1 (1978). Finally, while a court in the District of Columbia has stated that materiality is not an element of a defraud-clause conspiracy, *see Concord Mgmt. & Consulting LLC*, 347 F. Supp. 3d at 50 n.5, the Office was prepared to prove the materiality of Mr. Trump's deceptive statements and to offer a materiality instruction as another limitation on the scope of Section 371. Under that limitation, even conspirators who make knowingly false statements with an obstructive intent will not violate the defraud clause unless their statements are material.

All of these requirements for establishing a conspiracy to defraud under Section 371, taken collectively, ensure that common political conduct or political speech does not fall within the scope of the defraud clause. The evidence collected during the investigation met these requirements as to Mr. Trump's conduct.

B.   Obstruction and Conspiracy to Obstruct (18 U.S.C. § 1512(k) and (c)(2))

The federal statute prohibiting obstruction of an official proceeding makes it a crime to "corruptly (1) alter[], destroy[], mutilate[], or conceal[] a record, document, or other object, or attempt[] to do so, with the intent to impair the object's integrity or availability for use in an official proceeding; or (2) otherwise obstruct[], influence[], or impede[] any official proceeding, or attempt[] to do so." 18 U.S.C. § 1512(c). A separate provision defines the term "official proceeding" to include a "proceeding before the Congress." 18 U.S.C. § 1515(a)(1)(B).

In *Fischer v. United States*, 603 U.S. 480 (2024), decided during the pendency of Mr. Trump's immunity appeal, the Supreme Court clarified the scope of an obstruction offense under Section 1512(c)(2), holding that the statute applies only when a defendant impairs (or attempts to impair) "the availability or integrity for use in an official proceeding of records, documents, objects, or . . . other things used in the proceeding." *Id.* at 498. In language that applies directly to the allegations in the superseding indictment, the Supreme Court explained that Section 1512(c)(2)'s criminal prohibition includes "creating false evidence." *Id.* at 491. Before seeking the original indictment—which, like the superseding indictment, alleged that one component of Mr. Trump's and his co-conspirators' obstruction involved replacing valid elector certificates from the contested states with false ones they had manufactured—the Office anticipated the possibility of such a result in *Fischer* and confirmed that the evidence would prove Mr. Trump's guilt beyond a reasonable doubt even under a narrow interpretation of Section 1512(c)(2). *See* ECF No. 139 at 20-21. In construing Section 1512(c)(2) to reach impairing or attempting to impair the integrity or availability of records, documents, or other objects through "creating false evidence," the Supreme Court cited *United States v. Reich*, 479 F.3d 179, 183, 185-187 (2d Cir. 2007) (Sotomayor, J.), in which a defendant was convicted under Section 1512(c)(2) after he forged a court order and sent it to an opposing party intending to cause that party to withdraw a mandamus petition then pending before an appellate court. Just as the defendant in *Reich* violated Section 1512(c)(2) by "inject[ing] a false order into ongoing litigation to which he was a party," *id.* at 186, the evidence showed that the co-conspirators created fraudulent electoral

46

certificates that they intended to introduce into the congressional certification proceeding on January 6 to obstruct it.[167]

The Office was also prepared to prove that Mr. Trump willfully caused his supporters to obstruct and attempt to obstruct the proceeding by summoning them to Washington, D.C., and then directing them to march to the Capitol to cause the Vice President and legislators to reject the legitimate certificates and instead rely on the fraudulent electoral certificates.[168] *See* 18 U.S.C. § 2(b) (making a defendant criminally liable for "willfully caus[ing] an act to be done which if directly performed by him or another would be" a federal offense); *United States v. Hsia*, 176 F.3d 517, 522 (D.C. Cir. 1999) (upholding a conviction for willfully causing a violation of 18 U.S.C. § 1001). The Supreme Court's opinion in *Fischer* therefore did not undermine the viability of the Section 1512 counts.

Much of the evidence that supports the Section 371 conspiracy to defraud likewise proves that Mr. Trump and co-conspirators violated Section 1512(k) and Section 1512(c)(2). To demonstrate a violation of Section 1512(c)(2) following *Fischer*, the government must prove (1) the defendant obstructed, influenced, or impeded an official proceeding, or attempted to do so, (2) in the course of doing so, the defendant committed or attempted to commit an act that

---

[167] *See* ECF No. 252 at 48-49 & nn.251-254, 51-52 & n.274, 56-57 & nn.302-307, 58 & n.312, 65 & n.352; SCO-02341381 (Fraudulent "Arizona's Electoral Votes for President and Vice President"); SCO-02341386 (Fraudulent "Georgia's Electoral Votes for President and Vice President"); SCO-02341398 (Fraudulent "Michigan's Electoral Votes for President and Vice President"); SCO-02341415 (Fraudulent "Nevada's Electoral Votes for President and Vice President"); SCO-02341409 (Fraudulent "New Mexico's Electoral Votes for President and Vice President"); SCO-02341435 (Fraudulent "Pennsylvania's Electoral Votes for President and Vice President"); SCO-02341449 (Fraudulent "Wisconsin's Electoral Votes for President and Vice President"); SCO-00310626 (Co-Conspirator 5 memo 12/06/2020); SCO-00039408 (Email from Co-Conspirator 5 12/08/2020); SCO-00309946 (Email from Co-Conspirator 5 to Co-Conspirator 1 12/13/2020); SCO-12184337, SCO-12184338 (Email from Co-Conspirator 2 to Co-Conspirator 5 and Co-Conspirator 6, with attachment 12/23/2020) (memo); SCO-12101300, SCO-12101301 (Email from Co-Conspirator 2 to Co-Conspirator 6, with attachment 01/03/2021) (memo).

[168] *See* ECF No. 252 at 72-73 & nn.405-407, 74 & nn.411-414, 75 & n.422, 76-78 & nn.428-444, 80 & n.462; *see also, e.g.*, SCO-00455253, SCO-12987427 (Donald J. Trump Tweet 12/19/2020); SCO-00455068, SCO-12987393 (Donald J. Trump Tweet 01/01/2021); SCO-02244118 (Remarks by Mr. Trump at Save America Rally 01/06/2021).

impaired the integrity or rendered unavailable records, documents, objects, or other things for use in the official proceeding, (3) the defendant intended to impair the integrity of or render unavailable such records, documents, objects, or other things for use in the official proceeding, and (4) the defendant acted corruptly. *See United States v. Baez*, No. 21-cr-507, ECF No. 106 at 8 (D.D.C. Sept. 23, 2024) (describing elements required to establish a violation of Section 1512(c)(2) following *Fischer*).

Mr. Trump's conduct establishes each of these elements beyond a reasonable doubt. The congressional certification proceeding was an official proceeding for purposes of Section 1512, as every district court judge in the District of Columbia to have considered this question has concluded, *see United States v. Bingert*, 605 F. Supp. 3d 111, 120 (D.D.C. 2022), and as the D.C. Circuit has agreed, *see Fischer*, 64 F.4th at 342-343 (D.C. Cir. 2023), *vacated and remanded on other grounds*, 603 U.S. 480 (2024). The evidence described above supporting the Section 371 charge also establishes Mr. Trump's knowingly obstructive conduct. And as described above, Mr. Trump willfully caused others to attempt to obstruct the certification proceeding on January 6.

Finally, the Government was prepared to prove Mr. Trump's corrupt intent—under any definition—beyond a reasonable doubt. To act "corruptly" means (1) acting dishonestly, (2) intending the use of unlawful means, (3) violating a legal duty or causing or seeking to cause someone else to violate a legal duty, or (4) seeking an unlawful or improper benefit or advantage. Acting corruptly also means acting with consciousness of wrongdoing. *See United States v. Robertson*, 86 F.4th 355, 368-369 (D.C. Cir. 2023); *United States v. Morrison*, 98 F.3d 619, 630 (D.C. Cir. 1996); *Arthur Andersen LLP*, 544 U.S. at 706-707 (2005). Mr. Trump and co-conspirators used deceptive and dishonest means; he intended the use of independently criminal means to obstruct the congressional certification proceeding; he and co-conspirators plainly sought to cause state and federal officials to violate a legal duty; and Mr. Trump acted "with an intent to procure an unlawful benefit either for oneself or for some other person." *Fischer*, 64 F.4th at 352 (Walker, J., concurring) (citation and quotations omitted). Most basically, Mr. Trump sought "unlawfully [to] secure a professional advantage—the presidency," *id.* at 356 n.5—to which he was not lawfully entitled.

C.   Conspiracy Against Rights (18 U.S.C. § 241)

Section 241 makes it unlawful for two or more persons to "conspire to injure, oppress, threaten, or intimidate any person in any State, Territory, Commonwealth, Possession, or District in the free exercise or enjoyment of any right or privilege secured to him by the Constitution or laws of the United States." A violation of Section 241 requires proof of three elements: (1) Mr. Trump entered into a conspiracy, (2) to willfully injure, oppress, threaten, or intimidate a person in the United States, (3) in the exercise or enjoyment of a right secured by the Constitution or federal law. 18 U.S.C. § 241; *see, e.g., United States v. Epley*, 52 F.3d 571, 575-576 (6th Cir. 1995).

Mr. Trump's conduct meets each element.[169] The right to vote for President—based on the determination by state legislatures to appoint electors based on their constituents' votes—is "fundamental." *Bush v. Gore*, 531 U.S. 98, 104 (2000); *cf. Burdick v. Takushi*, 504 U.S. 428, 441 (1992) ("the right to vote is the right to participate in an electoral process that is necessarily structured to maintain the integrity of the democratic system"); *United States v. Robinson*, 813 F.3d 251, 255-256 (6th Cir. 2016) (Section 241 "prohibits interference with a voter's right to cast

---

[169] The Office further set forth its position on the applicability of Section 241 in response to Mr. Trump's motion to dismiss the charge in the district court. *See* ECF No. 139 at 22-25.

a ballot for his or her preferred candidate . . . and prohibits interference with the right of voters to have their votes free from dilution by unlawfully procured votes."). It is a right rooted in the principles of accountability to and consent by the governed, which has distinguished this nation from its founding. As the Supreme Court has recognized, "[t]he right to vote freely for the candidate of one's choice is of the essence of a democratic society, and any restrictions on that right strike at the heart of representative government." *Reynolds v. Sims*, 377 U.S. 533, 555 (1964); *see also Yick Wo v. Hopkins*, 118 U.S. 357, 370 (1886) (voting is "regarded as a fundamental political right, because [it is] preservative of all rights"); *Wesberry v. Sanders*, 376 U.S. 1, 17 (1964) ("No right is more precious in a free country than that of having a voice in the election of those who make the laws under which, as good citizens, we must live. Other rights, even the most basic, are illusory if the right to vote is undermined.").

Mr. Trump acknowledged that voting in a presidential election is a fundamental right under the Constitution. *See* ECF No. 163 at 23 (arguing that "urging States or Congress to use their power to select or to count electors does not affect the 'fundamental' right to vote because it does not arbitrarily 'value one person's vote over that of another,' *Bush*, 531 U.S. at 104-105, or restrict the exercise of that right; rather, it encourages the States and Congress to exercise their constitutional prerogatives a certain way"). Indeed, given that all states have made the popular vote an integral means of appointing electors, the right to vote in a presidential election is among the most precious federal rights protected by the Constitution. *Cf. United States v. Classic*, 313 U.S. 299, 314 (1941) (when a state makes a primary election "an integral part of the procedure for the popular choice of a Congressman," it becomes "a right established and guaranteed by the Constitution"); *see also Trump v. Anderson*, 601 U.S. 100, 115-116 (2024) (per curiam) (noting the "uniquely important national interest" in "a Presidential election" because "the President . . . represents all the voters in the Nation") (citation, quotations, and emphasis omitted).

This history of the Section 241 offense with which Mr. Trump was charged, along with courts' universal and longstanding recognition of the voting rights protected by that statute, confirm that protecting the right to vote is critical to the existence of the right. Section 241's predecessor statute was passed as part of the Enforcement Act of 1870, a Reconstruction-era law to address the "continued denial of rights" to Black citizens, "sometimes accompanied by violent assaults." *United States v. Price*, 383 U.S. 787, 801-802 (1966). That Act sought to combat widespread anti-Reconstruction violence, which included acts of terror aimed at disenfranchising Black voters. The same year as the Act's passage, Congress established the U.S. Department of Justice, and the Department zealously pursued its mission to enforce voting rights in the Reconstruction Era. Through the application and interpretation of Section 241 and its predecessor statute, courts have repeatedly underscored the importance of the right to vote. Courts have held that the right encompasses the ability to cast a vote, *Ex parte Yarbrough (The Ku-Klux Cases)*, 110 U.S. 651, 657-658 (1884) (protecting right of an emancipated person to vote), and to have that vote counted, *United States v. Mosley*, 238 U.S. 383, 386 (1915) ("We regard it as equally unquestionable that the right to have one's vote counted is as open to protection by Congress as the right to put a ballot in a box."). They have further confirmed that one's vote cannot lawfully be denied, destroyed, or diluted. *See, e.g., Classic*, 313 U.S. at 321-322 (holding that Section 241's predecessor statute applied to conspiracies to prevent the official counting of ballots in a primary election); *United States v. Saylor,* 322 U.S. 385 (1944) (Section 241 applies to prohibit conspiracies to dilute legitimate votes by stuffing the ballot box); *United States v. Pleva*, 66 F.2d 529, 530 (2d Cir. 1933) (board of elections inspectors charged with falsely tabulating ballots to favor certain candidates; convictions reversed on separate jury grounds); *United States v. Skurla*, 126 F. Supp. 713, 715 (W.D. Pa. 1954) (defendants charged for casting and causing to be cast false and forged ballots, causing an incorrect vote tally, and using unqualified individuals to impersonate lawful voters); *United States v. Townsley*, 843 F.2d 1070, 1073-1075 (8th Cir. 1988) (scheme to discard certain absentee ballots).

Mr. Trump and co-conspirators sought to deprive—that is, injure or oppress—citizens of their constitutional right to have their presidential election votes counted. The words "injure or oppress" in Section 241 are not used in any technical sense, but cover a variety of conduct intended to prevent, harm, inhibit, hinder, frustrate, obstruct, or interfere with the free exercise and enjoyment of a right. *See United States v. Handy*, No. 22-cr-96, 2023 WL 6199084, at *3 (D.D.C. Sept. 22, 2023); *United States v. Mackey*, 652 F. Supp. 3d 309, 336-337 (E.D.N.Y. 2023). Although they were not in a backroom altering the vote tallies in a local election, or stuffing falsified ballots into the ballot boxes, as alleged in prior cases charged under this statute, Mr. Trump and co-conspirators nonetheless sought the same result: to effectively cast aside legitimate votes in a manner that would have deprived citizens of their right to vote and have their votes counted. As Co-Conspirator 1 admitted, their primary objective was to "just flat out change the vote, deduct that number of votes from the – declare those votes, 300,000 votes in Philadelphia, illegal, unlawful. Reduce the number by 300,000."[170] Mr. Trump attempted to carry out this objective in multiple ways. He urged state officials to disregard the legitimate majority of votes for Mr. Biden and pressured and threatened Georgia's Secretary of State to "find" more than 11,000 votes to dilute Mr. Biden's vote count in the state.[171] And he urged Mr.

---

[170] SCO-06628582 at 13:07-13:22 (War Room episode 491 11/11/2020).

[171] *See* ECF No. 252 at 29 & n.137; SCO-12998394 at 12 (Tr. of Georgia Secretary of State Call 01/02/2021).

Pence to discard the legitimate electoral certificates that reflected millions of citizens' votes in the targeted states.[172] The evidence collected showed that Mr. Trump targeted this voting right with precision: he centered his false claims of election fraud on select states, or cities and counties within those states, with large numbers of voters who had not chosen to reelect him.

D.   Defenses

Before presenting the original indictment to the grand jury, the Office considered Mr. Trump's potential defenses to these charges, including a good faith defense, an advice of counsel defense, and constitutional defenses. The Office concluded that each of the defenses was legally or factually flawed and thus would not prevail.

First, it was expected that Mr. Trump would argue that he acted in good faith when he sought to stop the transfer of presidential power because he genuinely believed that outcome-determinative fraud had undermined the election's integrity and caused him to lose. As set forth above in Section II.A, the Office developed strong proof that Mr. Trump knew that his election fraud claims were false. For example, Mr. Trump made persistent claims of a large number of dead voters in Georgia—including in his speech at the Ellipse on January 6—even though his Senior Campaign Advisor and Georgia's Secretary of State had told him that the claims were untrue.[173] He spread lies—including in his Ellipse speech—of sinister, fraudulent "vote dumps" in Michigan, even after Michigan's Senate Majority Leader told him that nothing suspicious had occurred.[174]   And Mr. Trump repeatedly made provably false allegations about fraud in

---

[172] See ECF No. 252 at 66-67 & nn.361-365, 71 & nn.392-399; SCO-00014655 at 198-200.

[173] See ECF No. 252 at 21 & n.95, 30 & n.142; SCO-02244118 at 16 (Remarks by Mr. Trump at Save America Rally 01/06/2021); SCO-00011882 at 33-37; SCO-12998394 at 6 (Tr. of Georgia Secretary of State Call 01/02/2021).

[174] See ECF No. 252 at 32-33 & n.160; SCO-02244118 at 18 (Remarks by Mr. Trump at Save America Rally 01/06/2021); SCO-11545470 at 62-64 (Int. Tr.); SCO-00829361 at 16-17 (HSC Tr.).

Pennsylvania, despite having been told by the Chairman of the state Republican Party that the vote count was occurring as expected.[175]

Even if Mr. Trump maintained that he sincerely believed he won the election (a conclusion unsupported by the evidence collected in the investigation), it would not provide a defense to the Section 371 charge. A defendant may not use deceit to obstruct a government function even if he believes the function itself to be unconstitutional because "a claim of unconstitutionality will not be heard to excuse a voluntary, deliberate and calculated course of fraud and deceit." *Dennis*, 384 U.S. at 867. "One who elects such a course as a means of self-help may not escape the consequences by urging that his conduct be excused because the statute which he sought to evade is unconstitutional." *Id.* There are "appropriate and inappropriate ways to challenge" perceived illegalities. *Id.* Just as the president of a company may be guilty of fraud for using knowingly false statements of fact to defraud investors even if he subjectively believes that his company will eventually succeed, *see, e.g.*, *United States v. Arif*, 897 F.3d 1, 9-10 & n.9 (1st Cir. 2018); *United States v. Kennedy*, 714 F.3d 951, 958 (6th Cir. 2013); *United States v. Chavis*, 461 F.3d 1201, 1209 (10th Cir. 2006), Mr. Trump could be convicted of using deceit to obstruct the government function by which the results of the presidential election are collected, counted, and certified, even if he established that he subjectively believed that he had reason to do so because of his claims that the election was "rigged."

It bears emphasis that Mr. Trump's knowing deceit was pervasive throughout the charged conspiracies. This was not a case in which Mr. Trump merely misstated a fact or two in a handful of isolated instances. On a repeated basis, he and co-conspirators used specific and

---

[175] *See* ECF No. 252 at 37-38 & nn.187-190; SCO-02244118 at 11-12 (Remarks by Mr. Trump at Save America Rally 01/06/2021); SCO-00016926 at 20-24.

knowingly false claims of election fraud in his calls and meetings with state officials, in an effort to induce them to overturn the results of the election in their states;[176] to his own Vice President, to induce Mr. Pence to violate his duty during the congressional certification proceeding;[177] and on January 6, as a call to action to the angry crowd he had gathered at the Ellipse and sent to the Capitol to disrupt the certification proceeding.[178] Mr. Trump and co-conspirators used other forms of deceit as well—including when they falsely represented that the fraudulent electoral votes would be used only if Mr. Trump prevailed in pending contests in their states,[179] and when they caused the fraudulent electors to falsely swear that they were duly certified and send those false certifications to Congress.[180] Regardless of any claim that Mr. Trump subjectively believed the outcome of the election was unfair or "rigged," the Office concluded that these knowingly deceitful statements and acts would overcome any good faith defense.

The Office also expected that Mr. Trump might claim that his consultation with attorneys—several of whom were co-conspirators—should negate a finding that he acted with a

[176] *See* ECF No. 252 at 17 & nn.67-68, 18 & n.72, 29-30 & nn.139-144, 32 & n.159; SCO-12733339 at 4 (Int. Rep.); SCO-00767550 at 10-11 (HSC Tr.); SCO-11509251 at 41-42 (Int. Tr.); SCO-12998394 at 1-3 (Tr. of Georgia Secretary of State Call 01/02/2021); SCO-00829361 at 16-17 (HSC Tr.).

[177] *See* ECF No. 252 at 67 & n.365; SCO-00014655 at 155-158, 170-171; SCO-04982309 (Handwritten notes 12/29/2020); SCO-04982330 at 1 (Handwritten notes 01/04/2021).

[178] *See* ECF No. 252 at 75-76 & nn.423-428; SCO-02244118 at 6, 12-22 (Remarks by Mr. Trump at Save America Rally 01/06/2021).

[179] *See* ECF No. 252 at 50 & n.260, 53 & n.282; SCO-00009955 at 8-11; SCO-12949797 at 82-83 (Int. Tr.); SCO-00016926 at 48-50; SCO-00009540 at 15-19.

[180] *See* ECF No. 252 at 56 & n.301; SCO-02341381 (Fraudulent "Arizona's Electoral Votes for President and Vice President"); SCO-02341386 (Fraudulent "Georgia's Electoral Votes for President and Vice President"); SCO-02341398 (Fraudulent "Michigan's Electoral Votes for President and Vice President"); SCO-02341415 (Fraudulent "Nevada's Electoral Votes for President and Vice President"); SCO-02341409 (Fraudulent "New Mexico's Electoral Votes for President and Vice President"); SCO-02341435 (Fraudulent "Pennsylvania's Electoral Votes for President and Vice President"); SCO-02341449 (Fraudulent "Wisconsin's Electoral Votes for President and Vice President"). Even in Pennsylvania and New Mexico, where the fraudulent certificates contained future contingent language, the cover memoranda and envelopes sent to Congress represented that the documents were the state's "Electoral Votes for President and Vice President."

criminal state of mind. In pretrial litigation, the Court granted the Government's motion that Mr. Trump should be required to declare whether he intended to employ such a defense and, if he did, to produce the discovery required by the attendant waiver of Mr. Trump's attorney-client privilege. ECF No. 147. A defendant's claim that he relied in good faith on his attorney's advice is "not an affirmative defense that defeats liability even if the jury accepts the government's allegations as true," but functions instead as "evidence that, if believed, can raise a reasonable doubt in the minds of the jurors about whether the government has proved the required element of the offense that the defendant had an 'unlawful intent.'" *United States v. Scully*, 877 F.3d 464, 476 (2d Cir. 2017) (quoting *United States v. Beech-Nut Nutrition Corp.*, 871 F.2d 1181, 1194 (2d Cir. 1989)). Under D.C. Circuit law, an advice-of-counsel defense consists of two elements: the defendant (1) "'relied in good faith on the counsel's advice that his course of conduct was legal'" and (2) "'made full disclosure of all material facts to his attorney before receiving the advice at issue.'" *United States v. Gray-Burriss*, 920 F.3d 61, 66 (D.C. Cir. 2019) (quoting *United States v. DeFries*, 129 F.3d 1293, 1308 (D.C. Cir. 1997)).

The Office concluded that if Mr. Trump chose to raise such a defense, it would fail because an advice-of-counsel defense is not available "where counsel acts as an accomplice to the crime." *United States v. West*, 392 F.3d 450, 457 (D.C. Cir. 2004) (Roberts, J.). The evidence showed that the central attorneys on whom Mr. Trump may have relied for such a defense, such as Co-Conspirator 1 or Co-Conspirator 2, were "partner[s] in a venture," with the result that any advice-of-counsel defense necessarily would fail. *Id.* (citing *United States v. Carr*, 740 F.2d 339, 347 (5th Cir. 1984)); *cf. United States v. Cintolo*, 818 F.2d 980, 990 (1st Cir. 1987) ("A criminal lawyer has no license to act as a lawyer-criminal."). Co-Conspirator 1 assisted Mr. Trump in using knowingly false claims of election fraud in furtherance of the charged conspiracies. At press conferences,[181] at hearings before legislatures in the targeted states,[182] and directly with officials in the targeted states,[183] Co-Conspirator 1 made a wide range of specific (though ever-changing) false claims of election fraud. Co-Conspirator 1 continued to do so after his lies were publicly or directly debunked.[184] Co-Conspirator 1's involvement spanned from his insistence that Mr. Trump declare victory on election night[185] to the voicemails[186] that Co-Conspirator 1 left for Senators on the night of January 6, using false claims of election fraud to ask that the legislators further delay the certification. Co-Conspirator 2 was instrumental in Mr. Trump's efforts to organize his electors to cast fraudulent votes and send them to the Vice President, and then to pressure the Vice President to use the fraudulent electoral certificates to overturn the election results. Throughout his involvement in Mr. Trump's conspiracies, Co-Conspirator 2 conceded privately to other attorneys (both private attorneys and those responsible for advising Mr. Trump and the Vice President) that his plans violated federal law and would not withstand scrutiny in court.[187]

[181] See ECF No. 252 at 43 & nn.217-218; see, e.g., SCO-04976260 (Video of Four Seasons Total Landscaping Press Conference 11/07/2020); SCO-04976264 (Video of RNC Press Conference 11/19/2020).

[182] See ECF No. 252 at 19-20 & nn.83-85, 21 & n.97, 25 & nn.119-120, 39 & nn.195-197; SCO-04976265 at 15:52-30:00 (Video of Pennsylvania Hotel Hearing 11/25/2020); SCO-04976459 at 02:06:23-02:07:00 (Video of Arizona State Hearing 11/30/2020); SCO-04976326 at 25:00-31:05 (Video of Michigan House Committee Meeting 12/02/2020); SCO-04976332 at 01:04:50-01:10:25 (Video of Georgia Senate Judiciary Subcommittee Hearing 12/03/2020).

[183] See ECF No. 252 at 19 & nn.77-82, 33 & nn.163-164, 34 & nn.168-169; SCO-11545470 at 53 (Int. Tr.); SCO-00829361 at 20-22 (HSC Tr.); SCO-00312350 (Text messages from Co-Conspirator 1 12/07/2020); SCO-05390337-05390346 (Text messages 12/08/2020); SCO-11508370 at 62-64 (Int. Tr.).

[184] See ECF No. 252 at 14 & n.53, 23 & nn.105-106; see also, e.g., SCO-04976279 at 01:36:58-02:01:58 (Video of Georgia House Committee Hearing 12/10/2020); SCO-04952956 (Tweet 12/04/2020); SCO-04976277 at 08:44-09:10 (Video of Georgia Secretary of State Press Conference 12/07/2020); supra at n.12.

[185] See ECF No. 252 at 7 & n.15; SCO-00003548 at 61-62; SCO-00016750 at 31-35.

[186] See ECF No. 252 at 84 & nn.488-492; SCO-04134777 (Voicemail from Co-Conspirator 1 01/06/2021); SCO-06475675 (Voicemail from Co-Conspirator 1 01/06/2021).

[187] See ECF No. 252 at 61 & nn.324-326, 63 & n.336, 66 & n.356, 69 & n.384; SCO-00007167 at 66; SCO-02248764 at 3 (Email from Co-Conspirator 2 01/06/21); SCO-12245492 (Email from Co-Conspirator 2

Furthermore, Mr. Trump could not have succeeded in showing that he relied in good faith on legal advice from these attorneys. The evidence showed that Mr. Trump was not looking to Co-Conspirator 1 or Co-Conspirator 2 for legal advice; instead, Mr. Trump was the head of a conspiracy who sought legal cover from his co-conspirators. As Co-Conspirator 1 acted repeatedly in furtherance of the conspiracies, multiple advisors to Mr. Trump warned him that Co-Conspirator 1 would not successfully challenge the election results and was not acting in Mr. Trump's best interest; Mr. Trump ignored them all because he was not relying on Co-Conspirator 1 as an attorney.[188] Similarly, Co-Conspirator 2's willingness to advocate for actions that he knew and even privately conceded were unlawful demonstrates that both he and Mr. Trump understood his role was not that of an attorney offering legal advice on which Mr. Trump was acting.[189] For instance, in a lawsuit in Georgia, Co-Conspirator 2 filed a false certification by Mr. Trump after having written to other attorneys in an email that both he and Mr. Trump knew some of the allegations incorporated in the filing were inaccurate.[190] And Co-Conspirator 2's decision to advocate to the Vice President's counsel and chief of staff on January 5, 2021, that the Vice President should unlawfully reject legitimate electoral certificates—an act that Co-Conspirator 2 had previously recognized was not supported by the Constitution or federal

---

12/29/2020); SCO-00039087 (Text messages among Co-Conspirator 2, Co-Conspirator 5, and Co-Conspirator 6 12/28/2020).

[188] *See* ECF No. 252 at 11-12 & nn.32-35; SCO-12920242 at 1, 4, 7 (Int. Rep.); SCO-00006256 at 44-52; SCO-12945195 (Email 11/28/2020); SCO-00764172 at 26-27 (HSC Tr.); SCO-11532925 at 70-71 (Int. Tr.); SCO-00014655 at 68-73.

[189] *See* ECF No. 252 at 61 & nn.324-326, 63 & n.336, 66-67 & nn.356-364, 69-70 nn.382-385; *see, e.g.,* SCO-12245107 at 1-2 (Draft Letter from Co-Conspirator 2); SCO-00280481 at 2 (Memo from Co-Conspirator 2 to Co-Conspirator 6 12/23/2020); SCO-00006256 at 130-135; SCO-00007167 at 50-53, 60-63; SCO-00016118 at 72-80; SCO-00014442 at 38-39 (Pence, *So Help Me God* pp. 450-451); SCO-04982330 (Handwritten notes 01/04/2021); *Trump v. Kemp*, No. 20-cv-5310, ECF No. 21 at 27-29 (N.D. Ga. Jan. 5, 2021) (Transcript of Motions Hearing); SCO-04976350 at 56:53-57:36, 01:05:59-01:07:02, 01:19:12-1:27:28 (Video of HSC Testimony); SCO-04094748 (Handwritten notes 01/05/2021); SCO-00794788 at 108-115 (HSC Tr.).

[190] *See* ECF No. 252 at 27 & nn.127-130; *Kemp*, No. 20-cv-5310, ECF No. 1 at 33-34 (N.D. Ga. Dec. 31, 2020) (Complaint); SCO-00006256 at 205-206; SCO-00282435 at 1 (Email from Co-Conspirator 2 12/31/2020).

law [191]—was a sharp reversal from his position just one day earlier and happened only because Mr. Trump had made clear that it was his preferred strategy. [192] The Office was otherwise confident that it would be able to demonstrate that with respect to all attorneys, Mr. Trump could not meet the elements of the defense, such as the requirement that he make full disclosure to any attorneys of all relevant facts and then rely faithfully on their advice. *See Gray-Burriss*, 920 F.3d at 66.

Finally, the Office anticipated that Mr. Trump would claim that his conduct was protected by the First Amendment. As the district court recognized, "the First Amendment 'embodies our profound national commitment to the free exchange of ideas," and it bars the government from "'restrict[ing] expression because of its message, its ideas, its subject matter, or its content.'" ECF No. 171 at 31 (quoting *Ashcroft v. Am. Civ. Liberties Union*, 535 U.S. 564, 573 (2002), and *United States v. Stevens*, 559 U.S. 460, 468 (2010)). At the same time, "it is well established that the First Amendment does not protect speech that is used as an instrument of a crime." *Id.* "'Many long established' criminal laws permissibly 'criminalize speech that is intended to induce or commence illegal activities,' *United States v. Williams*, 553 U.S. 285, 298 (2008), such as fraud, bribery, perjury, extortion, threats, incitement, solicitation, and blackmail, *see, e.g.*, *Stevens*, 559 U.S. at 468–469 (fraud); *Williams*, 553 U.S. at 298 (incitement, solicitation); *Citizens United v. Fed. Election Comm'n*, 558 U.S. 310, 356 (2010) (bribery); *Rice v. Paladin Enters., Inc.*, 128 F.3d 233, 244 (4th Cir. 1997) (extortion, threats, blackmail, perjury)." ECF No. 171 at 31-32 (ellipsis omitted). "Prosecutions for conspiring, directing, and aiding and abetting do not run afoul of the Constitution when those offenses are 'carried out through

---

[191] *See* ECF No. 252 at 61 & nn.324-326; SCO-12245107 at 1-2 (Draft Letter from Co-Conspirator 2).

[192] *See* ECF No. 252 at 66-67 & nn.361-364, 69 & nn.382-384; SCO-00007167 at 51, 60-61; SCO-04976350 at 01:19:12-01:21:30 (Video of HSC Testimony); SCO-04094748 (Handwritten notes 01/05/2021).

speech.'" *Id.* at 32 (quoting *Nat'l Org. for Women v. Operation Rescue*, 37 F.3d 646, 655-656 (D.C. Cir. 1994), and citing *Williams*, 553 U.S. at 298).

Consistent with that precedent, the original and superseding indictments recognized that Mr. Trump "had a right, like every American, to speak publicly about the [2020 presidential] election and even to claim, falsely, that there had been outcome-determinative fraud during the election and that he had won." ECF No. 1 at ¶ 3; ECF No. 226 at ¶ 3. They charged Mr. Trump, however, with using knowingly false statements to defeat a government function, injure the right to vote, and obstruct an official proceeding. That is, he made "dozens of specific claims that there had been substantial fraud in certain states, such as that large numbers of dead, non-resident, non-citizen, or otherwise ineligible voters had cast ballots, or that voting machines had changed votes for the Defendant to votes for Biden." ECF No. 1 at ¶ 11; ECF No. 226 at ¶ 12. Those were factual claims that were verifiably false, and Mr. Trump knew that they were false. *See id.* Mr. Trump then used those lies as the instruments of his four criminal offenses. Because he used those knowingly false statements regarding specific facts to commit the crimes charged in the superseding indictment, they were not protected by the First Amendment. *See Stevens*, 559 U.S. at 468-469 (including "fraud" in the list of "well-defined and narrowly limited classes of speech, the prevention and punishment of which have never been thought to raise any Constitutional problem") (citation and quotations omitted); *United States v. Nordean*, 579 F. Supp. 3d 28, 53-54 (D.D.C. 2021) ("[B]y focusing on 'corrupt' actions, [Section 1512(c)(2)] does not even reach free speech."); *see also United States v. Alvarez*, 567 U.S. 709, 719-721 (2012) (plurality opinion) (explaining that while "falsity alone may not suffice to bring the speech outside the First Amendment," the First Amendment permits criminal laws that proscribe knowing or reckless falsehoods in connection with some "other legally cognizable harm," including "protect[ing] the integrity of Government processes").

In pretrial motions, Mr. Trump moved to dismiss the original indictment based on the First Amendment. *See* ECF No. 113 at 4-18. The Office filed an opposition brief, ECF No. 139 at 29-34, and the district court denied the motion, finding that the indictment "properly alleges Defendant's statements were made in furtherance of a criminal scheme," ECF No. 171 at 33. As the court explained, Mr. Trump was "not being prosecuted for his 'view' on a political dispute; he [was] being prosecuted for acts constituting criminal conspiracy and obstruction of the electoral process," *id.* at 34, and the fact that his "alleged criminal conduct involved speech does not render the Indictment unconstitutional," *id.* at 32. Because he was "not being prosecuted simply for making false statements, but rather for knowingly making false statements in furtherance of a criminal conspiracy and obstructing the electoral process," there was "no danger of a slippery slope in which inadvertent false statements alone are alleged to be the basis for criminal prosecution." *Id.* at 36 (citation omitted); *see generally id.* at 32-37 (rejecting other First Amendment claims).

E. Other Charges

The Office considered, but ultimately opted against, bringing other charges. One potential charge was 18 U.S.C. § 2383, sometimes referred to as the Insurrection Act, which provides that "[w]hoever incites, sets on foot, assists, or engages in any rebellion or insurrection against the authority of the United States or the laws thereof, or gives aid or comfort thereto, shall be fined under this title or imprisoned not more than ten years, or both; and shall be incapable of holding any office under the United States." 18 U.S.C. § 2383. Section 2383 originated during the Civil War, as part of the Second Confiscation Act of 1862. *See* Act of July 17, 1862, ch. 195, § 2, Pub. L. No. 37-160, 12 Stat. 589, 590.

Cases interpreting Section 2383 are scarce and arose in contexts that provided little guidance regarding its potential application in this case. *See, e.g.*, *United States v. Greathouse*, 26 F. Cas. 18, 23 (C.C.N.D. Cal. 1863) (construing the original version of the act to encompass treason, consisting of arming a vessel to commit hostilities against United States vessels, in the context of the rebellion by the confederate states); *United States v. Cathcart*, 25 F. Cas. 344, 345 (C.C.S.D. Ohio 1864) (rejecting legal argument that treason against the United States was legally impossible in the context of the rebellion by the confederate states); *In re Grand Jury*, 62 F. 834, 837-838 (S.D. Cal. 1894) (grand jury charge describing offense in the context of a labor dispute involving interference with transportation of the mail); *In re Charge to Grand Jury*, 62 F. 828, 829-830 (N.D. Ill. 1894) (grand jury charged that "[i]nsurrection is a rising against civil or political authority" and requires "such a number of persons as would constitute a general uprising in that particular locality" in the context of offense of obstructing the mails). It does not appear that any defendant has been charged with violating the statute in more than 100 years.

To establish a violation of Section 2383, the Office would first have had to prove that the violence at the Capitol on January 6, 2021, constituted an "insurrection against the authority of the United States or the laws thereof," and then prove that Mr. Trump "incite[d]" or "assist[ed]" the insurrection, or "g[ave] aid or comfort thereto." 18 U.S.C. § 2383.

Courts have found or described the attack on the Capitol as an insurrection. In *Anderson v. Griswold*, 543 P.3d 283, 329 (Colo. 2023), *rev'd on other grounds sub nom. Trump v. Anderson*, 601 U.S. 100 (2024) (per curiam), the Colorado Supreme Court found that Mr. Trump engaged in an insurrection as that term is used in Section Three of the Fourteenth Amendment. Federal courts in the District of Columbia have also used the term "insurrection" to describe the attack on the Capitol, but did so in cases where there was no criminal charge under Section 2383.

See, e.g., United States v. Chwiesiuk, No. 21-cr-536, 2023 WL 3002493, at *3 (D.D.C. Apr. 19, 2023) ("As this Court and other courts in the United States District Court for the District of Columbia have stated previously, what occurred on January 6, 2021 was in fact an insurrection and involved insurrectionists and, therefore, the terms to which Defendants object are accurate descriptors."); *United States v. Carpenter*, No. 21-cr-305, 2023 WL 1860978, at *4 (D.D.C. Feb. 9, 2023) ("What occurred on January 6 was in fact a riot and an insurrection, and it did in fact involve a mob."); *see also United States v. Munchel*, 991 F.3d 1273, 1279, 1281 (D.C. Cir. 2021) (using the term "insurrection" in a case that did not involve Section 2383). These cases, however, did not require the courts to resolve the issue of how to define insurrection for purposes of Section 2383, or apply that definition to the conduct of a criminal defendant in the context of January 6.

The Office recognized why courts described the attack on the Capitol as an "insurrection," but it was also aware of the litigation risk that would be presented by employing this long-dormant statute. As to the first element under Section 2383—proving an "insurrection against the authority of the United States or the laws thereof"—the cases the Office reviewed provided no guidance on what proof would be required to establish an insurrection, or to distinguish an insurrection from a riot. Generally speaking, an "[i]nsurrection is a rising against civil or political authority[]—the open and active opposition of a number of persons to the execution of law in a city or state." *In re Charge to Grand Jury*, 62 F. at 830; *see also Insurrection*, MERRIAM-WEBSTER 649 (11th ed. 2020) ("an act or instance of revolting against civil authority or an established government"); *Insurrection*, AMERICAN HERITAGE DICTIONARY 909 (4th ed. 2000) ("The act or an instance of open revolt against civil authority or a constituted government."); *Insurrection*, 7 THE OXFORD ENGLISH DICTIONARY 1060 (2nd ed. 1989) ("The action of rising in arms or open resistance against established authority or governmental restraint[.]"). Some sources distinguish an "insurrection" from a "'rout, riot, [or] offense connected with mob violence by the fact that in insurrection there is an organized and armed uprising against authority or operations of government, while crimes growing out of mob violence, however serious they may be and however numerous the participants, are simply unlawful acts in disturbance of the peace which do not threaten the stability of the government or the existence of political society.'" BLACK'S LAW DICTIONARY (12th ed. 2024) (quoting 77 C.J.S. *Riot; Insurrection* § 29, at 579 (1994)); *see also Anderson*, 543 P.3d at 329-336 (noting Mr. Trump's argument that "an insurrection is more than a riot but less than a rebellion" and agreeing that "an insurrection falls along a spectrum of related conduct").

In case law interpreting "insurrection" in another context, one court has observed that an insurrection typically involves overthrowing a sitting government, rather than maintaining power, which could pose another challenge to proving beyond a reasonable doubt that Mr. Trump's conduct on January 6 qualified as an insurrection given that he was the sitting President at that time. *Cf. CITGO Petroleum Corp. v. Starstone Ins. SE*, No. 21-cv-389, 2023 WL 2525651, at *13 (S.D.N.Y. Mar. 15, 2023) ("[I]n every case over the course of over sixty years to find the existence of an insurrection within the meaning of an insurance policy, the insurrection has occurred against—not by—the established, effective and de facto government.") (citation and quotations omitted); *Pan Am World Airways, Inc. v. Aetna Cas. & Sur. Co.*, 505 F.2d 989, 1017 (2d Cir. 1974) ("The district court held that the word insurrection means (1) a violent uprising by a group or movement (2) acting for the specific purpose of overthrowing the constituted government and seizing its powers.") (citation and quotations omitted); *accord, e.g., Home Ins. Co. of New York v. Davila*, 212 F.2d 731, 738 (1st Cir. 1954) (noting that if Puerto

Rican extremists had a "maximum objective" to "overthrow of the insular government" on the island, that group's uprising would constitute insurrection); *Hartford Fire Ins. Co. v. W. Union Co.*, 630 F. Supp. 3d 431, 435-437 (S.D.N.Y. 2022) (a Russian-backed separatist group's attack on a plane in service of overthrowing the current government in eastern Ukraine was an insurrectionary act); *Younis Bros. & Co., Inc. v. CIGNA Worldwide Ins. Co.*, 91 F.3d 13, 14-15 (3d Cir. 1996) (applying *Davila* in finding that, where individuals outside of the Liberian government "led their respective armies in a violent uprising" "against the Liberian government," damage to properties fell within an insurance contract's insurrection clause). The Office did not find any case in which a criminal defendant was charged with insurrection for acting within the government to maintain power, as opposed to overthrowing it or thwarting it from the outside. Applying Section 2383 in this way would have been a first, which further weighed against charging it, given the other available charges, even if there were reasonable arguments that it might apply.

As to the second element under Section 2383, there does not appear to have ever been a prosecution under the statute for inciting, assisting, or giving aid or comfort to rebellion or insurrection. The few relevant cases that exist appear to be based on a defendant directly engaging in rebellion or insurrection, but the Office's proof did not include evidence that Mr. Trump directly engaged in insurrection himself. Thus, however strong the proof that he incited or gave aid and comfort to those who attacked the Capitol, application of those theories of liability would also have been a first. *See* Alexander Tsesis, *Incitement to Insurrection and the First Amendment*, 57 WAKE FOREST L. REV. 971, 973 & n.6 (2022) ("The likelihood of conviction under the federal incitement to insurrection statute, 18 U.S.C. § 2383 . . . is fraught with uncertainty because no federal court has interpreted it.").

The Office determined that there were reasonable arguments to be made that Mr. Trump's Ellipse Speech incited the violence at the Capitol on January 6 and could satisfy the Supreme Court's standard for "incitement" under *Brandenburg v. Ohio*, 395 U.S. 444, 447 (1969) (holding that the First Amendment does not protect advocacy "directed to inciting or producing imminent lawless action and . . . likely to incite or produce such action"), particularly when the speech is viewed in the context of Mr. Trump's lengthy and deceitful voter-fraud narrative that came before it. For example, the evidence established that the violence was foreseeable to Mr. Trump, that he caused it, that it was beneficial to his plan to interfere with the certification, and that when it occurred, he made a conscious choice not to stop it and instead to leverage it for more delay. But the Office did not develop direct evidence—such as an explicit admission or communication with co-conspirators—of Mr. Trump's subjective intent to cause the full scope of the violence that occurred on January 6. Therefore, in light of the other powerful charges available, and because the Office recognized that the *Brandenburg* standard is a rigorous one, *see, e.g.*, *N.A.A.C.P. v. Claiborne Hardware Co.*, 458 U.S. 886, 902, 927-929 (1982) (speech delivered in "passionate atmosphere" that referenced "possibility that necks would be broken" and violators of boycott would be "disciplined" did not satisfy *Brandenburg* standard); *Brandenburg*, 395 U.S. at 446-447 (reversing conviction where Ku Klux Klan leader threatened "revengeance" for "suppression" of the white race), it concluded that pursuing an incitement to insurrection charge was unnecessary.

By comparison, the statutes that the Office did charge had been interpreted and analyzed in various contexts over many years. The Office had a solid basis for using Sections 371, 1512, and 241 to address the conduct presented in this case, and it concluded that introducing relatively untested legal theories surrounding Section 2383 would create unwarranted litigation risk.

Importantly, the charges the Office brought fully addressed Mr. Trump's criminal conduct, and pursuing a charge under Section 2383 would not have added to or otherwise strengthened the Office's evidentiary presentation at trial. For all of these reasons, the Office elected not to pursue charges under Section 2383.[193]

F. Co-Conspirator Liability

As described in the factual recitation above, Mr. Trump was charged with participating in crimes with at least six co-conspirators, and the Office's investigation uncovered evidence that some individuals shared criminal culpability with Mr. Trump. Following the original indictment on August 1, 2023, the Office continued to investigate whether any other participant in the conspiracies should be charged with crimes. In addition, the Office referred to a United States Attorney's Office for further investigation evidence that an investigative subject may have committed unrelated crimes.

Before the Department concluded that this case must be dismissed, the Office had made a preliminary determination that the admissible evidence could justify seeking charges against certain co-conspirators. The Office had also begun to evaluate how to proceed, including whether any potential charged case should be joined with Mr. Trump's or brought separately.

---

[193] The Office also considered, but decided not to pursue, charges under certain other federal criminal statutes, including 18 U.S.C. § 2101 (the Anti-Riot Act) and 18 U.S.C. § 372 (Conspiracy to Impede or Injure an Officer of the United States). The Office was aware that courts have struck down and limited various prongs of the Anti-Riot Act, *see United States v. Rundo*, 990 F.3d 709, 716-717 (9th Cir. 2021) (per curiam); *United States v. Miselis*, 972 F.3d 518, 535-539 (4th Cir. 2020). And as to Section 372, the Office had strong evidence that Mr. Trump and his co-conspirators agreed to use deceit to defeat the government function of collecting, counting, and certifying the results of the election, to obstruct the certification, and to injure the right of citizens to vote and have their votes counted. Further, as explained above, the Office also had strong evidence that the violence that occurred on January 6 was foreseeable to Mr. Trump, that he caused it, and that he and his co-conspirators leveraged it to carry out their conspiracies. But because the investigation did not develop proof beyond a reasonable doubt that the conspirators specifically agreed to threaten force or intimidation against federal officers, the Office did not pursue a charge under Section 372. After considering the facts, the law, and the Principles of Federal Prosecution, the Office concluded that the charges ultimately pursued would fully address Mr. Trump's criminal conduct, allow the Office to present the full scope of that conduct to a jury, and avoid unnecessary litigation. As a result, the Office decided not to seek any of these other potential charges.

Because the Office reached no final conclusions and did not seek indictments against anyone other than Mr. Trump—the head of the criminal conspiracies and their intended beneficiary—this Report does not elaborate further on the investigation and preliminary assessment of uncharged individuals. This Report should not be read to allege that any particular person other than Mr. Trump committed a crime, nor should it be read to exonerate any particular person.

III.   THE PRINCIPLES OF FEDERAL PROSECUTION

As set forth above, the Office concluded that Mr. Trump's conduct violated several federal criminal statutes and that the admissible evidence would be sufficient to obtain and sustain a conviction. Therefore, under the longstanding Principles of Federal Prosecution, the Office considered whether: (1) the prosecution would serve a substantial federal interest; (2) Mr. Trump was subject to effective prosecution in another jurisdiction; or (3) there existed an adequate non-criminal alternative to prosecution. U.S. Department of Justice, Justice Manual § 9-27.220. As described below, multiple substantial federal interests were served by Mr. Trump's prosecution, he was not subject to effective prosecution in another jurisdiction, and there was no adequate non-criminal alternative to prosecution. The Supreme Court's decision on presidential immunity, handed down after the initial decision to prosecute and analyzed below in Section V.D.2 did not alter the Office's view that the Principles of Federal Prosecution compelled prosecuting Mr. Trump; although that decision prevented use of certain evidence uncovered regarding Mr. Trump's misuse of presidential power, he also engaged in non-immune criminal conduct that is set forth in the superseding indictment. Accordingly, this section discusses only evidence that was not immunized—either because it involved Mr. Trump's private conduct or because the Office would have rebutted any presumption of immunity.

A.   Prosecuting Mr. Trump Served Multiple Substantial Federal Interests

Mr. Trump's prosecution served multiple federal interests, including the federal interest in the integrity of the United States' process for collecting, counting, and certifying presidential elections, and in a peaceful and orderly transition of presidential power; the federal interest in ensuring that every citizen's vote is counted; the federal interest in protecting public officials and government workers from violence; and the federal interest in the fair and even-handed enforcement of the law. All of these federal interests, which are rooted in the law, the Constitution, and our basic democratic values, are substantial and command protection from Mr. Trump's criminal design to subvert them.

1.   The substantial federal interest in protecting the integrity of the electoral process and the peaceful transfer of power was served by Mr. Trump's prosecution.

As set forth above, the investigation revealed that Mr. Trump and others conspired to use false claims of election fraud to attempt to disrupt the United States' electoral process and obstruct the congressional certification of the 2020 presidential election results. Prosecution for that conduct thus vindicated abiding federal interests in protecting the electoral process and the previously unbroken tradition—before Mr. Trump's charged conduct—of a peaceful transition of presidential power from one administration to the next. These federal interests are fundamental to our system of government, favoring no particular administration or political party. Indeed, electoral processes like selecting the president are "necessarily structured to maintain the integrity of the democratic system." *Burdick*, 504 U.S. at 441. "Preserving the integrity of the electoral process" and "preventing corruption . . . are interests of the highest importance." *First Nat. Bank of Boston v. Bellotti*, 435 U.S. 765, 788-789 (1978).

The Office was cognizant of Mr. Trump's free speech rights during the investigation and would not have brought a prosecution if the evidence indicated he had engaged in mere political exaggeration or rough-and-tumble politics. *See supra* at Section II.D (First Amendment defense discussion); Robert Jackson, *The Federal Prosecutor, Address Delivered at the Second Annual Conference of United States Attorneys* (April 1, 1940) ("In the enforcement of laws that protect our national integrity and existence, we should prosecute any and every *act* of violation, but only overt acts, not the expression of opinion, or activities such as the holding of meetings, petitioning of congress, or dissemination of news or opinions.") (emphasis in original). As set forth in the original and superseding indictments, Mr. Trump had "a right, like every American, to speak publicly about the election and even to claim, falsely, that there had been outcome-determinative fraud in the election and that he had won." ECF No. 1 at ¶ 3; ECF No. 226 at ¶ 3. He also had lawful recourse to challenge the election results, including through lawsuits, recounts, and audits. In fact, Mr. Trump and his allies vigorously pursued these methods of contesting the election results, but they were unsuccessful.

After election day, Mr. Trump or his Campaign were plaintiffs or intervenors in at least sixteen lawsuits seeking to change the outcome of the election,[194] and Mr. Trump's supporters

---

[194] *In re Enforcement of Election Laws and Securing Ballots Cast or Received after 7:00 p.m. on Nov. 3, 2020*, No. SPCV20-00982 (Chatham County, Ga. Super. Ct.); *Donald J. Trump for President Inc. v. Boockvar*, No. 602-md-2020 (Pa. Commw. Ct.); *Aguilera v. Fontes*, No. 20-cv-14083 (Maricopa County, Az. Super. Ct.); *Donald J. Trump for President Inc. v. Benson*, No. 20-000225-MZ (Mich. Ct. Cl.); *Donald J. Trump for President Inc. v. Philadelphia County Bd. of Elections*, No. 20-cv-5533 (E.D. Pa.); *Donald J. Trump for President Inc. v. Montgomery County Bd. of Elections*, No. 2020-18680 (Montgomery County, Pa. Ct. Com. Pls.); *Donald J. Trump for President Inc. v. Hobbs*, No. 2020-cv-014248 (Maricopa County Ariz. Super. Ct.); *Donald J. Trump for President Inc. v. Boockvar*, No. 20-cv-02078 (M.D. Pa.); *Donald J. Trump for President Inc. v. Benson*, No. 20-cv-1083 (W.D. Mich.); *Trump v. Evers*, No. 2020-AP-1971 (Wis. Sup. Ct.); *Trump v. Wisconsin Election Commission*, No. 20-cv-1785 (E.D. Wis.); *Trump v. Biden*, No. 2020-cv-7092, No. 2020-cv-2514 (Cir. Ct. Wis.); *Donald J. Trump for President Inc. v. Raffensperger*, No. 2020-cv-343255 (Fulton County, Ga. Super. Ct.); *Texas v. Pennsylvania*, 141 S. Ct. 1230 (2020); *Donald J. Trump for President Inc. v. Toulouse-Oliver*, No. 20-cv-01289-MV (D.N.M.); *Kemp*, No. 20-cv-5310 (N.D. Ga.).

filed dozens of other such lawsuits,[195] but all of these failed to change the outcome in any state. Mr. Trump pursued recounts in only two states—a statewide machine recount in Georgia and a recount in Wisconsin's Milwaukee and Dane Counties—and both served only to confirm the previously reported result (in Wisconsin, the recount increased Mr. Trump's margin of loss).[196] Following public requests, Secretaries of State in Georgia and Michigan ordered additional audits and recounts—in Georgia, a statewide hand recount and an audit in Cobb County, and in Michigan, a statewide audit and a hand recount in Antrim County, where Mr. Trump seized on claims of a clerk's temporary clerical error—but all merely confirmed previously reported results.[197]

The conduct of Mr. Trump and co-conspirators, however, went well beyond speaking their minds or contesting the election results though our legal system. Instead, Mr. Trump targeted a key federal government function—the process by which the United States collects, counts, and certifies the results of the presidential election—and sought to obstruct or defeat it through fraud and deceit. He did so using knowingly false claims of election fraud to attempt to induce state officials to reject citizens' votes and instead appoint Mr. Trump's electors; when he deceived his electors and caused them to falsify electoral certificates and submit them to Congress; when he attempted to enlist Mr. Pence with false claims of election fraud and pressure;

[195] See, e.g., Constantino v. City of Detroit, No. 20-14780 (Wayne County, Mich. Cir. Ct.); Republican Party of Arizona v. Fontes, No. 2020-cv-014553 (Maricopa County, Az. Super. Ct.); Law v. Whitmer, 20 OC 0016318B (First Jud. Ct. Carson City, Nev.); Ward v. Jackson, No. 2020-cv-015285 (Maricopa County, Az. Super. Ct.); Pearson v. Kemp, No. 18-cv-04809 (N.D. Ga.); King v. Whitmer, No. 20-cv-13134 (E.D. Mich.).

[196] See ECF No. 252 at 28 & n.131, 33-34 & n.167, 41 & n.207; SCO-12847178 (Georgia Secretary of State News Release 12/29/2020); SCO-03656876 (Wisconsin Order for Recount 11/19/2020); SCO-06613715 (Wisconsin Statement of Canvass 11/30/2020); Trump v. Biden, 394 Wis.2d 629, 633 (Wis. 2020).

[197] See ECF No. 252 at 12 & n.39, 28 & n.131, 46 & nn.241-243; SCO-04976281 at 03:22-04:16 (Video of Interview 01/02/2021); SCO-12847178 (Georgia Secretary of State News Release 12/29/2020); SCO-04957382 (Michigan Secretary of State News Release 12/17/2020); SCO-04952782 at 33 (Michigan Bureau of Elections, Audits of the November 3, 2020 General Election 04/21/2021).

and when he used, and attempted to leverage, an angry crowd of his supporters—fueled by Mr. Trump's lies—to stop the certification proceeding.

Mr. Trump did this in contravention of the Framers' intent to prevent a sitting President from perpetuating himself in power. "In free Governments," Benjamin Franklin explained, "the rulers are the servants, and the people their superiors & sovereigns." 2 *The Records of the Federal Convention of 1787*, at 120 (Max Farrand ed., 1911). Although the Framers recognized "the necessity of an energetic Executive," they justified and checked his power by ensuring that he always retained "a due dependence on the people." THE FEDERALIST NO. 70 (A. Hamilton); *see Seila Law LLC v. Consumer Financial Protection Bureau*, 591 U.S. 197, 223-224 (2020). As the Supreme Court noted in *Trump*, "[t]he President . . . plays no direct role in the process [of appointing electors], nor does he have authority to control the state officials who do. And the Framers, wary of 'cabal, intrigue and corruption,' specifically excluded from service as electors 'all those who from situation might be suspected of too great devotion to the president in office.'" 603 U.S. at 627-628 (quoting THE FEDERALIST NO. 68, at 459 (A. Hamilton) (J. Cooke ed., 1961)). Accordingly, Article II of the U.S. Constitution provides that "no Senator or Representative, or Person holding an Office of Trust or Profit under the United States, shall be appointed an Elector." U.S. CONST. art. II, § 1, cl. 2. The considerable federal interest in protecting the integrity of the United States' electoral process weighed in favor of proceeding with Mr. Trump's prosecution.

So too did the federal interest in defending from future harm the United States' exceptional tradition of peaceful transitions of presidential power. That tradition was initiated by George Washington when he announced in his September 1796 Farewell Address that he would decline to seek a third term, followed by John Adams when he relinquished the power of the presidency to his political rival Thomas Jefferson after the election of 1800, and continued by every sitting President until 2020—even through the turbulent Civil War and Reconstruction eras. And Congress and the courts have also recognized the federal interest in orderly presidential transitions. *See, e.g.,* Presidential Transition Act of 1963, Pub. L. 88-277, 78 Stat. 153, 153-154, § 2 (legislation "to promote the orderly transfer of the executive power" because "[a]ny disruption occasioned by the transfer of the executive power could produce results detrimental to the safety and well-being of the United States and its people"); *Trump v. Thompson*, 20 F.4th 10, 16-17 (D.C. Cir. 2021) (recognizing Congress's "unique legislative need" for documents "directly relevant to the . . . inquiry into an attack on the Legislative Branch and its constitutional role in the peaceful transfer of power"); *United States v. Tarrio*, 605 F. Supp. 3d 73, 78 (D.D.C. 2022) (when assessing "very serious" nature and circumstances of a January 6-related offense, court observed that "[t]hey involve, among other things, an alleged conspiracy to obstruct the certification of the Electoral College vote and thus to interfere with the peaceful transfer of power, one of our Nation's crown jewels").

In his first inaugural address, President Ronald Reagan remarked on the country's tradition of a peaceful transition of presidential power:

> To a few of us here today this is a solemn and most momentous occasion, and yet in the history of our nation it is a commonplace occurrence. The orderly transfer of authority as called for in the Constitution routinely takes place, as it has for almost two centuries, and few of us stop to think how unique we really are. In the eyes of many in the world, this every-4-year ceremony we accept as normal is nothing less than a miracle.

Inaugural Address (1981). In connection with preserving that tradition, Vice Presidents have presided over the certification of their own election losses. In 1961, then-Vice President Richard M. Nixon fulfilled his role as President of the Senate at the January 6 certification proceeding, announcing that John F. Kennedy had won the presidency. In so announcing his own defeat, Nixon stated,

> This is the first time in 100 years that a candidate for the Presidency announced the result of an election in which he was defeated and announced the victory of his opponent. I do not think we could have a more striking and eloquent example of the stability of our constitutional system and of the proud tradition of the American people of developing, respecting, and honoring institutions of self-government.

107 CONG. REC. 291 (Jan. 6, 1961). And in 2001, after a hard-fought legal dispute over the 2000 presidential election, Vice President Albert Gore Jr. similarly presided over the certification of his opponent, George W. Bush, as President-elect. *See* 147 CONG. REC. 101 (Jan. 6, 2001). Protecting the well-established American tradition of a peaceful transfer of power weighed in favor of prosecution.

2.   The substantial federal interest in counting every citizen's vote was served by Mr. Trump's prosecution.

Few federal interests are stronger in our representative democracy than that of protecting every eligible citizen's right to vote and to have that vote counted. The evidence establishes that in contravention of that right, Mr. Trump urged state officials to disregard the legitimate majority of votes for Mr. Biden and instead appoint Mr. Trump's electors; pressured and threatened Georgia's Secretary of State to "find" more than 11,000 votes to dilute the legitimate vote count and allow Mr. Trump to be declared the winner of the state; and urged Mr. Pence to discard the legitimate electoral certificates that reflected millions of citizens' votes in the targeted states.[198] An additional factor meriting Mr. Trump's prosecution therefore was the need to vindicate and protect the voting rights of these and all future voters.

---

[198] *See* ECF No. 252 at 19 & nn.77-82, 29 & n.137, 65 & n.349, 67 & n.364, 71 & nn.392-398, 73-74 & nn.410-411; *supra* at Section I; *see also, e.g.*, SCO-02295943 at 3 (Presidential Daily Diary 11/22/2020); SCO-00767550 at 9-12 (HSC Tr.); SCO-12998394 at 12 (Tr. of Georgia Secretary of State Call 01/02/2021).

The strength of the federal interest in protecting the right to vote is plain from the history of suffrage in America, as chronicled in the Constitution—which has been amended not fewer than five times to extend and protect the franchise for all adult citizens regardless of race, sex, age, and education, *see* U.S. CONST. amend. XIV, § 2 (providing that if a state failed to ensure all eligible citizens the right to vote, the state's proportional representation would be reduced); amend. XV, § 1 ("The right . . . to vote shall not be denied or abridged . . . on account of race, color, or previous condition of servitude."); amend. XIX (same "on account of sex"); amend. XXIV, § 1 (same "by reason of failure to pay any poll tax or other tax"); amend. XXVI, § 1 (same for citizens "who are eighteen years of age or older . . . on account of age")—and a consistent line of court decisions maintaining that suffrage "can neither be denied outright, nor destroyed by alteration of ballots," *Reynolds v. Sims*, 377 U.S. 533, 555 (1964) (citations omitted). The strength of the federal interest is further reflected by the history of the Section 241 offense with which Mr. Trump was charged, and, as set forth in Section II.C above, by courts' universal and longstanding recognition of the right protected by that statute. In attempting to disenfranchise voters who did not choose to reelect him, Trump targeted a bedrock fundamental right that the government has a strong interest in protecting.

3. The substantial federal interest in protecting election officials and other government officials from violence was served by Mr. Trump's prosecution.

Another federal interest that merited Mr. Trump's prosecution was addressing his resort, throughout the charged criminal conspiracies, to threats and encouragement of violence against his perceived opponents. Consistently, when elected officials refused to take improper actions that Mr. Trump urged, like discarding legitimate votes or appointing fraudulent electors, Mr. Trump attacked them publicly on Twitter, a social media application on which he had more than

80 million followers.[199] Inevitably, threats and intimidation to these officials followed.[200] For instance, after Mr. Trump targeted a Philadelphia City Commissioner in a Tweet criticizing the Commissioner for stating that there was no evidence of widespread election fraud in Philadelphia,[201] threats against the Commissioner grew more targeted, more detailed, and more graphic.[202] These threats extended to include highly personal information like the names and ages of the Commissioner's family members, as well as photos or the address of his home.[203] Fulton County, Georgia, election officials similarly reported receiving threats—including death threats—following Mr. Trump's false public accusations against Fulton County election workers.[204]

Mr. Trump also targeted private citizens who served as election workers. He took particular aim at a mother and daughter who worked at Atlanta's State Farm Arena counting ballots on election day; he and his co-conspirators spread pernicious false claims that these election workers had committed misconduct.[205] Although the lies were promptly and publicly

---

[199] *See* ECF No. 252 at 18 & nn.73-76, 20 & n.88, 26-27 & nn.123-126, 28 & n.132, 31 & n.146, 40 & n.206; *see, e.g.,* SCO-00456209, SCO-00715415 (Donald J. Trump Tweet 11/11/2020); SCO-00455691, SCO-12858431 (Donald J. Trump Retweet 11/30/2020); SCO-00455690, SCO-12987528 (Donald J. Trump Tweet 11/30/2020); SCO-00455536, SCO-12858636 (Donald J. Trump Retweet 12/06/2020).

[200] *See* ECF No. 252 at 21 & nn.92-93, 38 & nn.192-194; SCO-11545129 at 86-88 (Int. Tr.); SCO-00767550 at 52-54 (HSC Tr.).

[201] *See* ECF No. 252 at 38 & n.193; SCO-12876770 at 02:20-04:13 (Video of Interview with CNN 11/11/2020); SCO-00456209, SCO-12987659 (Donald J. Trump Tweet 11/11/2020).

[202] *See* ECF No. 252 at 38 & n.194; SCO-11545129 at 87 (Int. Tr.); SCO-04976349 at 02:03:17-02:04:10 (Video of HSC Hearing).

[203] *See* ECF No. 252 at 38 & n.194; SCO-11545129 at 87 (Int. Tr.); SCO-04976349 at 02:03:17-02:04:10 (Video of HSC Hearing).

[204] SCO-11507432 at 46-50, 57-62 (Int. Tr.); SCO-11528118 at 54-62 (Int. Tr.).

[205] *See* ECF No. 252 at 25-26 & nn.119-122; SCO-04976332 at 33:30-01:04:37 (Video of Georgia Senate Judiciary Subcommittee Hearing 12/03/2020); SCO-00455601, SCO-12987506 (Donald J. Trump Tweet 12/03/2020); SCO-04976279 at 01:36:58-02:01:58 (Video of Georgia House Committee Hearing 12/10/2020).

debunked,[206] Mr. Trump continued to repeat them,[207] and the election workers were subjected to vile threats. As one of the women explained, "when someone as powerful as the President of the United States eggs on a mob, that mob will come. They came for us with their cruelty, their threats, their racism, and their hats. They haven't stopped even today."[208] Mr. Trump persisted in publicly spreading false and harmful social media posts about the same election workers into 2023.[209] In 2024, Co-Conspirator 1 conceded in a defamation lawsuit filed by the election workers that his statements about them were "defamatory per se" and "false," and a jury awarded them damages of more than $145 million.[210]

Mr. Trump took aim at Mr. Pence when Mr. Pence repeatedly informed Mr. Trump that he could not in good conscience do as Mr. Trump asked. On January 6, this included Mr. Trump's retributive targeting of Mr. Pence during his Ellipse speech and the 2:24 p.m. Tweet attacking Mr. Pence that Mr. Trump issued even though he knew that the riot was ongoing at the Capitol. Taken together, these actions resulted in rioters at the Capitol on January 6 singling out Mr. Pence for their ire and chanting, "Where is Pence? Bring Him Out!"[211] and, "Hang Mike Pence!"[212]

---

[206] SCO-04952956 (Tweet 12/04/2020); SCO-04976277 at 08:44-09:10 (Video of Georgia Secretary of State Press Conference 12/07/2020).

[207] See ECF No. 252 at 26 & n.122; SCO-12998394 at 2 (Tr. of Georgia Secretary of State Call 01/02/2021).

[208] See ECF No. 252 at 25-26 & n.121; SCO-00783640 at 8 (HSC Tr.).

[209] See ECF No. 252 at 26 & n.122; SCO-04963742 (Donald J. Trump Truth Social Post 01/02/2023); SCO-04963743 (Donald J. Trump Truth Social Post 01/03/2023).

[210] Freeman v. Giuliani, No. 21-cv-3354, ECF No. 90 at 1-2 (D.D.C. Aug. 8, 2023) (Def. Stipulation), ECF No. 142 (D.D.C. Dec. 18, 2023) (Final Judgment).

[211] See ECF No. 1 at ¶ 113; see ECF No. 252 at 81 & n.467; SCO-12738318 (Video of Capitol Riot 01/06/2021).

[212] See ECF No. 1 at ¶ 113; see ECF No. 252 at 81 & n.466; SCO-12876211 (Video of Capitol Riot 01/06/2021).

In addition to prompting these threats against the targets of Mr. Trump's criticisms, Mr. Trump's words inspired his supporters to commit acts of physical violence. On January 6, Mr. Trump used his Ellipse speech to direct his supporters to "go[] to the Capitol" and "fight like hell."[213] He explicitly licensed them, not long after Co-Conspirator 1 had exhorted the crowd to engage in "trial by combat,"[214] to operate under "very different rules"[215] because fraud was allegedly involved. And he told them they were "not going to let it happen,"[216] urging them to stop the election certification proceeding that was about to begin.

The people who took Mr. Trump at his word formed a massive crowd that broke onto restricted Capitol grounds and into the building, violently attacking law enforcement officers protecting the Capitol and those inside. Officers have described being assaulted by rioters wielding bear spray, metal bats and flag poles, and other improvised weapons.[217] A Metropolitan Police Department (MPD) commander recounted that the scene was "a non-stop barrage of just strikes, with weapons and things being thrown, and pepper spray, and you name it. Everything being hurled at these [officers]. You could hear them yelling. You could hear them, screams and moans, and everything else."[218] Multiple officers stated that they feared for their lives when among the rioters that day. One MPD officer put that fear at "a hundred percent" from the moment he entered the crowd, and he explained that he thought he might die: "You know, you're

---

[213] See ECF No. 252 at 77 & nn.437, 440; SCO-02244118 at 22 (Remarks by Mr. Trump at Save America Rally 01/06/2021).

[214] SCO-04949418 at 02:22:07 (Video of Save America Rally 01/06/2021).

[215] SCO-02244118 at 20 (Remarks by Mr. Trump at Save America Rally 01/06/2021).

[216] Id. at 2.

[217] See ECF No. 252 at 82 & nn.475-476; SCO-11506096 at 125-126 (Int. Tr.); SCO-11506269 at 38-39 (Int. Tr.); SCO-12808448 at 127-128 (Int. Tr.); SCO-11520948 at 95-97 (Int. Tr.); SCO-12997436 at 64 (*United States v. Irwin & Richter*, No. 21-cr-589, Trial Day 1 Tr. 01/22/2024).

[218] SCO-11529214 at 98 (Int. Tr.).

getting pushed, kicked, you know, people are throwing metal bats at you and all that stuff. I was like, yeah, this is fucking it."[219] A U.S. Capitol Police officer similarly recalled thinking, "I think I might die today."[220] And in one instance, an MPD officer recounted that rioters dragged him into the crowd, where they beat and tased him while yelling things like, "I got one!" and, "Kill him with his gun!"[221]

The January 6 rioters assaulted at least 140 law enforcement officers that day, and at least 123 defendants have been charged with using a deadly or dangerous weapon or causing serious bodily injury to law enforcement.[222] This violence took a lasting toll. In addition to the significant physical injuries inflicted that day,[223] officers suffered "unseen injuries," including depression and other forms of psychological trauma.[224]

---

[219] *See* ECF No. 252 at 82 & nn.475-476; SCO-11506096 at 126 (Int. Tr.).

[220] SCO-12807683 at 106-107 (Int. Tr.).

[221] SCO-12919375 at 01:12:28-01:13:50 (Video of Interview from HBO's *Four Hours at the Capitol*, 10/20/2021).

[222] Press Release, U.S. Attorney's Office for the District of Columbia, Three Years Since the Jan. 6 Attack on the Capitol (Jan. 5, 2024), https://www.justice.gov/usao-dc/36-months-jan-6-attack-capitol-0.

[223] SCO-11506096 at 96-99, 134-135 (Int. Tr.) (MPD officer recounting knee injury and concussion from defending against rioters on January 6); SCO-12875808 at 228-230 (*United States v. McCaughey*, No. 21-cr-40, Trial Day 1 Tr. 08/29/2022) (MPD sergeant describing being "bruised, abrased," and "covered in chemical munitions" from January 6); *id.* at 229 (50 percent of sergeant's 30-person platoon injured); SCO-12997205 at 101 (*United States v. Sparks*, No. 21-cr-87, Trial Tr. 02/29/2024) (Capitol Police officer describing concern on January 6 for fellow officers he saw "still irritated from the tear gas, people still coughing, people limping, battered, bruised, bloody," and learning that a fellow officer "had passed away"); SCO-12997436 at 63-64 (*United States v. Irwin & Richter*, No. 21-cr-589, Trial Day 1 Tr. 01/22/2024) (Capitol Police Deputy Chief listing officers' injuries from rioters, including a "serious concussion" and a "near-career-ending leg injury"); SCO-12807683 at 124-125 (Int. Tr.) (Capitol Police officer describing jaw injury and concussion from rioter assault; *id.* at 135 (Capitol Police officer detailing lingering effects of Capitol siege injuries, including persistent migraines, fainting, and imbalance).

[224] SCO-12876218 at 08:53-09:45 (Video of Impact Statement) (MPD officer recounting that "there [were] a lot of unseen injuries," that MPD "has put a lot of effort and resources into getting these officers the help that they need for some of these emotional injuries," and that the events of January 6 had "definitely taken a toll on a lot of the officers over there that day"); SCO-11529214 at 116 (Int. Tr.) (MPD officer stating there were "some people that went through, like, you know, some depression and, like, really some soul-searching"); SCO-12807683 at 16 (Int. Tr.) (Capitol Police officer describing "survivor's guilt" and engaging in officer peer support program); *id.* at 143 (describing officer reactions to January 6, including "shell-shock" and inability to move on from that day); SCO-12919375 at 01:28:00-01:28:20 (Video of MPD Officer's Interview from HBO's *Four Hours at the Capitol*, 10/20/2021) (MPD officer describing that he had a mild heart attack and traumatic brain injury from rioter assaults

Officers at the Capitol understood that if the rioters reached the lawmakers and other staff inside the building violence would have been done to them as well.[225] Only through the heroism of the law enforcement officers who defended the Capitol were lawmakers and their staff protected from harm.[226] Many Members of Congress feared for their lives. Once the rioters breached the Capitol building, "elected representatives, congressional staff, and members of the press hid in terror from the mob" in barricaded offices or unmarked rooms as rioters roamed the hallways. *United States v. Chrestman*, 525 F. Supp. 3d 14, 19 (D.D.C. 2021).[227] For instance, in detailing his efforts to evacuate a U.S. Senator and her staff from an unmarked hiding spot, one

on January 6, but what he "most struggle[s] with is, you know, kind of, some of the emotional after-effects, or psychological trauma" of that day).

[225] SCO-11506096 at 107-108 (Int. Tr.) (MPD officer describing effort to keep rioters from entering the Capitol because, for staff inside, that would mean "possible death. People are getting killed, maimed," and adding that while officers "have gear on" and weapons, "someone who just showed up this morning to go to work, who was like a clerk or something, walked in their office . . . they're not ready for that, you know? And if one of these [rioters] get their hands on them, it's over with."); SCO-11529214 at 78-80 (Int. Tr.) (MPD officer describing seeing rioters "trying to beat [officers] up with such ferocity," and wondering, "What are they going to do to somebody else that's in here, that's maybe a staff or a congressman or somebody with the press? How are—what are they going to do to them? You know, like, we can take the beating. And I don't know if these other people can take the beating, too."); SCO-11544684 at 7 (Int. Rep.) (Capitol Police officer recalling that the rioters turned on Vice President Pence and being concerned for Pence's safety inside the Capitol if rioters breached the police line); *see also* SCO-12738295 (Video of Capitol Riot 01/06/2021) (rioters inside the Capitol yelling, "Where are the fucking traitors? Drag 'em out by their fucking hair!" and "Who's first?"); SCO-12738313 (Video of Capitol Riot 01/06/2021) (rioter yelling, "Bring Mitch out! Bring Pelosi out! Bring Schumer out!"); SCO-12738317 (Video of Capitol Riot 01/06/2021) (rioters chanting, "Pence is a traitor!" and, "Traitor Pence! Traitor Pence!"); SCO-12738306 (Video of Capitol Riot 01/06/2021) (rioter yelling, "We're coming for you, Nancy!"); SCO-12738312 at 00:59-01:40 (Video of Capitol Riot 01/06/2021) (rioter inside the Capitol yelling, "Nancy Pelosi! Where you at, Nancy?" and, "Nancy! Where are you, Nancy? We're looking for you!").

[226] *See* 167 CONG. RECORD S5686 (daily ed. Aug. 3, 2021) (statement of Sen. Klobuchar) ("The insurrection at the Capitol was more than an assault on democracy. . . . [I]t was also an actual life-or-death situation for the many brave law enforcement officers who show up here to do their work every day."); *id.* at S5687 (statement of Sen. Blunt) ("I am incredibly grateful for the heroic actions we saw that day [January 6] from the Capitol Police, from the Metropolitan Police, who . . . were here within 10 or 12 minutes of being called."); 167 CONG. RECORD H2790 (June 15, 2021) (statement of Rep. McHenry) ("[T]he brave men and women who stood and faced danger on January 6 deserve to be recognized for their actions. Without their courageous work and their dedication, many of us here today could have been seriously injured or worse.").

[227] *See also* SCO-12919375 at 29:44-30:52, 41:45-43:15 (Video of Interview from HBO's *Four Hours at the Capitol*, 10/20/2021) (Congressional staffer describing hiding under a table from rioters who had breached the Capitol building, hearing rioters banging on the door to the room in which she was barricaded, and fearing she would die that day).

U.S. Capitol Police officer described the Senator as "afraid for her life," "shaking," and "very, very—she was scared."[228] He added that the Senator later relayed to him that what the rioters did on January 6 had "scared and frightened everybody" and had "put a lot of people's lives in danger."[229]

The violence of January 6 was foreseeable to Mr. Trump, who had remarked just the evening before that his supporters were "angry"[230] and who—to cheers of, "Invade the Capitol building!" and, "Take the Capitol!"[231]—had told those supporters during his Ellipse speech to "show strength" and to "be strong."[232] When he told them "we're not going to let it happen," the crowd chanted, "Fight for Trump!"[233] And when he warned his gathered supporters that "if you don't fight like hell, you're not going to have a country anymore,"[234] the crowd marched to the Capitol in response. Indeed, officials and advisors close to Mr. Trump recognized and voiced their concerns over this high potential for election-related violence. On January 4, a Senior Advisor explicitly warned Co-Conspirator 2 that if Mr. Pence unilaterally rejected legitimate electoral votes, it would cause "riots in the streets."[235] Co-Conspirator 2 replied that there had previously been points in the nation's history where violence was necessary to protect the

---

[228] SCO-11520948 at 150-152 (Int. Tr.).

[229] Id. at 151.

[230] See ECF No. 1 at ¶ 98; SCO-00015613 at 155-156.

[231] See ECF No. 252 at 77-78 & n.443; SCO-12876144 at 00:28-00:43 (Rallygoer video 01/06/2021).

[232] See ECF No. 252 at 77-78 & n.442; SCO-02244118 at 6 (Remarks by Mr. Trump at Save America Rally 01/06/2021).

[233] See ECF No. 252 at 77 & nn.438-439; SCO-02244118 at 2 (Remarks by Mr. Trump at Save America Rally 01/06/2021).

[234] SCO-02244118 at 22 (Remarks by Mr. Trump at Save America Rally 01/06/2021).

[235] See ECF No. 252 at 66 & n.356; SCO-00006256 at 130-133; SCO-11522446 at 6 (Int. Rep.); SCO-00790949 at 26 (HSC Tr.).

republic.[236]   On January 5, after Mr. Trump told Mr. Pence that he would have to publicly criticize him, Mr. Pence's Chief of Staff was sufficiently concerned for Mr. Pence's safety that he alerted the head of the Vice President's protective detail.[237]   And a Counsel to the Vice President issued a prescient warning to Co-Conspirator 2 the same day, when he warned that the conspirators' plan would result in a "disastrous situation" where the election might "have to be decided in the streets."[238]   Indeed, as the riot at the Capitol unfolded on January 6, the Vice President's Counsel chided Co-Conspirator 2 that "whipping large numbers of people into a frenzy over something with no chance of ever attaining legal force through actual process of law, has led us to where we are."[239]

There is unquestionably a public interest in ensuring that elected officials and election workers can carry out their duties without fear of threats and retaliation. *See, e.g.*, Memorandum from Lisa Monaco, Deputy Attorney General, *Guidance Regarding Threats Against Election Workers* (June 25, 2021) ("The right to vote is the cornerstone of our democracy, the right from which all other rights ultimately flow. For this vital right to be effective, election officials must be permitted to do their jobs free from improper partisan influence, physical threats, or any other conduct designed to intimidate."). Accordingly, the need to promote this federal interest weighed in favor of proceeding against Mr. Trump.

---

[236] *See* SCO-00006256 at 133; SCO-11522446 at 6 (Int. Rep.); SCO-00790949 at 26 (HSC Tr.).

[237] SCO-11545613 at 165-171 (Int. Tr.).

[238] *See* ECF No. 252 at 69-70 & n.385; SCO-04976350 at 01:26:01-01:26:32 (Video of HSC Testimony).

[239] SCO-00256421 at 2 (Email to Co-Conspirator 2 01/06/2021).

4.   The substantial federal interest in the evenhanded administration of the law was served by Mr. Trump's prosecution.

There is a substantial federal interest in ensuring the evenhanded administration of the law with respect to accountability for the events of January 6, 2021, and the Office determined that interest would not be satisfied absent Mr. Trump's prosecution for his role. Multiple district court judges have recognized Mr. Trump's role in the events of January 6. *See United States v. Lolos*, No. 21-cr-242, ECF No. 37 at 55-56 (D.D.C. Nov. 19, 2021) (Transcript of Sentencing) (Court stating that Jan. 6 defendant was "called to Washington, D.C. by an election official; he was prompted to walk to the Capitol by an elected official" and telling defendant, "I think you were a pawn, you were a pawn in a game that was played and directed by people who should have known better"); *United States v. Peterson*, No. 21-cr-309, ECF No. 32 at 23 (D.D.C. Dec. 1, 2021) (Transcript of Sentencing) (Court stating that "incendiary" statements at the Ellipse rally "absolutely, quite clearly and deliberately, stoked the flames of fear and discontent and explicitly encouraged those at the rally to go to the Capitol and fight for one reason and one reason only, to make sure the certification did not happen"); *United States v. Barnard*, No. 21-cr-235, ECF No. 53 at 28 (D.D.C. Feb. 24, 2022) (Transcript of Sentencing) ("The events of January 6th involved a rather unprecedented confluence of events spurred by then President Trump and a number of his prominent allies who bear much responsibility for what occurred on that date."). To date, more than 1,500 people have been criminally charged for their roles in the January 6 attack on the United States Capitol. With that in mind, Mr. Trump's relative culpability weighed heavily in favor of charging him, as the individual most responsible for what occurred at the Capitol on January 6. *See* Justice Manual § 9-27.230.4 (requiring prosecutors to assess the "degree of the person's culpability in connection with the offense, both in the abstract and in comparison with any others involved in the offense").

Rioters have cited Mr. Trump as the reason they traveled to Washington, D.C., and went to the Capitol that day. In the weeks before January 6, Mr. Trump issued several Tweets calling his supporters to Washington, D.C., for his rally at the Ellipse, and they answered the call. In the days after Mr. Trump's December 19 Tweet promising that the rally would be "wild," for instance, Kelly Meggs—a member of the Oath Keepers group who was later convicted of seditious conspiracy among other charges—messaged associates that "[i]t's going to be wild. [Trump] wants us to make it wild. That's what he's saying." *United States v. Rhodes*, No. 22-cr-15, ECF No. 815 at 61 (D.D.C. Feb. 21, 2024) (Motion Hearing Tr.). Meggs added, "He called us all to the Capitol, . . . and he wants us to make it wild." *Id.* at 61-62. Rioter David Kuntz—a member of the Three Percenters militia group who would later plead guilty to charges related to breaching the Capitol building—planned travel to Washington, D.C., on January 6 in direct response to the December 19 Tweet. *United States v. Wilson*, No. 23-cr-427, ECF No. 47 at 6-7 (D.D.C. Apr. 17, 2024) (Superseding Indictment). Kuntz later shared Trump's December 27 Tweet, which told supporters, "See you in Washington DC, on January 6th. Don't miss it. Information to follow!" Kuntz commented, "He is asking us to be there," and, "Good he does need us im [sic] going armed period." *Id.* at 11; *see also Wilson*, No. 23-cr-427, ECF No. 95 at 8 (D.D.C. Dec. 2, 2024) (Statement of Offense).

In his Ellipse speech, Mr. Trump explicitly directed his supporters to march on the Capitol. At one point, in reply to a line in his speech that "[w]e will not let them silence your voices; we're not going to let it happen," a portion of the rally crowd chanted, "Fight for Trump! Fight for Trump!"[240] When he repeatedly exhorted his supporters to "walk down"[241] to the U.S.

---

[240] *See* ECF No. 252 at 77 & nn.438-439; SCO-02244118 at 2 (Remarks by Mr. Trump at Save America Rally 01/06/2021); SCO-00747921 at 03:18-03:47 (Rallygoer video 01/06/2021).

Capitol to help prevent Congress's planned certification, they listened. Law enforcement witnesses at and near the Capitol on January 6 describe large crowds descending upon Capitol grounds from the direction of the Ellipse rally.[241] And video and photographic evidence shows that hundreds of individuals in attendance at the Ellipse rally were later participants in the Capitol siege and in some cases were among the most violent of the rioters.[243]

During the siege, Mr. Trump's supporters continued to heed his words. Video evidence from that afternoon shows rioters, in real time, crediting Mr. Trump for their presence and conduct at the Capitol. For example, as the crowd sought to push past officers protecting the Capitol's East Front, one rioter shouted: "We were invited here! We were invited by the President of the United States!"[244] Inside, another rioter yelled at officers to "stand down. You're outnumbered. There's a fucking million of us out there. And we're listening to Trump—

your boss."[245] *United States v. Harris*, No. 21-cr-189, ECF No. 84 at 5 (D.D.C. Oct. 20, 2023). That rioter was later convicted of obstruction and of assaulting an officer, among other violations. *Id.* at 11. As the day wore on, rioters continued to obey Mr. Trump's commands. At 4:25 p.m.—just eight minutes after Mr. Trump's video Tweet telling supporters that they were "very special" but should "go home now"—rioter Edward Vallejo, a member of the Oath Keepers, posted to a group Signal chat that "our commander in chief has just ordered us to go home." *Rhodes*, ECF No. 822 at 55 (Sentencing Hearing Tr.). Another rioter, Jacob Chansley, played that video Tweet to a crowd at the Capitol and announced that "Donald Trump has asked everybody to go home."[246] Chansley left the Capitol at that point—having earlier breached the Senate chamber, taken a seat at the dais, and declared Vice President Pence to be "a fucking traitor." *United States v. Chansley*, No. 21-cr-3, ECF No. 81 at 10-11 (D.D.C. Nov. 9, 2021) (Gov't Sentencing Memorandum).[247]

After January 6, when rioters began to face accountability for their unlawful acts at the Capitol, many pointed to Mr. Trump in an attempt to excuse or mitigate their conduct. For example, following his arrest on charges stemming from the Capitol siege, rioter Alex Harkrider sought release from pretrial detention by arguing that "[l]ike thousands of others [at the Capitol], Mr. Harkrider was responding to the entreaties of the then Commander-in-Chief, former President Donald Trump." *United States v. Harkrider*, No. 21-cr-117, ECF No. 16 at 14 (D.D.C. Apr. 1, 2021) (Def.'s Motion to Revoke Order of Detention); *see also, e.g., United States v.*

---

[245] SCO-12876131 at 02:26-02:33 (Video of Capitol Riot 01/06/2021).

[246] SCO-12918754 at 24:47-27:22 (Video of Capitol Riot 01/06/2021); *id.* at 28:00-28:08 (rioter announcing that he was "going to do as Donald Trump has asked and [he was] going to go home"); SCO-12919861 at 01:55:29-01:55:45 (Video of Capitol Riot 01/06/2021); *id.* at 01:57:20-01:57:34 (rioter announcing that "Donald Trump asked everybody to go home. So what are we gonna do? We're going to obey our President; we're gonna do as he asked; and we're gonna go home."); SCO-12876155 (Video outside Capitol 01/06/2021).

[247] *See also* SCO-12916465 (Video of Senate Chamber 01/06/2021).

Hale-Cusanelli, No. 21-cr-37, ECF No. 13 at 17 (D.D.C. Mar. 2, 2021) (Def.'s Motion for Modification of Bond) (requesting pretrial release in part because defendant "was responding to the entreaties of the then commander in chief, President Trump"); *Chansley*, No. 21-cr-3, ECF No. 12 at 10 (D.D.C. Feb. 23, 2021) (Motion of Def. for Pretrial Release) (arguing that Chansley was "incited" by Mr. Trump and noting his unsuccessful request for a presidential pardon). In closing argument at trial on seditious conspiracy and other charges related to January 6, defense counsel unsuccessfully asked the jury to acquit Proud Boys leader Enrique Tarrio because, in part, "[i]t was [Mr. Trump's] anger that caused what occurred on January 6th" and "[i]t was not Enrique Tarrio." *United States v. Nordean et al.*, No. 21-cr-175, Trial Tr. at 19991 (D.D.C. Apr. 25, 2023). And, at sentencing in January 6 cases, many rioter defendants—whether expressing remorse or not—have sought leniency by blaming Mr. Trump both for their presence at the Capitol and their underlying belief "that the [2020 presidential] election was fraudulent and that they must take action to stop the transition of the presidency." *United States v. Palmer*, No. 21-cr-328, ECF No. 31 at 8 (D.D.C. Dec. 13, 2021) (Sentencing Memorandum and Motion for Downward Variance); *see also, e.g.*, *United States v. McCaughey*, 21-cr-40, ECF No. 528 at 2 (D.D.C. Feb. 17, 2023) (Def. David Mehaffie's Sentencing Statement); *United States v. Gruppo*, No. 21-cr-391, ECF No. 28-2 at 2 (D.D.C. Oct. 19, 2021) (Def.'s Letter) (citing language of Ellipse rally speech and stating, "I trusted the President and that was a big mistake").

B.   Mr. Trump Was Not Subject to Effective Prosecution in Another Jurisdiction

The next consideration, under the Principles of Federal Prosecution, is whether Mr. Trump was subject to effective prosecution in another jurisdiction. The Office concluded that a prosecution carried out by a single local authority could not effectively hold him accountable for his efforts targeting the only election for national office. Although Mr. Trump was theoretically subject to state criminal charges for his conduct, based on the scope and magnitude of Mr.

Trump's alleged crimes, no local prosecution could effectively hold Mr. Trump accountable for his attempts to overturn the valid results of the election, obstruct the congressional certification, and disenfranchise millions of voters. Indeed, all citizens, not just the citizens in the seven contested states that he targeted with his criminal plan, suffered the impact of Mr. Trump's crimes, warranting a federal prosecution accounting for all his conduct and the federal interests it implicated.

In addition, when the Office was making its charging decision in the summer of 2023, no other jurisdiction had initiated charges against Mr. Trump or co-conspirators. After the grand jury returned the original indictment against Mr. Trump in this case, however, he subsequently was also charged with a racketeering conspiracy in Georgia, *Georgia v. Trump*, 23sc188947, Indictment (Fulton County, Ga. Super. Ct. Aug. 14, 2023) (19-defendant case pending since August 2023 in Fulton County Superior Court). Although the forty-count indictment in Fulton County encompasses some of the same core conduct for which Mr. Trump was charged federally in the District of Columbia, its focus is on a conspiracy to commit fraud—that is, to change the outcome of the election—including through false statements to Georgia state legislators and other high-ranking state officials. *See id.* at 16-17. It does not fully address Mr. Trump's alleged criminal conduct in furtherance of a conspiracy to obstruct the January 6 certification proceeding or a conspiracy against voters' rights. As described above, there are strong federal interests in protecting the integrity of the certification proceeding and the right to vote and have one's vote counted.

C.   <u>There Was No Adequate Non-Criminal Alternative to Prosecution</u>

Given the strong federal interests in holding Mr. Trump accountable described above, the Office could not identify any adequate non-criminal alternative to prosecution. To be sure, because he was President at the time of his alleged offenses, Mr. Trump was subject to impeachment and was in fact impeached (though he was not convicted). Impeachment, however, was never intended to be a substitute for criminal prosecution. "[T]he Framers recognized that most likely there would be two sets of proceedings for individuals who commit impeachable offenses—the impeachment trial and a separate criminal trial." *Nixon v. United States*, 506 U.S. 224, 234 (1993). The Impeachment Judgment Clause itself expressly contemplates separate proceedings, stating that the punishment for impeachment and conviction "shall not extend further than to removal from Office, and disqualification to hold and enjoy any Office of honor, Trust or Profit under the United States: but the Party convicted shall nevertheless be liable and subject to Indictment, Trial, Judgment and Punishment, according to Law." U.S. CONST. art. I, § 3, cl. 7.

Not only are impeachment and prosecution separate and distinct proceedings, they apply different standards and pursue different objectives. When Congress decides whether a President should be impeached and convicted, that process does not depend on rigorously adjudicating facts and applying law, or on finding a criminal violation. Instead, the impeachment process is, by design, an inherently political remedy for the dangers to governance posed by an office holder who has committed "Treason, Bribery, or other high Crimes and Misdemeanors." U.S. CONST. art. II, § 4. Congress may decide not to impeach or convict for reasons that have little or no connection to the nature of the evidence of the officer's culpable conduct. For example, the political alignment of Congress may prevent impeachment and conviction, without regard to the officer's conduct. Indeed, prior to 2020, no Senator had ever voted to convict an impeached President of the same political party. And in cases like this one, where the President has left office by the time an impeachment trial occurs, Senators may question their authority to convict regardless of the egregiousness of the conduct at issue. *See, e.g.*, 167 CONG. REC. S736 (daily ed. Feb. 13, 2021) (statement of Sen. McConnell).

During Mr. Trump's impeachment trial, his counsel insisted that the outcome of the proceeding would have no bearing on any future criminal prosecution, stating, "Clearly, a former civil officer who is not impeached is subject to" criminal prosecution. 167 CONG. REC. S607 (daily ed. Feb. 9, 2021); *see id.* at S601 (noting that if a President "committed a criminal offense" then "[a]fter he is out of office, you go and arrest him," adding, "[t]he Department of Justice does know what to do with such people"). Senators who voted to acquit Mr. Trump expressed a similar view. *See, e.g.*, 167 CONG. REC. S736 (daily ed. Feb. 13, 2021) (statement of Sen. McConnell) (stating that Mr. Trump "is still liable for everything he did while he was in office, as an ordinary citizen," and noting that "[w]e have a criminal justice system in this country"). Thus, even if Mr. Trump had been convicted by the Senate, political accountability, in the form of impeachment, would not have been an adequate alternative for criminal accountability, especially considering the scope of Mr. Trump's offenses and the substantial federal interests they targeted.

D.   Mr. Trump's Conduct Had No Historical Analogue

During pretrial litigation, Mr. Trump contended that his conduct was materially indistinguishable from that of other actors throughout American history—including past Presidents and Vice Presidents—who had either claimed that an election was tainted by fraud or presided over a certification proceeding at the joint session where electoral votes were in dispute. Mr. Trump further argued that because those actors had not been prosecuted for their purportedly similar conduct, it would be unconstitutional to prosecute him for his conduct, because doing so would either violate his right to fair notice, *see* ECF No. 113 at 25-31; ECF No. 114 at 28-31, or result in selective or vindictive prosecution, *see* ECF No. 116 at 6-8. That is, even accepting that

Mr. Trump engaged in the conduct alleged in the indictment, and that such conduct violated the charged statutes, he maintained that prosecution was improper because it conflicted with historical practice.

The historical episodes that Mr. Trump invoked—arising from elections in 1800, 1824, 1876, 1960, 2000, 2004, and 2016—did not involve similar conduct and did not supply a valid reason to decline to bring charges here. In litigation, the Office addressed each historical episode he cited and explained why none was meaningfully similar to the charged conduct. *See* ECF No. 139 at 40-47; ECF No. 141 at 6-9. Taken together, those episodes showed that "[t]here have been times, as in 1800, 1876, and 1960, when genuine questions have arisen over which slate of electors from a particular state has been duly appointed"; "[t]here have also been times, as in 1824, when the failure of any candidate to obtain a majority of electoral votes has thrown the election to the House of Representatives"; and "there have been times, as in 2000, 2004, and 2016, when those dissatisfied with the results have sought to raise objections to the electoral vote count, resulting in either the objections being overruled or, in one case, a brief adjournment designed as an Ohio-focused protest vote without 'the hope or even the hint of overturning the victory of the President.'" ECF No. 139 at 46-47 (quoting 151 CONG. REC. 199 (Jan. 6, 2005)). But none of the historical episodes at issue involved "any attempt by any person to use fraud and deceit to obstruct or defeat the governmental function that would result in the certification of the lawful winner of a presidential election." *Id.* at 40-47; *see* ECF No. 141 at 6-9.

The district court found that there were no historical analogues to Mr. Trump's alleged criminal conduct. When Mr. Trump filed a motion to dismiss the indictment on a claim that he was being selectively prosecuted because of a historical "track record of similar, unprosecuted, efforts" to challenge elections, *see* ECF No. 116 at 6, the district court rejected it, explaining that

Mr. Trump was "not being prosecuted for publicly contesting the results of the election; he is being prosecuted for knowingly making false statements in furtherance of a criminal conspiracy and for obstruction of election certification proceedings." ECF No. 198 at 5-7. Likewise, in its opinion denying Mr. Trump's immunity motion, the district court found that "none of the contested elections" Mr. Trump "invokes is analogous to this case," as none involved "any allegation that any official engaged in criminal conduct to obstruct the electoral process." ECF No. 171 at 47.

IV.   INVESTIGATIVE PROCEDURE AND POLICY

Upon appointing the Special Counsel, the Attorney General explained that the appointment "underscores the Department's commitment to both independence and accountability in particularly sensitive matters. It also allows prosecutors and agents to continue their work expeditiously, and to make decisions indisputably guided only by the facts and the law." *See* Press Release, Office of Public Affairs, Department of Justice, Appointment of a Special Counsel (Nov. 18, 2022), https://www.justice.gov/opa/pr/appointment-special-counsel-0. The Attorney General also noted that, "[a]lthough the Special Counsel will not be subject to the day-to-day supervision of any official of the Department, he must comply with the regulations, procedures, and policies of the Department." *Id.* The Office conducted its work accordingly.

A.   The Investigative Process[248]

Employing traditional investigative tools, including voluntary interviews, grand jury subpoenas, and search warrants—and subject to the same legal requirements binding on all federal prosecutors—the Office, spanning the period predating the Special Counsel's

---

[248] The Appendix to this Report lists public information about key documents from significant litigation undertaken in the course of the investigation and prosecution.

appointment to the completion of its work, developed a thorough record of independently verified facts on which it based its prosecutive decisions in the Election Case. The investigative record comprised voluntary witness interviews and grand jury testimony from numerous individuals, [249] as well as voluminous records such as emails, text messages, encrypted messages, memoranda, and other documents. These records were obtained through both voluntary productions by dozens of witnesses and through compulsory process and court orders, including grand jury subpoenas directed to witnesses and entities, court orders for non-content information (such as sender, recipient, date, and time) from electronic communications accounts, and search warrants to obtain evidence from physical sources and/or locations, electronic devices, and email and iCloud accounts. [250] The Office also obtained records from other components of the Department of Justice, including the U.S. Attorney's Office for the District of Columbia, and other federal agencies, including the National Archives, Department of Homeland Security, Department of Defense, and Office of the Director of National Intelligence. [251] Further, the

---

[249] This record, including the period predating the Special Counsel's appointment, encompasses voluntary interviews of more than 250 individuals and grand jury testimony from more than 55 witnesses.

[250] Search warrants for electronic devices and accounts, as well as applications to obtain records of electronic communications, must be approved by a federal magistrate or district judge and are held to well-established standards of proof. To obtain a search warrant, for instance, the government must establish that there is probable cause to believe that the location, device, or account to be searched contains evidence of a crime. *See* U.S. CONST. amend. IV (search warrants require "probable cause, supported by Oath or affirmation, and particularly describing the place to be searched, and the persons or things to be seized"). Other court orders—for instance, those that give the government access to the non-content information described above regarding electronic communications— require a showing that there are reasonable grounds to believe that the information sought is relevant and material to an ongoing criminal investigation. *See* 18 U.S.C. § 2703(d).

[251] The Office's investigation included consideration of the report issued on December 22, 2022, by the U.S. House of Representatives' Select Committee to Investigate the January 6th Attack on the United States Capitol, as well as certain materials received from the Committee. Those materials comprised a small part of the Office's investigative record, and any facts on which the Office relied to make a prosecution decision were developed or verified through independent interviews and other investigative steps. During the prosecution of the Election Case, Mr. Trump alleged that the Select Committee and Special Counsel's Office were one and the same and sought additional discovery about the Select Committee's work. The district court rejected the claim. *See* ECF No. 263 at 47 (concluding that Mr. Trump has "not supplied an adequate basis to consider the January 6 Select Committee part of the prosecution team"). Regardless, the Office provided or otherwise made available to Mr. Trump in discovery all

Office collected more than one terabyte of data from publicly available sources such as social media postings and websites. All discoverable material was provided or made available to Mr. Trump in discovery during the prosecution of the Election Case.

Throughout its work, the Office complied with "the rules, regulations, procedures, practices and policies of the Department of Justice," 28 C.F.R. § 600.7(a), including consulting the Justice Manual, the Department's publicly available guidebook on policies and procedures, and consulting or obtaining requisite approvals from other Department components. For example, as required under the Justice Manual, the Office obtained approvals from the Criminal Division's Office of Enforcement Operations, which provides legal guidance on the use of sensitive law enforcement tools, such as certain subpoenas and search warrants involving attorneys. And as discussed more below, the Office consulted the Criminal Division's Public Integrity Section (PIN), which oversees the investigation and prosecution of federal crimes affecting government integrity, pursuant to Justice Manual requirements pertaining to the service of subpoenas and other process on Members of Congress, the use of election fraud charges, and the Department's Election Year Sensitivities Policy, a longstanding Department policy regarding the conduct of sensitive investigations during an election year.

Even when not required, in accordance with the best traditions of the Department, the Office actively sought advice and guidance from subject matter experts throughout the Department. For example, the Office requested assistance from the Civil Division and Office of Information Policy (OIP) on civil litigation for public access to investigative and prosecutive materials. And the Office conferred with the Office of the Solicitor General (OSG), which is

---

materials received from the Select Committee. *See* ECF No. 263 at 47 ("the Government states that it has already produced all the records it received from the Committee").

94

responsible for supervising and conducting government litigation in the United States Supreme Court, the Office of Legal Counsel (OLC), which provides binding legal advice to the Executive Branch, and the Criminal Division's Appellate Section, which conducts and oversees the Department's criminal appellate litigation, on complex statutory, constitutional, and other legal issues—including regarding charging decisions in the original and superseding indictments, *see supra* at Section II, Mr. Trump's challenge to the district court's order on extrajudicial statements, *see infra* at Section V.B, Mr. Trump's executive privilege claims, *see infra* at Section V.C, and Mr. Trump's immunity challenge to the indictment, *see infra* at Section V.D.

B.   Investigative and Prosecutive Procedures in an Election Year

Mr. Trump's announcement of his candidacy for President while two federal criminal investigations were ongoing presented an unprecedented challenge for the Department of Justice and the courts. Given the timing and circumstances of the Special Counsel's appointment and the Office's work, it was unavoidable that the regular processes of the criminal law and the judicial system would run parallel to the election campaign. Mr. Trump's position was that when the judicial process conflicted with his election campaign, the courts should always yield; as discussed below, the courts did not agree. Under these unique circumstances, the Department's actions would be criticized by one constituency or another, regardless of which path the investigations took. Accordingly, the Office leaned on established Department policy, practice, and wisdom, and focused on doing its job promptly and thoroughly.

From the outset and throughout its work, the Office recognized the weighty issues presented by the matters under its mandate and operated on the principle that the best interests of the Department and the nation required prompt investigation and decision-making. The Office's exceptional working pace ensured that its investigative work could be completed, charging decisions could be made, and any necessary indictments could be returned by the summer of

2023, long before the election. The Office had no interest in affecting the presidential election, and it complied fully with the letter and spirit of the Department's policy regarding election year sensitivities. It did so through fundamentally sound practices: moving its investigations swiftly, making charging decisions and returning indictments well before the election, litigating its cases on the timetables set by the courts, and consulting with PIN.

1.   The Department's Election Year Sensitivities Policy

The staff of the Office was deeply familiar with and committed to the Department's election year sensitivities policy, as it included fraud and public corruption prosecutors with many years of experience working in and leading PIN. The Special Counsel himself and one of his Counselors had served as Chief of PIN, two of the attorneys had been deputy chiefs in PIN, and two other attorneys in the Office had been trial attorneys in PIN. Collectively, prosecutors in the Office had many years of experience providing training, advice, and guidance to prosecutors and law enforcement agents throughout the Department on how to comply with the Department's election-related policies. In fact, the Counselor in the Office who had previously served as Chief of PIN was one of the drafters of the first election year sensitivities memorandum issued to Department attorneys.

The Department's policy regarding elections has two overlapping components. The first is focused on the prosecutor's purpose: it prohibits prosecutors from taking any action or timing any action for the purpose of affecting an election. Justice Manual § 9-27.260 and § 9-85.500. That flat prohibition applies to all actions by prosecutors and at all times during an investigation or prosecution. The second and overlapping component focuses on safeguarding the Department's reputation for fairness and nonpartisanship, requiring that prosecutors take particular care in an election year and consult with PIN when an action is "likely to raise an issue or the perception of an issue." Justice Manual § 9-85.500.[252]

These policies are well-established within the Department. In 2008, in the wake of allegations and investigations concerning politicization in the Department,[253] and recognizing that there was uncertainty regarding the terms of the Department's policies and practices in election years, the Criminal Division and PIN evaluated the feasibility of establishing a specific and definitive set of rules regarding the duty to avoid interference with elections in the run-up to an election. While prosecutors had long been advised to exercise particular care in politically sensitive cases in the two or three months immediately prior to an election, the Department had never had a formal 60-day or 90-day rule that governed such situations.[254] As part of its evaluation in 2008, the Department considered whether to codify a particular rule, but ultimately concluded that the best course was, instead, to provide guidance in the form of an Attorney General Memorandum addressing the need for particular care to protect the Department's reputation for impartiality in an election year, and setting forth in writing the core principle that prosecutors and agents may not act for a political purpose.

---

[252] The Department's election-related policies were first developed in the context of investigations involving ballot fraud, where PIN's Election Crimes Branch has for decades maintained a written non-interference policy that applies only in the context of ballot fraud investigations. *See Federal Prosecution of Election Offenses* (8th ed. 2017) at 84-85. That policy, which precludes certain investigative actions in a ballot fraud investigation until after the election to which the investigation relates is completed and certified, was codified in the Justice Manual in August 2022. *See* Justice Manual § 9-85.300. Because the 2020 presidential election had been completed and certified before our investigation began, the ballot fraud policy had no application to the Office's work.

[253] *See* Joint Report of the Department of Justice, Office of Professional Responsibility and Office of the Inspector General, *An Investigation of Allegations of Politicized Hiring by Monica Goodling and Other Staff in the Office of the Attorney General* (July 28, 2008), https://oig.justice.gov/sites/default/files/legacy/special/s0807/final.pdf.

[254] The background regarding the election year sensitivities policy and the so-called "60-day rule" was reviewed by the Department of Justice Office of the Inspector General in its June 2018 report, *A Review of Various Actions by the Federal Bureau of Investigation and the Department of Justice in Advance of the 2016 Election*, at 16-18, https://oig.justice.gov/sites/default/files/reports/18-04.pdf.

On March 5, 2008, Attorney General Michael Mukasey issued the first Election Year Sensitivities Memorandum setting forth this guidance. In relevant part, the Attorney General Memorandum stated:

> Department of Justice employees are entrusted with the authority to enforce the laws of the United States and with the responsibility to do so in a neutral and impartial manner. This is particularly important in an election year. Now that the election season is upon us, I want to remind you of the Department's existing policies with respect to political activities.
>
> ...
>
> The Department of Justice has a strong interest in the prosecution of election fraud and other election-related crimes, such as those involving federal and state campaign finance laws, federal patronage laws, and corruption of the election process. As Department employees, however, we must be particularly sensitive to safeguarding the Department's reputation for fairness, neutrality and nonpartisanship.
>
> Simply put, politics must play no role in the decisions of federal investigators or prosecutors regarding any investigations or criminal charges. Law enforcement officers and prosecutors may never select the timing of investigative steps or criminal charges for the purpose of affecting any election, or for the purpose of giving an advantage or disadvantage to any candidate or political party. Such a purpose is inconsistent with the Department's mission and with the Principles of Federal Prosecution.
>
> If you are faced with a question regarding the timing of charges or overt investigative steps near the time of a primary or general election, please contact the Public Integrity Section of the Criminal Division for further guidance.

Memorandum from Michael Mukasey, Attorney General, *Election Year Sensitivities* (Mar. 5, 2008).

Since 2008, Attorneys General have issued memoranda containing substantially the same guidance to prosecutors and agents in each election year.[255] In August 2022, just three months

---

[255] *See* Memorandum from William Barr, Attorney General, *Election Year Sensitivities* (May 15, 2020) (adding language to the Election Year Sensitivities memorandum to make clear that the policy applied not only to investigative and charging actions, but also to public statements by prosecutors and law enforcement agents).

before the Attorney General appointed the Special Counsel, the Department codified its election year policies in the Justice Manual:

> Federal prosecutors and agents may never select the timing of any action, including investigative steps, criminal charges, or statements, for the purpose of affecting any election, or for the purpose of giving an advantage or disadvantage to any candidate or political party. Such a purpose is inconsistent with the Department's mission and with the Principles of Federal Prosecution. *See* § 9-27.260. Any action likely to raise an issue or the perception of an issue under this provision requires consultation with the Public Integrity Section, and such action shall not be taken if the Public Integrity Section advises that further consultation is required with the Deputy Attorney General or Attorney General.

Justice Manual § 9-85.500; *see also id.* § 9-27.260 (adding the election year sensitivities policy to the Principles of Federal Prosecution).

Implementation of the election year sensitivities policy can raise challenging questions. Taking action may be viewed as hurting a candidate, while refraining from action may be viewed as helping that candidate. This challenging landscape counsels in favor of structuring and timing investigations in a manner that enables prosecutors and agents to avoid these issues as much as possible and do what they do best: focus on the needs of the case. Consistent with that, PIN often counsels prosecutors to move their investigations along promptly and avoid unnecessary delay that could needlessly place them in the position of deciding whether to take overt action or bring charges in the period immediately before an election. Because of the Office's deep familiarity and experience with these policies, it focused on completing both of its investigations promptly and making timely charging decisions, long before the election.

2. Pre-Indictment Procedures

During the investigation and prosecution of this case, the Office consulted regularly with PIN. For example, because the Election Case involved election fraud charges under 18 U.S.C. §§ 241 and 371, the Office consulted with PIN and its Election Crimes Branch prior to returning the Election Case indictment in the District of Columbia, as required by Justice Manual § 9-85.210 (Violations of Campaign Financing Laws, Federal Patronage Laws, and Corruption of Elections—Consultation Requirement). In addition, the Office consulted with PIN regarding investigative steps that involved gathering evidence connected to congressional staff, pursuant to Justice Manual § 9-85.110 (Investigations Involving Members of Congress). As discussed below in Section V.A.2, the Office also consulted PIN regarding issues that arose in litigation involving the Speech or Debate Clause, U.S. CONST. art. I, § 6, cl. 1, a unique constitutional protection that provides a form of immunity to legislative acts by Member of Congress and their staff. *See, e.g., In re Press Application for Access to Judicial Records Ancillary to Certain Grand Jury Proc. Concerning Former Vice President Mike Pence*, No. 23-mc-35, ECF No. 11-5 at 19 (D.D.C. June 9, 2023) (publicly released Mar. 27, 2023, Memorandum Opinion) (application of Speech or Debate privilege to Vice President when acting as President of the Senate); *In re Sealed Case*, 80 F.4th 355 (D.C. Cir. 2023) (application of Speech or Debate privilege to search of congressman's cell phone). However, because the Office proceeded expeditiously with its investigations and charging decisions, no election year sensitivities consultation with PIN was required prior to returning the original indictment in either the Classified Documents Case in June of 2023 or the Election Case in August of 2023.

3. Post-Indictment Procedures

The two components of the Department's election year sensitivities policy play out differently in the context of post-indictment litigation. First, the bedrock principle that prosecutors may not take any action for the purpose of affecting an election or providing an advantage or disadvantage to any candidate or party applies fully during post-indictment litigation. On this score, the Office did not take a single action at any time for any such purpose;

rather, the Office's mission was at all times to uphold the law and carefully follow the requirements of the criminal justice process.

Unlike the purpose-focused component of Department policy, the component that focuses on the Department's reputation for impartiality stands on a different footing with respect to pre-indictment and post-indictment activity. This component of the policy applies fully to the timing of actions by prosecutors prior to indictment—bringing charges, taking overt investigative steps, and making public statements. Justice Manual § 9-85.500. For such actions, prosecutors must take election year sensitivities into account, and they are required to consult with PIN. *Id.* However, once the case is charged, this component of the policy does not limit the ability to litigate according to the schedule set down by the court and does not require consultation with PIN for such litigation. Whether it is during an election year or any other time, the duty of prosecutors after indictment is to litigate their cases fully and zealously, consistent with the Constitution, United States Code, Federal Rules of Criminal Procedure, rules of professional responsibility, and dictates of the calendar set forth by the court. *See CNN This Morning, Garland Comments on Trump Case*, CNN.COM - TRANSCRIPTS (Jan. 19, 2024), https://transcripts.cnn.com/show/ctmo/date/2024-01-19/segment/02 [https://perma.cc/HD2R-6U8Y] (the "[p]rosecutor has urged speedy trials, with which I agree. And it's now in the hands of the judicial system, not in our hands."). Once a case is charged, no policy of the Department limits the ability of prosecutors to litigate effectively on the schedule set by the court, and that is what the Office did.

Consistent with the Department's policy, after indictment, the Office litigated the Election Case according to the schedules set down by the district court, the D.C. Circuit, and the

Supreme Court.[256] Given the gravity of the issues presented by the charges, the Office sought to move the case forward expeditiously for two central reasons unrelated to the election. First, the Speedy Trial Act mandates expeditious resolution of criminal cases, and it does so not only for the benefit of the accused, but in the best interest of the public. *See Zedner v. United States*, 547 U.S. 489, 501 (2006) ("[T]he [Speedy Trial] Act was designed with the public interest firmly in mind."); *Strunk v. United States*, 412 U.S. 434, 439 n.2 (1973) ("The public interest in a broad sense, as well as the constitutional guarantee, commands prompt disposition of criminal charges."); *Cobbledick v. United States*, 309 U.S. 323, 325 (1940) ("[E]ncouragement of delay is fatal to the vindication of the criminal law."). Second, those fundamental interests were heightened in this case, which raised matters of utmost gravity, urgency, and national concern, charging the former President with conspiring to thwart the peaceful transfer of power through lies that undermined the democratic process and ultimately fueled a violent attack on the United States Capitol. These criminal charges warranted prompt and fair disposition, and that is what the Office sought to achieve.

Both during the investigation and after the case was charged, however, Mr. Trump sought to delay the proceedings, taking the position that when the judicial process conflicted with his election campaign, the courts should always yield. *See, e.g.,* ECF No. 30 at 11 (proposing April

---

[256] The Office did the same in the Classified Documents Case in the Southern District of Florida, litigating the case according to the calendar set by the court. Trial had been set for May 20, 2024, but in late February, the court ordered the parties to submit proposals for a new schedule and held a conference to discuss them, including proposals for new trial dates. *See United States v. Trump*, No. 23-cr-80101, ECF No. 338 (S.D. Fla. Feb. 27, 2024); *Trump*, No. 23-cr-80101, ECF No. 369 (S.D. Fla. Mar. 1, 2024). Before responding to the court, the Office confirmed with PIN its own understanding that the election year sensitivities policy did not apply to post-indictment litigation or require an election year sensitivities consultation before requesting a new trial date. The Office then proposed a trial date of July 8, 2024, while Mr. Trump proposed August 12, 2024. But the court never set a new trial date. *See id.*, ECF Nos. 356 & 357 (S.D. Fla. Feb. 29, 2024). PIN later advised the Office that prosecutors who request a trial date closer in time to an election than the July date that the Office proposed could be required to consult with PIN. In any event, the Office consulted regularly with PIN, and PIN agrees that the Office complied fully with the election year sensitivities policy in both of its cases.

2026 trial date, emphasizing that "[n]o major party presidential candidate has ever been charged while in the middle of a campaign"); ECF No. 103 at 20 (Mr. Trump's counsel arguing, "The easiest solution to all of this is an obvious one. . . . and that is to adjourn the case after the presidential election. That's the solution."); ECF No. 242 at 7-8 (asking court to reconsider scheduling order, emphasizing that "President Trump is the leading candidate in the Presidential election, which is just weeks away").

The courts did not agree. They consistently rejected Mr. Trump's efforts to delay or stop the proceedings. The courts' words and actions throughout the litigation reflected their fundamental commitment to the operation of the judicial process, notwithstanding the election campaign. *See, e.g.*, ECF No. 38 at 53 ("the public has a right to a prompt and efficient resolution of this matter"); ECF No. 29 at 41 ("the fact that the defendant is engaged in a political campaign is not going to allow him any greater or lesser latitude than any defendant in a criminal case"); *id.* at 15 ("And so what the defendant is currently doing—you know, the fact that he's running a political campaign currently has to yield to the orderly administration of justice."); *id.* at 19 ("I cannot, and I will not, factor into my decisions the effect it's going to have on a political campaign for either side."); *United States v. Trump*, 88 F.4th 990, 1018 (D.C. Cir. 2023) ("Delaying the trial date until after the election, as Mr. Trump proposes, would be counterproductive, create perverse incentives, and unreasonably burden the judicial process."); *id.* at 1016 ("But there is another fundamental constitutional interest at stake here. The existence of a political campaign or political speech does not alter the court's historical commitment or obligation to ensure the fair administration of justice in criminal cases. A trial participant's engagement in political speech cannot degrade or diminish that essential judicial function."); *Trump*, No. 23-3228, Per Curiam Order (D.C. Cir. Dec. 13, 2023) (expediting briefing and oral argument); *Trump*, No. 23-3228, Judgment (D.C. Cir. Feb. 6, 2024) (accelerating the schedule for Mr. Trump to seek any further review).

The Office also sought to move the Election Case forward expeditiously in the Supreme Court based upon the public interest in a prompt resolution of the case and the precedent set by the Watergate Special Prosecutor in *United States v. Nixon*, 418 U.S. 683 (1974) (*Nixon*), where the Court "granted both the United States' petition for certiorari before judgment (No. 73-1766), and also the President's cross-petition for certiorari before judgment (No. 73-1834), because of the public importance of the issues presented and the need for their prompt resolution . . . ." *Id.* at 686-687 (citations omitted). The Office filed a petition for certiorari before judgment, which would have moved the Election Case directly to the Supreme Court from the district court, and argued that the Court should follow the *Nixon* model. The Supreme Court did not grant the Office's petition for certiorari before judgment. However, like the D.C. Circuit, the Supreme Court ultimately expedited its consideration of the case, further confirming the Office's emphasis on the strong public interest in a prompt resolution.[257]

Following the Supreme Court's immunity decision, the Office again proceeded in a manner that was fully consistent with the letter and spirit of the Department's election year

---

[257] After the D.C. Circuit issued its opinion affirming the district court, Mr. Trump filed a motion in the Supreme Court to stay the Circuit's issuance of its mandate until he could file, and the Supreme Court could resolve, a petition for certiorari that he intended to file in the Supreme Court. *See Trump v. United States*, No. 23A745, Application for a Stay of the D.C. Circuit's Mandate Pending the Filing of a Petition for Writ of Certiorari (U.S. Feb. 12, 2024). In response to that motion, the Office again pointed to the significant public interest in a prompt resolution of the case, and argued that the Supreme Court should either deny the stay or, as an alternative manner of moving the case promptly, treat Mr. Trump's motion as a petition for certiorari, grant the petition, and set the case for expedited briefing and argument. *See Trump*, No. 23A745, Resp. in Opp'n to Application for a Stay of the Mandate of the United States Court of Appeals for the D.C. Circuit (U.S. Feb. 14, 2024). The Supreme Court adopted the Office's alternative proposal and set an argument and briefing schedule to complete the litigation in the October Term, which ended on July 1, 2024. *See Trump*, No. 23-939, Order Granting Petition (U.S. Feb. 28, 2024). Briefing was completed by April 15, 2024, the Supreme Court held oral argument on April 25, 2024, and the Supreme Court issued its immunity opinion remanding for further proceedings on July 1, 2024. *See Trump*, 603 U.S. at 642.

sensitivities policy: litigating the case according to the schedule established by the district court, taking action based upon the law and the best interests of the case, and consulting with PIN. Upon receiving the decision, the Office immediately began a multi-faceted process to determine the best way forward, including (1) a thorough evaluation of the opinion itself; (2) an exhaustive and detailed review of the evidence and the allegations in the original indictment to determine whether there was sufficient non-immune evidence to support the charges in light of the opinion; (3) once the Office determined that there was sufficient non-immunized evidence, an evaluation of whether to litigate the case based on the existing grand jury record and indictment or instead, seek a superseding indictment that would be presented to a grand jury that had not heard any immunized evidence; and (4) given the timing, evaluate whether all of the necessary steps could be undertaken consistent with the election year sensitivities policy. The Office determined that that there was sufficient non-immunized evidence to support the charges and that the best course of action for the case was to obtain a superseding indictment that implemented the Supreme Court's holding in *Trump*, and present that new indictment to a grand jury that had not heard evidence of immunized conduct. *See* ECF No. 228 (Notice of Superseding Indictment). Before doing so, the Office consulted with PIN for two purposes: (1) to obtain PIN's concurrence regarding the proposed election fraud charges under 18 U.S.C. §§ 241 and 371, as required by Justice Manual § 9-85.300; and (2) given the timing of the superseding indictment, to consult with PIN regarding election year sensitivities, pursuant to Justice Manual § 9-85.500 and the Attorney General's Election Year Sensitivities Memorandum. PIN concurred with the return of the superseding indictment, which was returned by the grand jury on August 27, 2024.

Following the superseding indictment, and consistent with the district court's instructions, on August 30, 2024, the parties submitted their positions regarding the schedule for pretrial proceedings. ECF No. 229. The Office proposed that it file an opening brief regarding immunity in which it would provide detailed information without which the court could not undertake the factbound analysis that was required by the Supreme Court's remand. The Office argued that its filing would include the information that the defense would need to address and that the district court would need to make its immunity determinations—regarding both the allegations in the superseding indictment and the evidence that the Office would introduce at trial—in a manner that would avoid the prospect of multiple interlocutory appeals. *Id.* at 2-3. Were the defense to file first on remand, it would leave a large gap in the analysis that the district court was required to undertake because only the Office could identify all of the evidence upon which the charges were based and upon which it would rely at trial. *See* ECF No. 232 at 12-15 (Transcript of Hearing). The Office did not propose a particular date for filing its immunity brief or a schedule for conducting the immunity litigation. It left those matters to the court's discretion. Mr. Trump proposed that the immunity litigation should not begin until December 2024.

The district court issued an order setting a new schedule for pretrial litigation and directing the Office to file its opening immunity brief on September 26, 2024. *See* ECF No. 233. Prior to filing its immunity brief, the Office again confirmed with PIN that the election year sensitivities policy did not apply to conducting such post-indictment litigation according to the court's schedule and that the Justice Manual did not require consultation with PIN regarding such litigation. And after the Office filed its immunity brief and Mr. Trump attempted to delay its public disclosure, the district court again rejected his attempt to conflate the election and the criminal justice process:

> In addition to the assertions discussed above, Defendant's opposition brief
> repeatedly accuses the Government of bad-faith partisan bias. *See* Def.'s Opp'n

at 2, 5-6. These accusations, for which Defendant provides no support, continue a pattern of defense filings focusing on political rhetoric rather than addressing the legal issues at hand. *See* Oversized Brief Order at 2-3 (identifying two recent instances of this pattern). Not only is that focus unresponsive and unhelpful to the court, but it is also unbefitting of experienced defense counsel and undermining of the judicial proceedings in this case.

ECF No. 251 at 7.[258]

Throughout its work, the Office was focused entirely on its mandate to uphold the law, and nothing more. The career prosecutors in the Office conducted its investigation and prosecution in a manner that complied fully with the Department's policies regarding election year sensitivities.

V.   INVESTIGATIVE CHALLENGES AND LITIGATION ISSUES

In a corruption or conspiracy investigation, it is not unusual for a subject or target of the investigation to continue to wield significant influence over, or command strong loyalty from, potential witnesses, often complicating the ability of prosecutors to obtain evidence. That dynamic was amplified in this case given Mr. Trump's political and financial status, and the prospect of his future election to the presidency. As described below, one company resisted a lawful court order issued during the Office's investigation, and important witnesses made the choice to assert privileges against providing evidence based on their own official positions in the government. In addition, after his indictment, Mr. Trump used his considerable social media presence to make extrajudicial comments—sometimes of a threatening nature—about the case, and the Office was forced to pursue litigation to preserve the integrity of the proceeding and

---

[258] On October 17, 2024, Mr. Trump filed a motion, ECF No. 264, to delay public disclosure of the Office's appendix to its immunity brief until after Mr. Trump had filed his own appendix on November 14, nine days after the 2024 presidential election, such that both appendices would be released publicly simultaneously. Because Mr. Trump filed his motion before obtaining the Office's position, the Office emailed the district court's chambers, copying defense counsel, to inform the court that the Office did not object to that procedure.

prevent witness intimidation. Mr. Trump also was able to raise claims of executive privilege and presidential immunity. This section discusses each of those challenges and how the Office addressed them.

A.   Pre-Indictment Litigation with Third Parties

1.   The Twitter/X Search Warrant

Mr. Trump's public statements—and specifically, his posts on the social media application Twitter—constituted important potential evidence of his criminal conduct and intent. Accordingly, on January 17, 2023, the Office applied for, and the district court authorized, a search warrant requiring Twitter to provide certain information regarding Mr. Trump's Twitter account. *In re Twitter Search Warrant*, No. 23-sc-31, ECF No. 32 at 1-2 & n.1, 5 (D.D.C. Mar. 3, 2023) (Twitter Decision). At the same time, as is common in non-public criminal investigations to prevent individuals under investigation from destroying evidence or otherwise hampering the process, the Office asked the district court to issue a non-disclosure order (NDO), which would direct Twitter that it could not inform Mr. Trump that the Office was seeking information regarding his account. *Id.* at 6. The district court granted the request and issued the NDO. *Id.*

The search warrant required Twitter's compliance within ten days of its issuance, but the day before that deadline, its Senior Director of Legal informed the Office that "it would not comply with the Warrant by the next day." *Id.* at 7-9. Shortly thereafter, Twitter's Senior Director of Legal further informed the Office that it would not comply with the warrant "without changes to the NDO" permitting Twitter to notify Mr. Trump of the warrant. *Id.* at 9. Twitter claimed that the NDO impinged on its First Amendment interests in communicating with the former President, which, according to Twitter, were heightened because the warrant purportedly could implicate issues of executive privilege though it conceded that it had no standing to raise any privilege issues. *Id.* at 24. The district court later described Twitter's actions as "extraordinary" and noted that its resistance to the NDO appeared to be a first in the company's history. *Id.* at 1 ("For what appears to be the first time in their nearly seventeen-year existence as a company . . . [Twitter] seeks to vacate or modify an order, issued under the Stored Communications Act . . . commanding that the company not disclose the existence of a search warrant for a user's Twitter account, and further seeks to condition any compliance by the company with that search warrant on the user (or user's representatives) first being notified about the warrant and given an opportunity to stop or otherwise intervene in execution of the warrant.").

The Office promptly moved in district court to have Twitter show cause why it should not be held in contempt of court, asking the district court to impose a penalty that doubled with each day of non-compliance, starting at $50,000. *Id.* at 9, 12. In rejecting Twitter's basis for refusing to comply with the warrant, the district court emphasized that the search warrant and NDO had been "issued by this Court after being apprised of extensive reasons sufficient to establish probable cause for issuance of the warrant and to meet the statutory requirements for an NDO, to which reasons Twitter is neither privy nor entitled to be privy." *Id.* at 2. The district court rejected Twitter's contentions, finding that there existed compelling government interests to maintain the NDO to preserve the integrity of the investigation, *id.* at 17-26, and that as a practical matter, "[i]f accepted, Twitter's argument would invite repeated litigation by Twitter and other [electronic communication services] providers to challenge NDOs in order to alert users to [Stored Communications Act] orders, particularly for high profile, highly placed users, such as current or former government officials, with whom the providers might want to curry favor, with concomitant and inevitable delays in execution of [Stored Communications Act] orders and resultant frustration in expeditiously conducting criminal investigations," *id.* at 11.

The district court ultimately held that the NDO lawfully prohibited Twitter from notifying Mr. Trump about the warrant and fined Twitter $350,000 for failing to comply with the court-ordered search warrant in a timely fashion, finding that Twitter failed to show good faith and substantial compliance in response to the warrant. *Id.* at 30-34. The sanction and NDO were both upheld by the D.C. Circuit, and the Supreme Court declined to review the case. *In re Sealed Case*, 77 F.4th 815, 830 (D.C. Cir. 2023), *cert. denied sub nom. X Corp. v. United States*, 2024 WL 4426628 (U.S. Oct. 7, 2024) (upholding NDO where the order was narrowly tailored and "the district court specifically found reason to believe that disclosure of the warrant would jeopardize the criminal investigation"); *id.* at 836 (holding that the "sanction ultimately imposed was not unreasonable, given Twitter's $40-billion valuation and the court's goal of coercing Twitter's compliance").

2. Legislative Privilege Under the Speech or Debate Clause

The Speech or Debate Clause provides that "for any Speech or Debate in either House, [Senators and Representatives] shall not be questioned in any other Place." U.S. CONST. art. I, § 6, cl. 1. The Clause affords members of Congress a number of distinct protections, including a testimonial privilege that guarantees that a member "may not be made to answer" questions about his or her legislative acts. *Gravel v. United States*, 408 U.S. 606, 616 (1972). During the investigation, former Vice President Pence (in his capacity as President of the Senate) invoked his privilege under the Speech or Debate Clause. Through litigation over the scope and applicability of the claimed privilege, the Office obtained important evidence.

After the grand jury subpoenaed Mr. Pence to testify about Mr. Trump's alleged efforts to overturn the results of the 2020 election, Mr. Pence moved to quash the subpoena, invoking the at 2, 5-6. These accusations, for which Defendant provides no support, continue a pattern of defense filings focusing on political rhetoric rather than addressing the legal issues at hand. *See* Oversized Brief Order at 2-3 (identifying two recent instances of this pattern). Not only is that focus unresponsive and unhelpful to the court, but it is also unbefitting of experienced defense counsel and undermining of the judicial proceedings in this case.

ECF No. 251 at 7.[258]

Throughout its work, the Office was focused entirely on its mandate to uphold the law, and nothing more. The career prosecutors in the Office conducted its investigation and prosecution in a manner that complied fully with the Department's policies regarding election year sensitivities.

V. INVESTIGATIVE CHALLENGES AND LITIGATION ISSUES

In a corruption or conspiracy investigation, it is not unusual for a subject or target of the investigation to continue to wield significant influence over, or command strong loyalty from, potential witnesses, often complicating the ability of prosecutors to obtain evidence. That dynamic was amplified in this case given Mr. Trump's political and financial status, and the prospect of his future election to the presidency. As described below, one company resisted a lawful court order issued during the Office's investigation, and important witnesses made the choice to assert privileges against providing evidence based on their own official positions in the government. In addition, after his indictment, Mr. Trump used his considerable social media presence to make extrajudicial comments—sometimes of a threatening nature—about the case, and the Office was forced to pursue litigation to preserve the integrity of the proceeding and

---

[258] On October 17, 2024, Mr. Trump filed a motion, ECF No. 264, to delay public disclosure of the Office's appendix to its immunity brief until after Mr. Trump had filed his own appendix on November 14, nine days after the 2024 presidential election, such that both appendices would be released publicly simultaneously. Because Mr. Trump filed his motion before obtaining the Office's position, the Office emailed the district court's chambers, copying defense counsel, to inform the court that the Office did not object to that procedure.

B.   Threats and Harassment of Witnesses

A significant challenge that the Office faced after Mr. Trump's indictment was his ability and willingness to use his influence and following on social media to target witnesses, courts, and Department employees, which required the Office to engage in time-consuming litigation to protect witnesses from threats and harassment.

Mr. Trump's resort to intimidation and harassment during the investigation was not new, as demonstrated by his actions during the charged conspiracies. A fundamental component of Mr. Trump's conduct underlying the charges in the Election Case was his pattern of using social media—at the time, Twitter—to publicly attack and seek to influence state and federal officials, judges, and election workers who refused to support false claims that the election had been stolen or who otherwise resisted complicity in Mr. Trump's scheme. After Mr. Trump publicly assailed these individuals, threats and harassment from his followers inevitably followed. *See* ECF No. 57 at 3 (one witness identifying Mr. Trump's Tweets about him as the cause of specific and graphic threats about his family, and a public official providing testimony that after Mr. Trump's Tweets, he required additional police protection). In the context of the attack on the Capitol on January 6, Mr. Trump acknowledged that his supporters "listen to [him] like no one else."[260]

Representative Perry a copy of the contents of his phone so that he had an opportunity to claim the Speech or Debate privilege over the materials before the Government accessed them. *Id.* After Representative Perry did so, and after litigation in both the district court and the D.C. Circuit, *see generally id.*; *see also In re Sealed Case*, No. 23-3001, Doc. 2031508 (D.C. Cir. Dec. 14, 2023), and *In re Scott Perry Cell Phone Search Warrant*, No. 22-sc-2144, Memorandum Opinion at 1 (D.D.C. Dec. 19, 2023), https://www.dcd.uscourts.gov/sites/dcd/files/22-sc-2144%20-%20Opinion.pdf [https://perma.cc/5PPD-JH68], the Government obtained records—including encrypted messages between Representative Perry and Co-Conspirator 4—that it intended to use at trial prior to the Supreme Court's decision on presidential immunity. *See, e.g.*, SCO-12946533 (Signal messages between Co-Conspirator 4 and Perry 01/02/2021). Irrespective of that decision, the records would have been admissible in a trial of Mr. Trump's co-conspirators.

[260] SCO-04958191 at 7 (CNN Town Hall Tr. 05/10/2023); SCO-04976309 at 13:28-14:35 (CNN Town Hall Video 05/10/2023).

The same pattern transpired after Mr. Trump's indictment in the Election Case. As the D.C. Circuit later found, Mr. Trump "repeatedly attacked those involved in th[e] case through threatening public statements, as well as messaging daggered at likely witnesses and their testimony," *Trump*, 88 F.4th at 1010. Those attacks had "real-time, real-world consequences," exposing "those on the receiving end" to "a torrent of threats and intimidation" and turning their lives "upside down." *Id.* at 1011-1012. The day after his arraignment, for example, Mr. Trump posted on the social media application Truth Social, "IF YOU GO AFTER ME, I'M COMING AFTER YOU!" *Id.* at 998. The next day, "one of his supporters called the district court judge's chambers and said: 'Hey you stupid slave n[****]r[.] * * * If Trump doesn't get elected in 2024, we are coming to kill you, so tread lightly b[***]h. * * * You will be targeted personally, publicly, your family, all of it.'" *Id.*[261] Mr. Trump also "took aim at potential witnesses named in the indictment," *id.* at 998-999, and "lashed out at government officials closely involved in the criminal proceeding," as well as members of their families, *id.* at 1010-1011.

To protect the integrity of the proceedings, on September 5, 2023, the Office filed a motion seeking an order pursuant to the district court's rules restricting certain out-of-court statements by either party. *See* ECF No. 57; D.D.C. LCrR 57.7(c). The district court heard argument and granted the Office's motion, finding that Mr. Trump's public attacks "pose a significant and immediate risk that (1) witnesses will be intimidated or otherwise unduly influenced by the prospect of being themselves targeted for harassment or threats; and (2) attorneys, public servants, and other court staff will themselves become targets for threats and harassment." ECF No. 105 at 2. Because no "alternative means" could adequately address these

---

[261] *See also United States v. Shry*, 23-cr-413 (S.D. Tex.) (threats made against the district court judge presiding over the Election Case).

"grave threats to the integrity of these proceedings," the court prohibited the parties and their counsel from making public statements that "target (1) the Special Counsel prosecuting this case or his staff; (2) defense counsel or their staff; (3) any of this court's staff or other supporting personnel; or (4) any reasonably foreseeable witness or the substance of their testimony." *Id.* at 3. The court emphasized, however, that Mr. Trump remained free to make "statements criticizing the government generally, including the current administration or the Department of Justice; statements asserting that [he] is innocent of the charges against him, or that his prosecution is politically motivated; or statements criticizing the campaign platforms or policies of [his] current political rivals." *Id.* at 3.

Mr. Trump appealed, and the D.C. Circuit affirmed in large part, finding that Mr. Trump's attacks on witnesses in this case posed "a significant and imminent threat to individuals' willingness to participate fully and candidly in the process, to the content of their testimony and evidence, and to the trial's essential truth-finding function," with "the undertow generated by such statements" likely to "influence other witnesses" and deter those "not yet publicly identified" out of "fear that, if they come forward, they may well be the next target." *Trump,* 88 F.4th at 1012-1013. Likewise, "certain speech about counsel and staff working on the case poses a significant and imminent risk of impeding the adjudication of th[e] case," since "[m]essages designed to generate alarm and dread, and to trigger extraordinary safety precautions, will necessarily hinder the trial process and slow the administration of justice." *Id.* at 1014.

The court of appeals explained that the district court's order "involve[d] the confluence of two paramount constitutional interests: the freedom of speech guaranteed by the First Amendment and the federal courts' vital Article III duty to ensure the fair and orderly administration of justice in criminal cases." *Id.* at 996. Balancing these interests, the court explained, required consideration of three related questions: "(1) whether the Order is justified by a sufficiently serious risk of prejudice to an ongoing judicial proceeding; (2) whether less restrictive alternatives would adequately address that risk; and (3) whether the Order is narrowly tailored, including whether the Order effectively addresses the potential prejudice." *Id.* at 1007. Because "the record amply support[ed]" the district court's finding that, "'when [Mr. Trump] has publicly attacked individuals including on matters related to this case, those individuals are consequently threatened and harassed,'" *id.* at 1012 (quoting ECF No. 105 at 2), and because "[n]o less-speech-restrictive alternative could viably protect against the imminent threat to the participation of witnesses, trial participants, and staff in this criminal matter, or the full, fair, and unobstructed receipt of relevant evidence," *id.* at 1017, the court affirmed the decision to "impose[] some limitation on trial participants' speech," *id.* at 1016. Indeed, "[g]iven the record in this case, the [district] court had a duty to act proactively to prevent the creation of an atmosphere of fear or intimidation aimed at preventing trial participants and staff from performing their functions within the trial process." *Id.* at 1014. The court of appeals therefore affirmed the district court's order to the extent that it prohibited parties and their counsel from making "public statements about known or reasonably foreseeable witnesses concerning their potential participation in the investigation or in this criminal proceeding," or "public statements about—(1) counsel in the case other than the Special Counsel, (2) members of the court's staff and counsel's staffs, or (3) the family members of any counsel or staff member—if those statements are made with the intent to materially interfere with, or to cause others to materially interfere with, counsel's or staff's work in this criminal case, or with the knowledge that such interference is highly likely to result." *Id.* at 1027-1028. To ensure that going forward the order was as narrowly tailored as possible, the court vacated the district court order "to the extent it cover[ed] speech beyond those specified categories." *Id.* at 1028.

C.   Mr. Trump's Claims of Executive Privilege

A time-consuming investigative challenge that the Office faced was Mr. Trump's broad invocation of executive privilege to try to prevent witnesses from providing evidence on a wide variety of topics. Mr. Trump asserted a form of executive privilege known as the presidential-communications privilege—a special privilege belonging to Presidents that the Supreme Court has found derives from the Constitution's design of the Executive Branch and separation of powers, *see Nixon v. GSA*, 433 U.S. 425, 446-447 (1977) (*GSA*); *Nixon*, 418 U.S. at 708—with respect to fourteen Executive Branch officials.   Mr. Trump's repeated assertion of the presidential-communications privilege as a basis to withhold evidence required extensive pre-indictment litigation that delayed the Office's receipt of important testimony and other evidence, including testimony from senior White House staff and Executive Branch officials about topics such as Mr. Trump's knowledge that he had lost the election and the pressure campaign Mr. Trump waged against the Vice President to convince him to reject legitimate elector slates at the January 6 certification proceeding.

The courts uniformly rejected Mr. Trump's privilege assertions seeking to deny the grand jury from hearing evidence from Executive Branch employees, *see* Media Access ECF No. 32-2 (No. 22-gj-25, Memorandum Opinion, Sept. 28, 2022);[262] Media Access ECF No. 32-6 (Memorandum Opinion, Nov. 19, 2022); Media Access ECF No. 32-11 (No. 22-gj-39, Memorandum Opinion, Dec. 9, 2022); Media Access ECF No. 32-15 (No. 23-gj-12,

---

[262] "Media Access ECF" refers to previously sealed documents that were made public in redacted form in *In re Application of the New York Times*, 22-mc-100 (D.D.C.), litigation brought by the media for access to materials from the executive-privilege litigation.

Memorandum Opinion, Mar. 15, 2023); Media Access ECF No. 32-17 (No. 23-gj-13, Memorandum Opinion, Mar. 25, 2023), finding that the evidence was "directly relevant, important, and essential" to the Office's investigation, as well as unavailable elsewhere, *e.g.*, Media Access ECF No. 32-15 at 33, 45. In each instance, the courts determined that the "importance and unavailability" of that "vital" evidence "outweigh[ed]" the qualified privilege for presidential communications and ordered that it be produced promptly to the grand jury. Media Access ECF No. 32-2 at 30. And when Mr. Trump tried to delay the investigation even further by seeking to stay orders denying his executive privilege claims pending appeal, district and appellate courts rejected all of them. In so doing, one court held that Mr. Trump was engaging in an "obvious" effort to delay the investigation and impede the grand jury from carrying out its constitutional responsibilities, Media Access ECF No. 32-4 at 6-8 (No. 22-gj-25, Memorandum Opinion, Oct. 6, 2022), and separately observed that staying proceedings risked indefinite delay, *see* Media Access ECF No. 32-8 at 9 (No. 22-gj-33, Memorandum Opinion, Dec. 18, 2022) ("The Court thus declines to further pause the grand jury's constitutionally protected work, particularly in the absence of any reassurance that the former president's delay tactics will cease."). Another court concluded that Mr. Trump's claim that the impact of delay on the investigation would be "nominal" was a "vast understatement," noting instead that it "would be . . . serious and deleterious" and would "harm[] the public interest." Media Access ECF No. 32-16 at 34 (No. 23-gj-12, Hearing Transcript, Apr. 3, 2023).

The presidential-communications privilege covers evidence "that reflect[s] presidential decisionmaking and deliberations and that the President believes should remain confidential." *In re Sealed Case*, 121 F.3d 729, 744 (D.C. Cir. 1997). The law on the presidential-communications privilege derives from the Supreme Court's decision in *Nixon*. There, the Court recognized a "presumptive privilege for Presidential communications," which it described as "fundamental to the operation of Government and inextricably rooted in the separation of powers under the Constitution." 418 U.S. at 708. But the Court held that the privilege is qualified, not absolute, *id.* at 706-707, emphasizing "our historic commitment to the rule of law," which is "nowhere more profoundly manifest than in our view that the twofold aim of criminal justice is that guilt shall not escape or innocence suffer," *id.* at 708-709 (citation, quotations, and alterations omitted). Specifically, the Court "weigh[ed] the importance of the general privilege of confidentiality of Presidential communications in performance of the President's responsibilities against the inroads of such a privilege on the fair administration of criminal justice," *id.* at 711-712, and it concluded that "[t]he generalized assertion of privilege must yield to the demonstrated, specific need for evidence in a pending criminal trial," *id.* at 713. The D.C. Circuit has applied the same general standard to grand jury subpoenas. *See In re Sealed Case*, 121 F.3d at 756.

Most of the executive privilege litigation in this case took place in five sealed proceedings between August 2022 and March 2023 concerning the testimony of fourteen witnesses in total. *See* Media Access ECF No. 32 (notice attaching district court orders and memorandum opinions). In August 2022, before the Special Counsel was appointed, the Government began to seek evidence from two former Executive Branch employees of Mr. Trump's, including by issuing subpoenas for testimony before the grand jury. *See* Media Access ECF No. 32-2. Although the Government believed it unlikely that the information that it sought from these witnesses was subject to the presidential-communications privilege because it did not concern presidential decision-making, in an abundance of caution given the unprecedented circumstance of investigating the former President, the Government made certain notifications to determine whether executive privilege would be a contested issue.

Specifically, with the district court's permission, the Government notified Mr. Trump and the incumbent President about the subpoenas to ascertain whether either would assert executive privilege and identified certain potential topics of investigative inquiry.[263] The Government chose to notify both the sitting and former Presidents even though it was unsettled under *GSA* whether a former President's view about potential harm to Executive Branch confidentiality interests could supersede the sitting President's. *See GSA*, 433 U.S. at 449. The incumbent President responded through the White House Counsel's Office that he did not intend to assert executive privilege.[264] Mr. Trump instructed the two witnesses that they should not provide testimony about any privileged communications, and he specifically identified the presidential-communications privilege. *See* Media Access ECF No. 32-2 at 9-10.[265]

After the witnesses withheld testimony pursuant to Mr. Trump's instruction, the Government filed a motion to compel with the Chief Judge of the United States District Court for the District of Columbia. Given that the investigation focused largely on Mr. Trump's activities as a candidate seeking office, not his official activities as President, the Government believed that it was likely that many if not all the communications at issue were not subject to the presidential-communications privilege because they were not made in the process of arriving at

---

[263] *See, e.g.*, SCO-11533730 (Letter to Trump Attorney) (identifying topics covering, among other things, potential fraud or irregularities regarding the 2020 presidential election, the January 6 rally at the Ellipse, the congressional certification on January 6, and co-conspirators).

[264] *See* SCO-00007123 at 2 (Letter from the White House Counsel's Office to U.S. Attorney for the District of Columbia 06/27/2022). Throughout its existence, the Office conducted its work in full compliance with the Department's Policy on Communications with the White House. *See, e.g.*, Memorandum from Merrick Garland, Attorney General, *Department of Justice Communications with the White House* (July 21, 2021).

[265] *See* SCO-12921102, SCO-11545866 at 2 (Letters from Trump Attorney to Witness Counsel).

presidential decisions. *See* Media Access ECF No. 32-2 at 17. As the Supreme Court has explained, the presidential-communications privilege "is limited to communications in performance of a President's responsibilities of his office and made in the process of shaping policies and making decisions." *GSA*, 433 U.S. at 449 (citation, quotations, and alterations omitted). But the Government's position was that the district court did not have to decide whether the communications at issue were subject to the privilege and instead could assume that the communications were privileged and find that the Government had overcome any privilege that would apply to presidential communications because it had made the showing of need for the evidence required under *Nixon*. Under D.C. Circuit precedent, to make the required showing of need, the Government had to establish that the testimony withheld by the witnesses likely contained important evidence that was not available to the grand jury with due diligence elsewhere. *In re Sealed Case*, 121 F.3d at 754.

After briefing and argument, the district court granted the Government's motion to compel. *See* Media Access ECF No. 32-1 (Order, Sept. 28, 2022). The court found that the witnesses possessed "unique and inimitable evidence," Media Access ECF No. 32-2 at 28-29, that was "important and relevant to the grand jury's investigation," Media Access ECF No. 32-1 at 2. The court concluded that the witnesses possessed "vital evidence for the grand jury, the importance and unavailability of which outweigh the presidential-communications privilege in this case." *Id.* at 30. The district court subsequently denied a motion by Mr. Trump for a stay pending appeal. Media Access ECF No. 32-4 at 6-8 (No. 22-gj-25, Memorandum Opinion, Oct. 6, 2022); *see* Media Access ECF No. 32-3 (No. 22-gj-25, Order, Oct. 6, 2022). The court of appeals also denied a stay pending appeal and later dismissed the appeal as moot. *See* Docket, *In re Sealed Case*, No. 22-3073 (D.C. Cir. 2023).

In the following months, the Government filed two more motions to compel testimony from three additional witnesses. *See* Media Access No. 32-6 (No. 22-gj-33, Memorandum Opinion, Nov. 19, 2022); Media Access No. 32-11 (No. 22-gj-39, Memorandum Opinion, Dec. 9, 2022). The district court granted the motions, making findings with respect to each witness that the Government had made a showing of need to overcome the qualified privilege for presidential communications. *See* Media Access ECF Nos. 32-5, 32-6 (No. 22-gj-33, Order and Memorandum Opinion, Nov. 19, 2022); Media Access ECF Nos. 32-10, 32-11 (No. 22-gj-39, Order and Memorandum Opinion, Dec. 9, 2022). The district court also denied stays pending appeals. *See* Media Access ECF Nos. 32-7, 32-8 (No. 22-gj-33, Order and Memorandum Opinion, Dec. 18, 2022); Media Access ECF Nos. 32-12, 32-13 (No. 22-gj-29, Order and Memorandum Opinion, Jan. 10, 2023).

After the appointment of the Special Counsel, it became clear—given the scope of the grand jury's investigation and the need to obtain evidence from a number of former Executive Branch officials—that seeking to compel testimony from one or two witnesses at a time would be inefficient and would unduly delay the investigation. The Office therefore decided to consolidate the proceedings to the extent possible and filed two additional motions to compel that covered the remaining eight Executive Branch officials who had communicated through their attorneys that they would withhold testimony from the grand jury based on executive privilege. The district court granted the motions, making findings with respect to each individual witness that, as noted above, they "possess[ed] vital evidence for the grand jury, the importance and unavailability of which outweigh[ed] the presidential communications privilege." Media Access ECF No. 32-15 at 45; Media Access ECF No. 32-17 (No. 23-gj-13, Memorandum Opinion, Mar. 25, 2023). The district court also denied stays pending appeals. *See* Media

Access ECF No. 32-16; Media Access ECF No. 32-18 (23-gj-13, Transcript of Hearing, Apr. 10, 2023). Subsequently, the court of appeals denied stays pending appeals in both cases, dismissed one of the appeals as moot, and granted Mr. Trump's motion to voluntarily dismiss the other appeal. *See* Docket, *In re Sealed Case*, No. 23-3043 (D.C. Cir. 2023); Docket, *In re Sealed Case*, No. 23-3049 (D.C. Cir. 2023).

        D.   Presidential Immunity

Before this case, no court had ever found that Presidents are immune from criminal responsibility for their official acts, and no text in the Constitution explicitly confers such criminal immunity on the President. As set forth below, prior criminal investigations by the Department of Justice, whether conducted through special prosecutors, independent counsels, or special counsels, had examined whether Presidents had violated federal criminal law through use of their official powers, and none of those investigations had regarded former Presidents as immune from criminal liability for their official acts. The Office proceeded from the same premise.

Soon after the original indictment issued in the Election Case, Mr. Trump raised a claim of immunity in a motion to dismiss the indictment. The district court denied the immunity motion, and the court of appeals affirmed. The Supreme Court, however, vacated the court of appeals' judgment based on its conclusion that Presidents have absolute immunity for core official conduct that Congress lacks power to regulate; at least presumptive immunity for other official presidential acts; and no immunity for unofficial conduct. The Court then applied that test to hold that certain conduct alleged in the indictment was immune, while remanding for application of its legal framework to the remaining allegations. *Trump*, 603 U.S. at 593. The Office responded by obtaining a superseding indictment to comply with the Court's decision and

The Jack Smith Report

by seeking district court rulings that the charged conduct and expected evidence at trial was not shielded by immunity.

This section summarizes the chronology of the immunity litigation and key findings of the courts throughout. Because the immunity litigation unfolded on the public record, this discussion provides an overview; the Office's briefs and judicial decisions contain more detailed analysis.

1.   Prosecutorial Decisions During the Charging Stage

This Office conducted its investigation against the background of the Department's prior legal determinations with respect to the potential criminal liability of a former President for official acts. The longstanding view of the Department was that the Constitution's separation of powers precludes prosecution of a sitting President for official or unofficial acts. *See* Memorandum from Randolph D. Moss, Assistant Attorney General, Office of Legal Counsel, *A Sitting President's Amenability to Indictment and Criminal Prosecution*, 24 Op. O.L.C. 222 (Oct. 16, 2000) (2000 OLC Opinion); Memorandum from Robert G. Dixon, Jr., Assistant Attorney General, Office of Legal Counsel, *Amenability of the President, Vice President and other Civil Officers to Federal Criminal Prosecution while in Office* (Sept. 24, 1973) (1973 OLC Opinion). But that same legal conclusion recognizes that former Presidents could be held criminally liable for conduct undertaken while in office. 2000 OLC Opinion at 255 & n.32, 257. The Department's constitutional analysis of the "temporary" immunity of a sitting President, *id.*, drew no distinction between official acts and unofficial conduct.

Consistent with that analysis, former Department of Justice prosecutors had historically investigated presidential conduct based on the understanding that no criminal immunity would bar prosecution if the President had used his official powers to violate federal criminal law. Significantly, no President whose conduct was investigated (other than Mr. Trump) ever claimed absolute criminal immunity for all official acts. During the Watergate investigation, for example, prosecutors examined whether President Nixon was liable for the obstruction-of-justice conspiracy charged against the Watergate conspirators. Although President Nixon was not indicted, the grand jury named him as a co-conspirator, *United States v. Nixon*, 418 U.S. 683, 687 (1974), and in the Supreme Court, President Nixon acknowledged his exposure to prosecution after leaving office, *see United States v. Nixon*, Nos. 73-1766, 73-1834, 1974 WL 174855, Resp. Brief at *98 (U.S. June 21, 1974) ("While out of necessity an incumbent President must not be subject to indictment in order for our constitutional system to operate, he is not removed from the sanction of the law. He can be indicted after he leaves office at the end of his term or after being 'convicted' by the Senate in an impeachment proceeding."). Similarly, President Ford's pardon of President Nixon rested on both Presidents' understanding that President Nixon was exposed to criminal liability. *See Trump v. United States*, No. 23-939, 2024 WL 1592669, Brief for the United States at 15-16 (U.S. Apr. 8, 2024) (Gov't Sup. Ct. Brief) (collecting sources). Later, Independent Counsel Lawrence Walsh and Special Counsel Robert S. Mueller III conducted investigations into presidential conduct. 1 Lawrence E. Walsh, *Final Report Of The Independent Counsel For Iran/Contra Matters: Investigations and Prosecutions*, ch. 27 (Aug. 1993); 2 Robert S. Mueller III, Special Counsel, *Report On The Investigation Into Russian Interference In The 2016 Presidential Election* (Mar. 2019) (Mueller Report). Neither investigation reflected the view that presidents, after leaving office, were immune from prosecution for their official acts. *See* Mueller Report at 168-181 (analyzing constitutional separation-of-powers issues and statutory clear-statement issues before concluding that the President was not categorically exempt from criminal law for his official acts); *see also* Gov't Sup. Ct. Brief at 17 (quoting Walsh Report: "a past President" can be "subject to prosecution in appropriate cases"). And counsel for former President Trump stated at his second Senate impeachment trial that declining to convict him on the article of impeachment alleging conduct related to January 6 would not place him in "any way above the law" because a former President "is like any other citizen and can be tried in a court of law." 2 Proceedings of the U.S. Senate in the Impeachment Trial of Donald John Trump, S. Doc. No.117-2, at 144 (2021); 167 Cong. Rec. S667, S693 (daily ed. Feb. 12, 2021) ("[T]he text of the Constitution . . . makes very clear that a former President is subject to criminal sanction after his Presidency for any illegal acts he commits."). This Office made its investigative and prosecutorial decisions based on the same understanding.

The conduct at issue in the Election Case involved both unofficial and official conduct. Much of the former President's alleged conduct involved actions in his private capacity as a defeated candidate for reelection seeking to overturn the result—e.g., his coordinated conduct with his personal attorneys, campaign staff, and other private advisors. Such private conduct does not implicate constitutional functions of the presidency. Other alleged conduct, however, did involve the former President's misuse of official authority—including using the power of the presidency directly by exercising his authority over agencies and personnel in the Executive Branch. In determining to bring charges in the Election Case, the Office therefore examined the former President's amenability to prosecution for that conduct through the lens of two doctrines: the separation of powers under the Constitution and clear-statement principles that limit the application of criminal statutes to presidential conduct in certain circumstances. The Office concluded that neither the separation of powers nor clear-statement principles barred prosecution for the limited instances of official conduct at issue.[266]

That determination was consistent with similar conclusions reached by Special Counsel Mueller after detailed constitutional and statutory analysis; his report concluded that "Congress can validly regulate the President's exercise of official duties to prohibit actions motivated by a corrupt purpose" and that clear-statement principles of statutory interpretation did not apply to preclude application of criminal obstruction statutes to corrupt presidential conduct. Mueller Report at 168-181. Based on the same principles and legal frameworks, the Office's analysis determined that the potential charges—conspiracy to defraud the United States, conspiracy and substantive obstruction-of-justice offenses, and conspiracy to deprive citizens of voting rights— would not entail application of the statutes in a manner that burdened presidential prerogatives, and thus that the application of criminal law triggered neither clear-statement principles nor separation-of-powers concerns.

    2.   Immunity Litigation

On October 5, 2023, Mr. Trump filed a motion to dismiss the indictment based upon a sweeping claim of presidential immunity for all official conduct during his presidency. ECF No. 74. After briefing, on December 1, 2023, the district court rejected Mr. Trump's claim of immunity, concluding that "[t]he Constitution's text, structure, and history" do not support the contention that the President is absolutely immune from prosecution for criminal acts performed within his official responsibilities and that "[n]o court—or any other branch of government—has ever accepted" such a contention. *United States v. Trump*, 704 F. Supp. 3d 196, 206 (D.D.C.

---

[266] The Office addressed separation of powers and clear-statement principles in the district court, *see* ECF No. 109 at 32-34, and the Supreme Court, *see Trump*, No. 23-939, Brief for the United States at 26-31. Neither the district court nor the majority opinion in the Supreme Court addressed the application of clear-statement principles to the charges in the case.

2024). The court held that a former President "may be subject to federal investigation, indictment, prosecution, conviction and punishment for any criminal acts undertaken while in office," *id.*, that "[e]xempting former Presidents from the ordinary operation of the criminal justice system" would "undermine the foundation of the rule of law," *id.* at 217, and that Mr. Trump's "four-year service as Commander in Chief did not bestow on him the divine right of kings to evade the criminal responsibility that governs his fellow citizens," *id.* at 219.

The district court reasoned that the prospect of federal criminal liability for a former President did not impair the Executive's ability to perform its constitutionally mandated functions, "either by imposing unacceptable risks of vexatious litigation or otherwise chilling the Executive's decision-making process," and that "it is likely that a President who knows that their actions may one day be held to criminal account will be motivated to take greater care that the laws are faithfully executed." *Id.* at 210. With respect to the possible chilling effect that criminal liability might have on a President, the court concluded that "the possibility of future criminal liability might encourage the kind of sober reflection that would reinforce rather than defeat important constitutional values. If the specter of subsequent prosecution encourages a sitting President to reconsider before deciding to act with criminal intent, that is a benefit, not a defect." *Id.* at 213.

Mr. Trump appealed the district court's ruling. The D.C. Circuit heard oral argument on January 9, 2024. In a telling exchange, counsel for Mr. Trump acknowledged that, under his theory of immunity, a President could not be criminally prosecuted for ordering SEAL Team Six to assassinate a political rival unless Congress had first impeached and convicted that President for the same conduct. *See* Sup. Ct. J.A. 131-132. Less than a month after argument, the court of appeals affirmed the district court's decision, stating, "We cannot accept that the office of the

Presidency places its former occupants above the law for all time thereafter." *Trump*, 91 F.4th at 1200. In a unanimous opinion, the court stated that "our analysis is 'guided by the Constitution, federal statutes and history,' as well as 'concerns of public policy.'" *Id.* at 1189 (quoting *Nixon v. Fitzgerald*, 457 U.S. 731, 747 (1982) (*Fitzgerald*)). "Relying on these sources," the court rejected each of Mr. Trump's "potential bases for immunity both as a categorical defense to federal criminal prosecutions of former Presidents and as applied to this case in particular." *Id.* With respect to the case before it, the court stated that "former President Trump's alleged efforts to remain in power despite losing the 2020 election were, if proven, an unprecedented assault on the structure of our government." *Id.* at 1199. As such, it "would be a striking paradox if the President, who alone is vested with the constitutional duty to 'take Care that the Laws be faithfully executed,' were the sole officer capable of defying those laws with impunity." *Id.* at 1198 (quoting U.S. CONST. art II, § 3, cl. 1).

Like the district court, the court of appeals found that "the risk of criminal liability chilling Presidential action appears to be low" and that "[i]nstead of inhibiting the President's lawful discretionary action, the prospect of federal criminal liability might serve as a structural benefit to deter possible abuses of power and criminal behavior." *Id.* at 1196 (citing with approval the district court's observation that "[e]very President will face difficult decisions; whether to intentionally commit a federal crime should not be one of them"). Based on the safeguards in place to prevent baseless indictments applicable to all citizens, the court similarly found that "the risk that former Presidents will be unduly harassed by meritless criminal prosecutions appears slight." *Id.* at 1197.

More broadly, the court of appeals' evaluation of our system of separated powers led it to conclude "that there is no functional justification for immunizing former Presidents from federal prosecution in general or for immunizing former President Trump from the specific charges in the Indictment." *Id.* at 1200. Because it concluded that Mr. Trump did not have immunity for the crimes or conduct charged in the case, the court of appeals did not decide whether every allegation in the indictment constituted an official act. However, the court noted that "because the President has no official role in the certification of the Electoral College vote, much of the misconduct alleged in the Indictment reasonably can be viewed as that of an office-*seeker*—including allegedly organizing alternative slates of electors and attempting to pressure the Vice President and Members of the Congress to accept those electors in the certification proceeding." *Id.* at 1205 n.14 (emphasis in original). The court therefore found it "doubtful that all five types of conduct alleged in the indictment constitute official acts." *Id.*

In a divided decision, the Supreme Court vacated the court of appeals' judgment and remanded the case for further proceedings. *Trump*, 603 U.S. at 642.[267] The Supreme Court weighed the competing constitutional considerations differently than the lower courts. While the lower courts and the dissenting Justices placed greater emphasis on rule of law considerations, the majority found that the need for Presidents to act "boldly and fearlessly" in executing their duties of office was of paramount importance. *Id.* at 640.

---

[267] Justice Sotomayor, who authored a dissenting opinion joined by Justices Kagan and Jackson, described the majority opinion as follows:

> The Court effectively creates a law-free zone around the President, upsetting the status quo that has existed since the Founding. This new official-acts immunity now "lies about like a loaded weapon" for any President that wishes to place his own interests, his own political survival, or his own financial gain, above the interests of the Nation. *Korematsu v. United States*, 323 U.S. 214, 246 (1944) (Jackson, J., dissenting). The President of the United States is the most powerful person in the country, and possibly the world. When he uses his official powers in any way, under the majority's reasoning, he now will be insulated from criminal prosecution. Orders the Navy's Seal Team 6 to assassinate a political rival? Immune. Organizes a military coup to hold onto power? Immune. Takes a bribe in exchange for a pardon? Immune. Immune, immune, immune.

Trump, 603 U.S. at 684-685 (Sotomayor, J., dissenting).

The Court reasoned that there "'exists the greatest public interest' in providing the President with 'the maximum ability to deal fearlessly and impartially with the duties of his office,'" "free from undue pressures and distortions." *Id.* at 610, 615 (citation and quotations omitted). The Court found that "[c]riminally prosecuting a President for official conduct undoubtedly poses a far greater threat of intrusion on the authority and functions of the Executive Branch than simply seeking evidence in his possession" and that the threat of a criminal prosecution was "plainly more likely to distort Presidential decisionmaking" than a civil suit. *Id.* at 613. In responding to the dissenting Justices' concerns that the vast immunity that the Court provided opened the door to lawless behavior by Presidents in violation of their duty to faithfully execute the law, the Court assessed that a President who uses official power to violate the law was a less likely "prospect" than "an Executive Branch that cannibalizes itself, with each successive President free to prosecute his predecessors, yet unable to boldly and fearlessly carry out his duties for fear that he may be next." *Id.* at 640.

The Court rejected the lower courts' view that established safeguards such as the Department of Justice's "longstanding commitment to the impartial enforcement of law," a neutral grand jury, the requirement in criminal law that the Government must prove its case beyond a reasonable doubt, courts enforcing "existing principles of statutory construction and as-applied constitutional challenges," and certain President-specific defenses like the "public-authority defense or the advice of the Attorney General," would adequately protect a former President charged with criminal wrongdoing. *Id.* at 635-637. Instead, the Court placed greater weight on the risk to the administration of government from excessive caution by a President who might face criminal accountability for official acts, reasoning that "[w]ithout immunity, such types of prosecutions of ex-Presidents," for example over claims of insufficient enforcement of federal law, "could quickly become routine," thus "enfeebling" the presidency through "such a cycle of factional strife." *Id.* at 640.

In conducting its balancing, the majority placed greater weight than did the dissents or the lower courts on the importance of protecting the independence and fearlessness of the President as opposed to the risk that immunity would encourage lawless behavior. *Contrast id.* at 614 ("Such an immunity is required to safeguard the independence and effective functioning of the Executive Branch, and to enable the President to carry out his constitutional duties without undue caution.") *with* 91 F.4th at 1198 ("The risks of chilling Presidential action or permitting meritless, harassing prosecutions are unlikely, unsupported by history and 'too remote and shadowy to shape the course of justice.'" (citing *Clark v. United States*, 289 U.S. 1, 16 (1933))) *and* 704 F. Supp 3d at 213 ("Consequently, to the extent that there are any cognizable 'chilling effects' on Presidential decision-making from the prospect of criminal liability, they raise far lesser concerns than those discussed in the civil context of *Fitzgerald*. Every President will face difficult decisions; whether to intentionally commit a federal crime should not be one of them.").

Ultimately, the Supreme Court ruled that for official powers entrusted exclusively to the President, a President is entitled to absolute criminal immunity and that for other acts "within the outer perimeter of his official responsibility" he is entitled to at least presumptive immunity. *Id.* at 613-614. Specifically, the Court divided presidential acts into three categories: (1) core presidential conduct that Congress has no power to regulate and for which a former President has absolute immunity; (2) other official presidential acts for which the President has at least presumptive immunity; and (3) unofficial conduct for which the President has no immunity. *Id.* at 606, 642. Applying those principles to the original indictment, the Supreme Court concluded that Mr. Trump is "absolutely immune from prosecution for the alleged conduct involving his discussions with Justice Department officials" and involving his "threatened removal of the Acting Attorney General." *Id.* at 620-621. The Court also concluded that several conversations between Mr. Trump and the Vice President constituted official conduct, but remanded for consideration of whether the Office could rebut the presumption of immunity. *Id.* at 624-625. As to several other allegations—involving interactions with state officials, private parties, and the public—the Court remanded for the lower courts to determine whether the conduct was undertaken in an official capacity or, alternatively, constituted a private scheme with private actors, as the Office contended. *Id.* at 625-627.

The Court also added an evidentiary rule to its immunity framework: official conduct for which the President is immune may not be used as evidence in a prosecution for non-immune conduct. *Id.* at 630-632. The Court was concerned that "jurors' deliberations will be prejudiced by their views of the President's policies and performance while in office." *Id.* at 631. Justice Barrett joined the dissenters in disagreeing with that rule, noting, "The Constitution does not require blinding juries to the circumstances surrounding conduct for which Presidents *can* be held liable." *Id.* at 655 (emphasis in original) (Barrett, J., concurring in part). Standard evidentiary rules, she explained, "are equipped to handle that concern [about prejudice from admitting evidence of a President's official acts] on a case-by case-basis." *Id.* at 656. "I see no need," she wrote, "to depart from that familiar and time-tested procedure here." *Id.*

3.   Unresolved Issues Regarding Presidential Immunity

The Supreme Court's decision raises several issues about the scope of presidential immunity that the lower courts, and ultimately the Supreme Court, would likely have had to address before the prosecution could have proceeded to trial. The following discussion illustrates some of the issues that the Court's immunity decision left open and that remain unresolved given the required dismissal of the superseding indictment.

First, while the Court determined that certain core exercises of presidential power are absolutely immune and gave several examples, *see* 603 U.S. at 608-609 (pardon power; power to remove presidential appointees; power to recognize foreign nations), 620-621 (supervision of criminal investigations and prosecutions), it left undefined the full scope of that category. *Compare id.* at 620 (relying in part on the President's responsibility to "take Care that the Laws be faithfully executed" (U.S. CONST. art II, § 3) to find that his investigative and prosecutorial decision-making, and threats to remove the Acting Attorney General, were absolutely immune) *with id.* at 651 n.1 (Barrett, J., concurring) ("I do not understand the Court to hold that all exercises of the Take Care power fall within the core executive power"). The Office's position was that none of the allegations in the superseding indictment implicated core presidential powers.

Second, the Court's decision accorded at least presumptive immunity to all non-core official presidential conduct. 603 U.S. at 614-615. That holding left unresolved whether, at some future point, the Court will determine that absolute immunity is required for that category of official acts as well. It also left unresolved the manner of applying its test for overcoming presumptive immunity: *i.e.*, that the government must "show that applying a criminal prohibition to that act would pose no 'dangers of intrusion on the authority and functions of the Executive Branch.'" *Id.* at 615 (quoting *Fitzgerald*, 457 U.S. at 754); *cf.* 603 U.S. at 667 (Sotomayor, J., dissenting) ("According to the majority, however, any incursion on Executive power is too much. When presumptive immunity is this conclusive, the majority's indecision as to 'whether [official-acts] immunity must be absolute' or whether, instead, 'presumptive immunity is sufficient,' hardly matters.") (citation omitted). In its one concrete discussion of that test, the Court described competing arguments about communications between the President and the Vice

President about the certification proceeding, noting that the Vice President presides as President of the Senate, not in any Executive Branch capacity, and that the President has "no direct constitutional or statutory role" in the certification proceeding. *See id.* at 622-625. But the Court stopped short of deciding whether any Executive Branch functions were in danger of potential intrusion in that setting and, if so, the nature of such functions. It also did not address whether de minimis intrusions would preclude rebutting the presumption, and how courts should make predictive judgments about potential intrusions (for example, by looking to history, speculating about future presidential behavior, or relying solely on legal materials).

Following the remand to the district court, the Office argued that, with respect to the presumptive immunity test, "[t]he analysis should first identify the specific alleged act at issue, and then determine whether criminal liability for the act intrudes on a relevant Executive Branch authority or function, taking care not to 'conceive[] of the inquiry at too high a level of generality.'" ECF No. 252 at 87 (quoting *Banneker Ventures, LLC v. Graham*, 798 F.3d 1119, 1141 (D.C. Cir. 2015) (reversing district court in civil immunity case)). The Office's brief emphasized that this approach "recognizes that Executive authority has limits—boundaries imposed by constitutional text, the separation of powers, and precedent—and that application of criminal law to the President's official conduct does not *per se* intrude impermissibly on Executive Branch authority and functions." *Id.* at 87-88. With regard to the communications between the President and the Vice President, the Office submitted that "[b]ecause the Executive Branch has no role in the certification proceeding—and indeed, the President was purposely excluded from it by design—prosecuting the defendant for his corrupt efforts regarding Pence poses no danger to the Executive Branch's authority or functioning." *Id.* at 89-90.

Third, in discussing the process of separating official from unofficial conduct, the Court wrote that the analysis is "fact specific and may prove to be challenging." 603 U.S. at 629. The Court's discussion of a President's public communications illustrates those challenges. The Court directed that the status of a President's public communications should be assessed through an "objective analysis of 'content, form, and context.'" *Id.* (quoting *Snyder v. Phelps*, 562 U.S. 443, 453 (2011)). It also cautioned that "most of a President's public communications are likely to fall comfortably within the outer perimeter of his official responsibilities" while stating that there "may" be contexts in which a President "speaks in an unofficial capacity—perhaps as a candidate for office or party leader." *Id.* The Court's analysis recognized that, in principle, there is a line between a President's official and nonofficial communications, but the Court gave little detail about when an incumbent President crosses the line between his official role and his candidate role. *Cf.* 603 U.S. at 667 (Sotomayor, J., dissenting) ("In fact, the majority's dividing line between 'official' and 'unofficial' conduct narrows the conduct considered 'unofficial' almost to a nullity."). Upon remand, the Office argued that "[a]t its core, the defendant's scheme was a private one," ECF No. 252 at 88, and that in proving the case the Office would rely on "public Campaign speeches, Tweets, and other public statements and comments" that Mr. Trump made "not as President but as a candidate for office." *Id.* at 115.

Finally, as noted, the Court's decision that presidential immunity precludes the introduction of evidence of immune official acts even in a prosecution for unofficial conduct left open substantive and procedural questions. 603 U.S. at 630-632. In responding to Justice Barrett's disagreement with the Court's evidentiary holding, in which she highlighted her concern about excluding official act evidence in, for example, a bribery prosecution, *id.* at 655-656 (Barrett, J., concurring in part), the Court wrote in a footnote that in a bribery prosecution, "of course the prosecutor may point to the public record to show the fact that the President performed the official act." *Id.* at 632 n.3 (majority opinion). "What the prosecutor may not do, however, is admit testimony or private records of the President or his advisors probing the official act itself." *Id.* Those statements create uncertainty regarding which types of evidence of official acts can be used and which cannot. A further procedural issue involved the scope of any interlocutory appeal from the district court's rulings on immunity. The Supreme Court had emphasized that immunity issues should be "addressed at the outset of a proceeding," 603 U.S. at 636, and presupposed that "a district court's denial of immunity would be appealable before trial," *id.* at 635. While the parties and the district court agreed that whether the superseding indictment states an offense based on non-immune conduct would be subject to a pretrial interlocutory appeal, the evidentiary component of the Court's immunity ruling left open the question of whether evidentiary determinations regarding potentially immune evidence could be appealed before trial. Further proceedings on remand likely would have provided guidance on this and the other issues described above.

VI.   CONCLUSION

On remand from the Supreme Court's decision in *Trump*, the district court set a litigation schedule whereby the parties would submit briefs regarding whether any material in the superseding indictment was subject to presidential immunity. ECF No. 233. The parties were in the middle of that process when the results of the presidential election made clear that Mr. Trump would be inaugurated as President of the United States on January 20, 2025. As described above, it has long been the Department's interpretation that the Constitution forbids the federal indictment and prosecution of a sitting President, but the election results raised for the first time the question of the lawful course when a private citizen who has already been indicted is then elected President. The Department determined that the case must be dismissed without prejudice before Mr. Trump takes office, and the Office therefore moved to dismiss the indictment on November 25, 2024. *See* ECF No. 281. The district court granted the motion the same day. ECF No. 283.

The Department's view that the Constitution prohibits the continued indictment and prosecution of a President is categorical and does not turn on the gravity of the crimes charged, the strength of the Government's proof, or the merits of the prosecution, which the Office stands fully behind. Indeed, but for Mr. Trump's election and imminent return to the Presidency, the Office assessed that the admissible evidence was sufficient to obtain and sustain a conviction at trial.

APPENDIX: KEY FILINGS IN SIGNIFICANT LITIGATION

DISTRICT COURT CRIMINAL LITIGATION

	*United States v. Donald J. Trump*, Case No. 23-cr-257 (D.D.C.)
ECF No.	Date	Document Description
1	8/1/2023	Indictment
10	8/4/2023	Government's Motion for Protective Order
12	8/5/2023	Government's Opposition to Defendant's Motion for Extension of Time
15	8/7/2023	Government's Reply in Support of Motion for Protective Order
16	8/3/2023	Transcript of Initial Appearance (issued 8/8/2023)
23	8/10/2023	Government's Response to Court's August 3, 2023 Minute Order (Proposed Trial Date)
26	8/10/2023	Government's Response in Opposition to Defendant's Motion for Exclusion of Time Under Speedy Trial Act
28	8/11/2023	Court Protective Order Governing Discovery and Authorizing Disclosure of Grand Jury Testimony
29	8/11/2023	Transcript of Hearing on Protective Order
32	8/21/2023	Government's Reply to Defendant's Response in Opposition to Government's Proposed Trial Calendar
38	8/28/2023	Transcript of Status Hearing
39	8/28/2023	Court Pretrial Order
54	9/14/2023	Government's Response in Opposition to Defendant's Motion for Recusal of District Judge Pursuant to 28 U.S.C. Section 455(a)
57	9/15/2023	Government's Opposed Motion to Ensure that Extrajudicial Statements Do Not Prejudice These Proceedings
61	9/27/2023	Court Memorandum Opinion & Order (Defendant's Motion for Recusal of District Judge)
64	9/29/2023	Government's Reply in Support of Opposed Motion to Ensure that Extrajudicial Statements Do Not Prejudice These Proceedings
65	10/2/2023	Government's Opposition to Defendant's Motion for Access to CIPA Section 4 Filing and an Adjournment of the CIPA Section 5 Deadline
66	10/2/2023	Government's Response in Opposition to Defendant's Motion for Extension of Time to File Pretrial Motions
82	10/6/2023	Court Opinion & Order (Defendant's Motion for Access to CIPA Section 4 Filing and an Adjournment of the CIPA Section 5 Deadline)
97	10/10/2023	Government's Opposed Motion for Fair and Protective Jury Procedures

ECF No.	Date	Document Description
		United States v. Donald J. Trump, Case No. 23-cr-257 (D.D.C.)
98	10/10/2023	Government's Motion for Formal Pretrial Notice of the Defendant's Intent to Rely on Advice-of-Counsel Defense
103	10/16/2023	Transcript of Hearing (Government's Motion on Extrajudicial Statements)
105	10/17/2023	Court Opinion & Order (Government's Motion to Ensure that Extrajudicial Statements Do Not Prejudice These Proceedings)
108	10/18/2023	Government's Opposition to Second Defense Motion for Access to CIPA Section 4 Filing
109	10/19/2023	Government's Response in Opposition to Defendant's Motion to Dismiss on Presidential Immunity Grounds
117	10/25/2023	Government's Reply in Support of Motion for Fair and Protective Jury Procedures
118	10/25/2023	Government's Reply in Support of Motion for Formal Pretrial Notice of the Defendant's Intent to Rely on Advice-of-Counsel Defense
119	10/25/2023	Government's Opposition to Defendant's Motion for Pre-Trial Rule 17(c) Subpoenas
120	10/25/2023	Government's Response in Opposition to Defendant's Motion to Stay
124	10/29/2023	Court Opinion & Order (Denying Defendant's Motion to Stay)
126	11/1/2023	Court Opinion & Order (CIPA Section 4 Motions)
130	11/2/2023	Court Order (Government's Motion for Fair and Protective Jury Procedures)
137	11/3/2023	Government's Opposition to Defendant's Motion for Extension of Time to File Pretrial Motions Related to Discovery and Subpoenas
139	11/6/2023	Government's Omnibus Opposition to Defendant's Motions to Dismiss the Indictment on Statutory and Constitutional Grounds
140	11/6/2023	Government's Opposition to Defendant's Motion to Strike Inflammatory Allegations from the Indictment
141	11/6/2023	Government's Opposition to Defendant's Motion to Dismiss for Selective and Vindictive Prosecution
142	11/6/2023	Government's Opposition to Defendant's Motion to Stay Case Pending Resolution of Motion to Dismiss Based on Presidential Immunity
146	11/7/2023	Court Opinion & Order (Defendant's Motion for Extension of Time to File Pretrial Motions Related to Discovery and Subpoenas)
147	11/8/2023	Court Opinion & Order (Government's Motion for Formal Pretrial Notice of Advice of Counsel Defense)

ECF No.	Date	Document Description
		United States v. Donald J. Trump, Case No. 23-cr-257 (D.D.C.)
	ECF No.	Date	Document Description
151	11/13/2023	Government's Opposition to Defendant's Motion for Extension of Time to File Reply Briefs
152	11/13/2023	Court Order (Defendant's Motion for Extension of Time to File Reply Briefs)
158	11/17/2023	Court Opinion & Order (Defendant's Motion to Strike)
165	11/27/2023	Court Opinion & Order (Defendant's Motion for Pretrial Rule 17(c) Subpoenas)
171, 172	12/1/2023	Court Memorandum Opinion & Order (Defendant's Motions to Dismiss Based on Presidential Immunity and Constitutional Grounds)
176	12/5/2023	Government's Notice Pursuant to Federal Rule of Evidence 404(b)
181	12/9/2023	Government's Opposition to Defendant's Discovery Motions
182	12/10/2023	Government's Opposition to Defendant's Motion to Stay Proceedings Pending Appeal
183	12/11/2023	Government's Summary of Anticipated Expert Testimony
186	12/13/2023	Court Opinion & Order (Defendant's Motion to Stay Proceedings Pending Appeal)
188	12/18/2023	Government's Notice of Service (Government's Draft Exhibit List)
191	12/27/2023	Government's Motion *in Limine*
193	1/5/2024	Government's Opposition to Defendant's Motion for Order to Show Cause
195	1/18/2024	Court Opinion & Order (Defendant's Motion to Show Cause)
198, 199	8/3/2024	Court Memorandum Opinion & Order (Defendant's Motion to Dismiss for Selective and Vindictive Prosecution)
226	8/27/2024	Superseding Indictment
228	8/27/2024	Government's Notice of Superseding Indictment
229	8/30/2024	Joint Status Report (Pretrial Schedule)
232	9/5/2024	Transcript of Arraignment and Status Conference
233	9/5/2024	Court Order (Pretrial Schedule)
246	9/27/2024	Government's Motion for Leave to File Unredacted Motion Under Seal, and to File Redacted Motion on Public Docket
249	10/1/2024	Government's Sur-Reply to Defendant's Discovery Motions
251	10/2/2024	Court Opinion & Order (Government's Motion for Leave to File Unredacted Motion Under Seal, and to File Redacted Motion on Public Docket)
252	10/2/2024	Government's Motion for Immunity Determinations

United States v. Donald J. Trump, Case No. 23-cr-257 (D.D.C.)		
ECF No.	Date	Document Description
262	10/16/2024	Government's Response in Opposition to the Defendant's Supplement to His Motion to Dismiss on Statutory Grounds
263	10/16/2024	Court Memorandum Opinion & Order (Defendant's Motions to Compel Discovery and for an Order Regarding the Scope of Prosecution Team)
265	10/17/2024	Court Opinion & Order (Defendant's Motion to Continue Stay of Order)
266	10/18/2024	Government Appendix to Motion for Immunity Determinations
277	10/31/2024	Government's Response in Opposition to the Defendant's Proposed Motion to Dismiss and for Injunctive Relief Based on the Appointments and Appropriations Clauses
278	11/8/2024	Government's Unopposed Motion to Vacate Briefing Schedule
281	11/25/2024	Government's Motion to Dismiss Without Prejudice
282, 283	11/25/2024	Court Opinion & Order (Government's Motion to Dismiss Without Prejudice)

PRESIDENTIAL IMMUNITY APPELLATE LITIGATION

United States v. Trump, No. 23-3228 (D.C. Cir.)		
Doc. No.	Date	Document Description
2030867	12/11/2023	Government's Opposed Motion for Expedited Appellate Review
2031335	12/13/2023	Government's Reply in Support of Motion for Expedited Appellate Review
2031419	12/13/2023	Court Order (Expediting Appeal and Setting Briefing Schedule)
2033810	12/30/2023	Government's Answering Brief (Presidential Immunity)
2034942	1/9/2024	Oral Argument[268]
2038999, 2039001	2/6/2024	Court Judgment & Opinion[269]

---

[268] *Oral Argument Recordings Archive*, United States Court of Appeals for the District of Columbia Circuit (Jan. 9, 2024), https://media.cadc.uscourts.gov/recordings/bydate/2024/1 [https://perma.cc/9523-TRZ9].

[269] *See United States v. Trump*, 91 F.4th 1173 (D.C. Cir. 2024).

United States v. Trump, No. 23-624 (U.S.)		
Doc. No.	Date	Document Description
1	12/11/2023	Government's Petition for a Writ of Certiorari Before Judgment (Presidential Immunity)
2	12/11/2023	Government's Motion to Expedite Briefing on the Petition for a Writ of Certiorari Before Judgment and for Expedited Merits Briefing If the Court Grants the Petition
3	12/11/2023	Court Order (Government's Motion to Expedite)
7	12/21/2023	Government's Reply Brief in Support of Motion to Expedite (Presidential Immunity)
8	12/22/2023	Court Order (Petition for a Writ of Certiorari Before Judgment)

Trump v. United States, No. 23-939 (U.S.)		
Doc. No.	Date	Document Description
6	2/14/2024	Government Response in Opposition to Application for a Stay of the Mandate of the United States Court of Appeals for the District of Columbia Circuit (Presidential Immunity) (originally filed in Trump v. United States, No. 23A745 (U.S.))
15, 16	2/28/2024	Court Order (Application for Stay/Petition for Certiorari) (originally filed in Trump v. United States, No. 23A745 (U.S.))
47	4/8/2024	Government's Brief (Presidential Immunity)
65	4/25/2024	Oral Argument[270]
66, 67	7/1/2024	Court Opinion & Judgment (Presidential Immunity)[271]

RULE 57.7(c) APPELLATE LITIGATION

United States v. Trump, No. 23-3190 (D.C. Cir.)		
Doc. No.	Date	Document Description
2026922	11/14/2023	Government's Answering Brief (Rule 57.7(c))
2027866	11/20/2023	Oral Argument[272]

---

[270] *Transcript of Oral Argument in Case No. 23-939*, Supreme Court of the United States (Apr. 25, 2024), http://www.supremecourt.gov/oral_arguments/argument_transcripts/2023/23-939_3fb4.pdf [https://perma.cc/XQ7N-E33J].

[271] *See Trump v. United States*, 603 U.S. 593 (2024).

[272] *Oral Argument Recordings Archive*, United States Court of Appeals for the District of Columbia Circuit (Nov. 20, 2023), https://media.cadc.uscourts.gov/recordings/bydate/2023/11 [https://perma.cc/5J2E-PDT6].

United States v. *Trump*, No. 23-3190 (D.C. Cir.)		
Doc. No.	Date	Document Description
2032665	12/20/2023	Court Public Opinion (Rule 57.7(c)) (decided 12/8/2023)[273]
2033815	12/31/2023	Government's Response in Opposition to Rehearing
2037003	1/23/2024	Court Order (Petition for Rehearing)

SELECTED GRAND JURY LITIGATION
(PARTIALLY UNSEALED)[274]

Case No.	Case Name
No. 22-gj-25 (D.D.C.)	*In re Grand Jury Subpoenas*
No. 22-3073 (D.C. Cir.)	*In re Sealed Case*
No. 22-gj-33 (D.D.C.)	*In re Grand Jury Subpoenas*
No. 23-3002 (D.C. Cir.)	*In re Sealed Case*
No. 22-gj-39 (D.D.C.)	*In re Grand Jury Subpoena*
No. 23-3003 (D.C. Cir.)	*In re Sealed Case*
No. 23-gj-12 (D.D.C.)	*In re Grand Jury Subpoenas*
No. 23-3043 (D.C. Cir.)	*In re Sealed Case*
No. 23-gj-13 (D.D.C.)	*In re Grand Jury Subpoena*
No. 23-3049 (D.C. Cir.)	*In re Sealed Case*

---

[273] *See United States v. Trump*, 88 F.4th 990, 1018 (D.C. Cir. 2023).

[274] As of the date of this Report, certain documents from selected grand jury litigation have been made available to the public through related litigation. *See In re Application of the New York Times*, No. 22-mc-100, ECF No. 32 (D.D.C.); *In re Press Application*, No. 23-mc-35, ECF No. 11 (D.D.C.); *see also Former Vice President Michael R. Pence's Motion to Quash Subpoena*, United States District Court for the District of Columbia (Mar. 3, 2023), https://www.dcd.uscourts.gov/sites/dcd/files/Attachment%201.pdf [https://perma.cc/5LNK-72DG]; *Government's Opposition to Former Vice President Pence's Motion to Quash Subpoena*, United States District Court for the District of Columbia (Mar. 10, 2023), https://www.dcd.uscourts.gov/sites/dcd/files/Attachment%202.pdf [https://perma.cc/C8VM-E2PV]; *Former Vice President Michael R. Pence's Reply in Support of His Motion to Quash Subpoena*, United States District Court for the District of Columbia (Mar. 17, 2023), https://www.dcd.uscourts.gov/sites/dcd/files/Attachment%203.pdf [https://perma.cc/Z5DJ-7Y2K]; *Order*, United States District Court for the District of Columbia (Mar. 27, 2023); https://www.dcd.uscourts.gov/sites/dcd/files/Attachment%204.pdf [https://perma.cc/L7TS-L6AQ]; *Memorandum Opinion*, United States District Court for the District of Columbia (Mar. 27, 2023), https://www.dcd.uscourts.gov/sites/dcd/files/Attachment%205.pdf [https://perma.cc/FR8G-S3SJ]; *Sealed Proceeding Before the Honorable James E. Boasberg*, United States District Court for the District of Columbia (Mar. 23, 2023), https://www.dcd.uscourts.gov/sites/dcd/files/Attachment%206.pdf [https://perma.cc/J2C6-K35S].

PERRY SEARCH WARRANT LITIGATION

ECF No.	Date	Document Description
In re Scott Perry Cell Phone Search Warrant, No. 22-sc-2144 (D.D.C.)		
(Partially Unsealed)[275]		
41[276]	11/4/2022	Court Memorandum Opinion & Order (Applicability of the Speech or Debate Clause)
42, 43[277]	12/28/2022	Court Memorandum Opinion & Order (Perry's Motion for Non-Disclosure to the Government)
44[278]	1/4/2023	Court Memorandum Opinion & Order (Perry's Emergency Motion to Stay)
45[279]	2/24/2023	Court Memorandum & Order (Unsealing)
Sealed[280]	12/19/2023	Court Memorandum Opinion & Order (Applicability of the Speech or Debate Clause)

Doc. No.	Date	Document Description
In re Sealed Case, No. 23-3001 (D.C. Cir.)		
2031508 (Att. 2)	1/9/2023	Government's Opposition to Emergency Motion for Stay Pending Appeal
1983102	1/25/2023	Court Order (Perry's Motion for Stay Pending Appeal)

---

[275] Additional filings in this matter have been made publicly available in *In re Sealed Case*, No. 23-3001 (D.C. Cir.), Doc. No. 2031508, Attachment 10 (Joint Appendix).

[276] *Memorandum Opinion and Order*, United States District Court for the District of Columbia (Nov. 4, 2022), http://www.dcd.uscourts.gov/sites/dcd/files/Redacted%20November%204%2C%202022%20Memorandum%20Opinion%20and%20Order.pdf [https://perma.cc/6CLJ-BETZ].

[277] *Memorandum Opinion*, United States District Court for the District of Columbia (Dec. 28, 2022), https://www.dcd.uscourts.gov/sites/dcd/files/Redacted%20December%2028%2C%202022%20Memorandum%20Opinion%2C%20ECF%20No%2043.pdf [https://perma.cc/7Z37-SRA4]; *Order*, United States District Court for the District of Columbia (Dec. 28, 2022), https://www.dcd.uscourts.gov/sites/dcd/files/Redacted%20December%2028%2C%202022%20Order%2C%20ECF%20No%2042.pdf [https://perma.cc/AYF7-ECBD].

[278] *Memorandum Opinion and Order*, United States District Court for the District of Columbia (Jan. 4, 2023), https://www.dcd.uscourts.gov/sites/dcd/files/Redacted%20January%204%2C%202023%20Memorandum%20Opinion%20and%20Order%2C%20ECF%20No%2044.pdf [https://perma.cc/38NW-EXV3].

[279] *Memorandum and Order*, United States District Court for the District of Columbia (Feb. 4, 2023), https://www.dcd.uscourts.gov/sites/dcd/files/Memorandum%20and%20Order%20February%2024%2C%202023.pdf [https://perma.cc/7PZQ-NZK6].

[280] *Memorandum Opinion*, United States District Court for the District of Columbia (Dec. 19, 2023), https://www.dcd.uscourts.gov/sites/dcd/files/22-sc-2144%20-%20Opinion.pdf [https://perma.cc/5PPD-JH68]; *Order*, United States District Court for the District of Columbia (Dec. 19, 2023), https://www.dcd.uscourts.gov/sites/dcd/files/22-sc-2144%20-%20Order.pdf [https://perma.cc/C3E5-JQXK].

In re Sealed Case, No. 23-3001 (D.C. Cir.)		
Doc. No.	Date	Document Description
2031508 (Att. 12)	2/16/2023	Government's Brief
---	2/23/2023	Oral Argument[281]
2015233	9/5/2023	Court Judgment
2016705	9/13/2023	Court Opinion (decided 9/5/2023)[282]

TWITTER SEARCH WARRANT LITIGATION

In re Twitter Search Warrant, No. 23-sc-31 (D.D.C.)		
ECF No.	Date	Document Description
5	2/2/2023	Government's Motion for an Order to Show Cause Why Twitter Inc. Should Not Be Held in Contempt for Failure to Comply with a Search Warrant
11	2/6/2023	Government's Reply in Further Support of Motion for an Order to Show Cause Why Twitter Inc. Should Not Be Held in Contempt for Failure to Comply with a Search Warrant
50	2/7/2023	Transcript of Hearing (Government's Motion for an Order to Show Cause)
---	2/7/2023	Court Minute Order Granting Government's Motion for Order to Show Cause and Directing Twitter to Comply
50	2/9/2023	Transcript of Hearing (Twitter's Non-Compliance with Warrant)
19	2/13/2023	Government's Notice Regarding Accrued Sanction
50	2/16/2023	Government's Opposition to Twitter Inc.'s Motion to Vacate or Modify Non-Disclosure Order and Stay Twitter's Compliance with Search Warrant
29, 32	3/3/2023	Court Memorandum Opinion & Order (Twitter's Motion to Vacate or Modify and Stay)
36	3/9/2023	Government's Opposition to Motion for Stay Pending Appeal
39	3/10/2023	Court Opinion & Order (Twitter's Motion for a Stay)
50	8/15/2023	Court Order (Unsealing)

---

[281] *Oral Argument Recordings Archive*, United States Court of Appeals for the District of Columbia Circuit (Feb. 23, 2023), https://media.cadc.uscourts.gov/recordings/bydate/2023/2 [https://perma.cc/YS57-HMYW].

[282] *See In re Sealed Case*, 80 F.4th 355 (D.C. Cir. 2023).

In re Sealed Case, No. 23-5044 (D.C. Cir.)		
Doc. No.	Date	Document Description
1989703	3/10/2023	Government's Response in Opposition to Twitter's Motion for Stay
1991524	3/23/2023	Court Order (Twitter's Motion for Stay)
2017103	4/21/2023	Government's Answering Brief (filed with redactions on 9/15/2023)
---	5/19/2023	Oral Argument[283]
2011549	8/9/2023	Court Amended Redacted Opinion (decided 7/18/2023)[284]
2018981	9/26/2023	Government's Response in Opposition to Rehearing En Banc
2035679	1/16/2024	Court Order (Petition for Rehearing)

X Corp. v. United States, No. 23-1264 (U.S.)		
Doc. No.	Date	Document Description
5	7/3/2024	Government's Opposition (Petition for Writ of Certiorari)
9	10/7/2024	Court Order (Petition for Writ of Certiorari)[285]

---

[283] *Oral Argument Recordings Archive*, United States Court of Appeals for the District of Columbia Circuit (May 19, 2023), https://media.cadc.uscourts.gov/recordings/bydate/2023/5 [https://perma.cc/SR2Z-GL5B].

[284] *See In re Sealed Case*, 77 F.4th 815, 830 (D.C. Cir. 2023).

[285] *See X Corp. v. United States*, 2024 WL 4426628 (U.S. Oct. 7, 2024).

ADDENDUM

TODD BLANCHE
ToddBlanche@blanchelaw.com
(212) 716-1250

January 6, 2025

Via Email
The Honorable Merrick Garland
Attorney General of the United States
c/o Brad Weinsheimer
Associate Deputy Attorney General

Re: Draft "Final Report" By Jack Smith

Dear Attorney General Garland:

We write on behalf of President Trump to demand that Smith terminate all efforts toward the preparation and release of this report (the "Draft Report").[1]

As you know, Courts in Florida and the District of Columbia have now dismissed both of Jack Smith's failed cases against President Trump. Rather than acknowledging, as he must, President Trump's complete exoneration, Smith now seeks to disseminate an extrajudicial "Final Report" to perpetuate his false and discredited accusations. Consistent with the bad-faith crusade that Smith executed on behalf of the Biden-Harris Administration from the moment he was appointed, we were only permitted to review the Draft Report in person in the District of Columbia, including prohibitions on the use of any outside electronic devices in the room where the Draft Report was made available. Smith's team likewise demanded, in advance of any review, that we delete prior discovery productions, preventing us from reviewing any of those underlying documents cited in the Draft Report. Nevertheless, it is clear, as has been the case with so many of the other actions of Smith and his staff, that the Draft Report merely continues Smith's politically-motivated attack, and that his continued preparation of the Report and efforts to release it would be both imprudent and unlawful.

First, Smith lacks authority under our Constitution to issue a report because he was not validly appointed, and the plain terms of the permanent indefinite appropriation that he has pillaged for more than $20 million clearly do not apply to his politically-motivated work. The preparation and release of a report, therefore, would extend and perpetuate Smith's violations of the Appointments Clause and the Appropriations Clause.

Second, the Draft Report violates fundamental norms regarding the presumption of innocence, including with respect to third parties unnecessarily impugned by Smith's false claims. Releasing the report to the public without significant redactions (that would render its release meaningless) would violate prohibitions on extrajudicial statements by prosecutors and Rule 6(e). This is particularly problematic with respect to ongoing proceedings relating to Waltine Nauta and Carlos De Oliveira, as well as others who Smith and his staff falsely characterize as co-conspirators in the Draft Report.

---

[1] Should these demands be improperly rejected, contrary to law, we respectfully request that this letter be appended to and addressed in any report by Smith that is issued to the public.

Third, preparing a report and releasing it to the public would violate the Presidential Transition Act and the Presidential immunity doctrine. The Act prohibits *all* officers and those acting as such, including the Attorney General and Smith, at least in his own view of himself, from interfering with the ongoing transition process. Presidential immunity, which Smith conceded required pre-inauguration dismissal of his prosecutions, likewise prohibits criminal processes, including disclosures of any prosecutorial reports or statements, that would exacerbate stigma and public opprobrium surrounding the Chief Executive and otherwise divert from the time and attention that is necessary to complete the transition and run the County. Accordingly, releasing a report regarding Smith's failed and abandoned election-interference efforts would violate the Act and Presidential immunity.

Finally, the release of any confidential report prepared by this out-of-control private citizen unconstitutionally posing as a prosecutor would be nothing more than a lawless political stunt, designed to politically harm President Trump and justify the huge sums of taxpayer money Smith unconstitutionally spent on his failed and dismissed cases. Under such circumstances, releasing Smith's report is obviously not in the public interest—particularly in light of President Trump's commanding victory in the election and the sensitive nature of the ongoing transition process.

Accordingly, because Smith has proposed an unlawful course of action, you must countermand his plan and remove him promptly. If Smith is not removed, then the handling of his report should be deferred to President Trump's incoming attorney general, consistent with the expressed will of the People. Finally, should you disagree with the positions set forth below, we respectfully request notice of that decision prior to the unlawful release of any report so that we can pursue injunctive and other relief to protect the rights of President Trump, others unfairly implicated by Smith's work, and the people of this great Nation who elected President Trump to run the government and put an end to the weaponization of the justice system.

I. Background

You are no doubt familiar with the history of the unethical election-interference and lawfare by the Special Counsel's Office, as you have publicly commented on some of those efforts while they were ongoing. This letter concerns Smith's most recent improper activities.

During the week of December 9, 2024, we learned from members of the media that Smith was preparing a report, which would include a purported analysis relating to classified information at issue in the dismissed Florida prosecution. We were surprised to learn of such a plan because, among other reasons, Smith had insisted up to that point that his work was not concluded, Smith and his Office refused to disclose details regarding this alleged analysis prior to the dismissal of his Florida prosecution against President Trump, and the Biden-Harris Administration has suggested that they wish to facilitate an orderly and collegial transition process.

On December 11, 2024, we contacted a supervisor with the Special Counsel's Office to express concerns about reports we were hearing from the press. We asked whether the Office was preparing a report and, if so, whether we would be allowed to review it prior to completion. Initially, Smith's position was that: (1) we would only be permitted to access a draft of the report in Washington, D.C. between December 23 and December 29, 2024, the week of Christmas; (2) we would only be permitted to take handwritten notes during our review; and (3) any comments or objections to the draft would have to be submitted in writing by the close of business on December 29, 2024. Aside from all counsel living outside D.C. and planning on spending time with family that week, as Smith and his team knew, Smith's proposal afforded zero opportunity for President Trump to assist counsel in reviewing and preparing any response to the report, given the irrational conditions imposed. Apparently working under a self-imposed deadline, Smith's team informed us, implausibly, that permitting defense review of Smith's unlawful Draft Report during the first week of January 2025 would be "too late to allow us to complete our work." Subsequently Smith walked back those now clearly false claims and permitted defense counsel to review the two-volume Draft Report in a conference room at Smith's office between January 3 and January 6, 2025, without allowing counsel to access the Internet or use their own electronic devices while in the room with supposedly sensitive documents that the press has known about for weeks by virtue of Smith's leaks.

II. Preparation And Release Of A Report Would Violate Existing Law

Preparation and public release of a report by Smith would violate the Constitution and existing law, including the Appropriations and Appointments Clauses, the Special Counsel Regulations, the Presidential Transition Act, and the Presidential immunity doctrine. Collectively, these considerations distinguish the circumstances surrounding the release of reports by prior Special Counsels. Here, release of an unlawful report would *not* "comply with applicable legal restrictions" or "be in the public interest." 28 C.F.R. § 600.9(c); *see also id.* § 600.7(a) ("A Special Counsel shall comply with the rules, regulations, procedures, practices and policies of the Department of Justice."). Therefore, you must countermand Smith's proposed course of action, *id.* § 600.7(b), and he should be removed for "dereliction of duty" and "good cause," § 600.7(d).

Smith was not validly appointed, and Congress did not provide funding for his improper mission. No statute authorized you to deploy a private attorney against President Trump and others, and Smith functioned as a principal officer acting without the necessary Senate confirmation. In addition, the DOJ permanent indefinite appropriation Smith relied upon was—and still is—inapplicable. The only judge to have examined the particulars of Smith's appointment reached these conclusions in an extremely thorough and well-reasoned opinion. *See generally United States v. Trump*, 2024 WL 3404555, at *46 (S.D. Fla. July 15, 2024). On appeal, Smith's prosecutors failed to identify any meritorious reason for questioning Judge Cannon's treatment of these issues, and then abandoned the appeal as to President Trump. Therefore, Smith lacks authority to issue a report regarding his activities while masquerading as a prosecutor, and his Office lacks authority to expend any public funds in furtherance of preparing or issuing such a report. Indeed, because Smith abandoned the 11th Circuit appeal as to President Trump, Judge Cannon's decision is a final judgment with issue-preclusive effect on these issues. *See, e.g., Bravo-Fernandez v. United States*, 580 U.S. 5, 7-8 (2016) (cleaned up) ("In criminal prosecutions, as in civil litigation, the issue-preclusion principle means that when an issue of ultimate fact has once been determined by a valid and final judgment, that issue cannot again be litigated between the same parties in any future lawsuit."); *Bobby v. Bies*, 556 U.S. 825, 834 (2009) (same).

Preparation and release of a report would also be improper under the Special Counsel Regulations. Those Regulations only call for "Closing documentation," in the form of a "confidential report," to be prepared "[a]t the *conclusion* of the Special Counsel's work." 28 C.F.R. § 600.8(c) (emphasis added). In light of the violations of the Appointments Clause and the Appropriations Clause, Smith has no lawful "work" to conclude. Moreover, by Smith's own repeated admission, Smith has not concluded his mission.

Rather, Presidential immunity based on the national mandate arising from President Trump's overwhelming victory in the election has made it impossible for Smith to proceed, and rightly so.

Smith's representations in the District of Columbia regarding his dismissed prosecution of President Trump reinforce these points and make clear that no "Closing documentation" is warranted. 28 C.F.R. § 600.8(c). Smith wrongly relied on the claim that Presidential immunity is "temporary," which is not the case, to ask that the charges against President Trump only be dismissed "without prejudice."[2] The plain implication of Smith's position, which Judge Chutkan adopted, is that he does not believe his work targeting President Trump has reached its "conclusion." 28 C.F.R. § 600.8(c). Thus, taking a contrary position in order to justify preparation of one last long-winded, inaccurate, and unlawful smear of the President-elect and others would violate the Special Counsel Regulations.

Public release of a report by Smith would also disrupt the ongoing transition process and violate the Presidential Transition Act. "[T]he orderly transfer of the executive power is one of the most important public objectives in a democratic society. The transition period insures that the candidate will be able to perform effectively the important functions of his or her new office as expeditiously as possible." Memorandum from Randolph D. Moss, Assistant Attorney General, OLC, *Definition of "Candidate" Under 18 U.S.C. §207(j)*, 2000 WL 33716979, at *4 (Nov. 6, 2000) (cleaned up). "One of the top priorities of any presidential administration is to protect the country from foreign and domestic threats. While a challenge at all times, the country is especially vulnerable during the time of presidential transitions . . . ."[3] Thus, the transition process is "an integral part of the presidential administration," in the "national interest," and part of President Trump's "public function," as he prepares to govern. Memorandum from Randolph D. Moss, Assistant Attorney General, OLC, *Reimbursing Transition-Related Expenses Incurred Before The Administrator Of General Services Ascertained Who Were The Apparent Successful Candidates For The Office Of President And Vice President*, 2001 WL 34058234, at *3 (Jan. 17, 2001).

Congress passed the Presidential Transition Act to protect these critical functions. The purpose of the Act is "to promote the orderly transfer of the executive power in connection with the expiration of the term of office of a President and the inauguration of a new President." 3 U.S.C. § 102 note, § 2. "Any disruption" of the transition "could produce results detrimental to the safety and well-being of the United States and its people." *Id.* Consequently, under the Act, "all officers of the Government"—including the Attorney General and, according to his claims, Smith—are required to "conduct the affairs of the Government for which they exercise responsibility and authority" in a manner that "promote[s] orderly transitions in the office of President." *Id.* This includes, *inter alia*, "tak[ing] appropriate lawful steps to avoid or minimize disruptions that might be occasioned by the transfer of the executive power." *Id.*

Creating and releasing a prejudicial report to the public would violate these commands by giving rise to a media storm of false and unfair criticism that President Trump would be required to address while preparing to assume his Article II responsibilities. Equally problematic and inappropriate are the draft's

---

[2] ECF No. 281 at 6, *United States v. Trump*, No. 23 Cr. 257 (D.D.C. Nov. 25, 2024).

[3] Center for Presidential Transition, *Presidential Transitions are a Perilous Moment for National Security* (Aug. 16, 2023), https://presidentialtransition.org/reports-publications/presidential-transitions-are-a-perilous-moment-for-national-security.

baseless attacks on other anticipated members of President Trump's incoming administration, which are an obvious effort to interfere with upcoming confirmation hearings, and Smith's pathetically transparent tirade about good-faith efforts by X to protect civil liberties, which in a myriad other contexts you have claimed are paramount.

A one-sided, improper report by Smith, particularly if publicly released, would also violate the Presidential immunity principles that Smith has conceded foreclose him from proceeding against President Trump. Indeed, footnote 1 of "Volume 1" of the Draft Report concedes that Smith has brazenly included "conduct for which the Supreme Court later held [President] Trump to be immune from prosecution," and subsequently further highlights the incredible hubris that has clouded the judgment of Smith and his staff from the outset by falsely claiming that the Supreme Court's decision is ambiguous with respect to holdings and reasoning that Smith simply does not like. Based on guidance from OLC—which Smith's staff subsequently informed us that the Office improperly failed to document in any way, in violation of, *inter alia*, DOJ policy regarding the handling of exculpatory information—Smith has acknowledged that Presidential immunity is "categorical," and that it applies while President Trump is the President-elect prior to his inauguration.[4] A public report by Smith would unnecessarily and unjustly add to the inappropriate "peculiar public opprobrium" that has resulted from Smith's unlawful activities thus far. *Trump v. United States*, 603 U.S. 593, 613 (2024). OLC explained previously that such "public stigma and opprobrium" could "compromise the President's ability to fulfill his constitutionally contemplated leadership role with respect to foreign and domestic affairs." Memorandum from Randolph D. Moss, Assistant Attorney General, OLC, *A Sitting President's Amenability to Indictment and Criminal Prosecution*, 2000 WL 33711291, at *19 (Oct. 16, 2000). "[T]he stigma arising . . . from the need to respond to such charges through the judicial process would seriously interfere with [the President's] ability to carry out his constitutionally assigned functions." *Id.* at *22. The release of a report would also pose an unconstitutional risk of diverting President Trump's "*personal* time and energy, and [would] inevitably entail a considerable if not overwhelming degree of mental preoccupation." *Id.* at *25 (emphasis in original). A "single prosecutor" such as Smith should not, and must not, be afforded "the practical power to interfere with the ability of a popularly elected President to carry out his constitutional functions." *Id.* at *19. "The Framers' design of the Presidency did not envision such counterproductive burdens on the vigor and energy of the Executive." *Trump*, 603 U.S. at 614 (cleaned up).

In sum, the same legal principles and logic that required Smith to dismiss his prosecutions of President Trump require that his activities be terminated without further action. Preparation and release of "Closing documentation" would violate the Constitution and existing law, harm the activities of the transition, and weaken the federal government that you have sworn an oath to support. The collective application of these circumstances make this situation entirely unlike any prior Special Counsel report. Preparation and release of a report is therefore not "in the public interest." 28 C.F.R. § 600.9(c). To the contrary, the course of action Smith proposes would further solidify the well-founded perception of partisanship created by Smith's violation of DOJ policies in connection with decisions based on his ultimately failed attempt to influence the outcome of the 2024 Presidential election. For all of these reasons, you must countermand Smith's proposed course of action, remove him, and stop the preparation and/or dissemination of the Draft Report.

---

[4] ECF No. 281 at 6, *United States v. Trump*, No. 23 Cr. 257 (D.D.C. Nov. 25, 2024) ("[T]he Department's position is that the Constitution requires that this case be dismissed before the defendant is inaugurated.").

III.   Smith's Report Violates The Presumption of Innocence

The presumption of innocence is "the undoubted law, axiomatic and elementary." *Coffin v. United States*, 156 U.S. 432, 453 (1895). It is "vital and fundamental" to our Constitutional system, *id.* at 460, and "its enforcement lies at the foundation of the administration of our criminal law," *id.* at 453; *see also Cool v. United States*, 409 U.S. 100, 104 (1972) (holding violation of defendant's "constitutionally rooted presumption of innocence" required reversal).

"The presumption serves as a reminder to the jury that the prosecution has the burden of proving every element of the offense beyond a reasonable doubt," *United States v. Starks*, 34 F.4th 1142, 1158 (10th Cir. 2022), and thus, may be "extinguished only upon the *jury's* determination that guilt has been established beyond a reasonable doubt," *Mahorney v. Wallman*, 917 F.2d 469, 471 n.2 (10th Cir. 1990) (emphasis in original) (collecting cases).

Consistent with *these* bedrock principles, the Justice Manual prohibits prosecutors from publicly declaring a defendant's guilt prior to a jury verdict, or otherwise disseminating statements inconsistent with the presumption of innocence. Justice Manual §§ 1.7.500; 1-7.600; 28 C.F.R. § 600.7(a) ("A Special Counsel shall comply with the rules, regulations, procedures, practices and policies of the Department of Justice."). Rather, prosecutors must limit their statements to "[t]he substance of the charge, as contained in the complaint, indictment, information, or other public documents" and any "release issued before a finding of guilt should state that the charge is merely an accusation, and the defendant is presumed innocent until proven guilty." Justice Manual § 1.7.500. Moreover, "DOJ personnel should refrain from disclosing" *inter alia,* "[a]ny opinion as to [a] defendant's guilt" or any other "[o]bservations about a defendant's or party's character" "except as appropriate *in the proceeding or in an announcement after a finding of guilt.*" Justice Manual § 1-7.610 (emphasis added).

These restrictions ensure that the Department's statements do not "prejudice the rights of a defendant; or unfairly damage the reputation of a person." Justice Manual § 1-7.100; *see also* 32 C.F.R. § 776.47 ("Except for statements that are necessary to inform the public of the nature and extent of the trial counsel's actions and that serve a legitimate law enforcement purpose, refrain from making extrajudicial comments that have a substantial likelihood of heightening public condemnation of the accused."); D.C. Bar Rule 3.8 (same).

The Draft Report violates every one of these core requirements. Despite Smith's decision to dismiss his cases against President Trump, and his complete failure to obtain a "*jury's* determination that guilt has been established beyond a reasonable doubt," *Mahorney*, 917 F.2d at 471 n.2 (emphasis in original), his Draft Report repeatedly, and falsely, claims that President Trump, Carlos De Oliveria, Waltine Nauta, and others have committed crimes and otherwise engaged in purported "criminal conduct." For example, Volume I of the Draft Report falsely asserts, without any jury determination, that President Trump and others "engaged in an unprecedented criminal effort," was "the head of the criminal conspiracies," and harbored a "criminal design." Draft Report, Vol. I at 2, 68, 69. These false accusations of criminality, which Smith again utterly failed to prove in Court, repeat throughout Volume I. *See, e.g., id.* at 3, 52, 60, 64, 67, 88, 108. Likewise, Volume II asserts, without any supporting verdict, "that Mr. Trump violated multiple federal criminal laws," and that he and others engaged in "criminal conduct." Vol. II at 60, 88; *see also, e.g., id.* at 89, 121. Moreover, the Draft Report makes these allegations despite

January 6, 2025
Page 7

the ongoing prosecutions of DeOliveira and Nauta, which would cause gravely unconstitutional prejudice if released.

Neither the Constitution nor applicable regulations or ethical rules allow Smith to make public, extrajudicial claims that purport to reflect conclusive determinations of guilt backed by the imprimatur of DOJ. It is the role of the jury, not the Special Counsel, to weigh the facts and determine guilt. Other Special Counsels have recognized this foundational fact. For example, Special Counsel Hur carefully cabined his observations to what some "jurors could," "might," "may well," or, at most, "would likely" conclude. *See, e.g., Hur Report* at 4, 5, 9, 10, 204, 206-211, 214, 216, 218, 220, 233, 235, 240-42, 246-47. At all points, Hur's focus was on whether "jurors assessing Mr. Biden's guilt and intent w[ould] be persuaded," *id.* at 241, and not on the Special Counsel's unilateral views or opinions regarding Biden's obvious guilt.

Likewise, Special Counsel Mueller expressly declined to "apply an approach" to his report "that could potentially result in a judgment that the President committed crimes," where, as here, "no charges c[ould] be brought." *Mueller Report*, Vol. II at 2. In Special Counsel Mueller's view, "[f]airness concerns counseled against" any kind of public accusation because:

> [t]he ordinary means for an individual to respond to an accusation is through a speedy and public trial, with all the procedural protections that surround a criminal case. An individual who believes he was wrongly accused can use that process to seek to clear his name. In contrast, a prosecutor's judgment that crimes were committed, but that no charges will be brought, affords no such adversarial opportunity for public name-clearing before an impartial adjudicator.

Id. Moreover, Special Counsel Mueller warned that a public disclosure of a prosecutor's unilateral judgment would only heighten these dangers. *Id.* ("[T]he possibility of the report's public disclosure and the absence of a neutral adjudicatory forum to review its findings counseled against potentially determining 'that the person's conduct constitutes a federal offense.' Justice Manual § 9-27.220."). For these reasons, Special Counsel Mueller's report "did not draw ultimate conclusions about the President's conduct," *id.* at 182, but "[i]nstead for each of the relevant actions investigated, . . . set[] out evidence on both sides of the question. . . ." Ltr. from Attorney General William Barr at 3 (Mar. 24, 2019).

To the extent Special Counsel Smith possesses any authority to draft a report (and he does not) he should have applied the same principles as Special Counsels Hur and Mueller, which the Constitution, the Justice Manual, and applicable regulations and ethical rules all require. That is—providing a dispassionate description of the relevant facts, free of any gratuitous commentary regarding President Trump's conduct, let alone direct accusations of guilt. Smith failed to do so. Instead, he chose to construct the Draft Report as a partisan weapon, designed to "unfairly damage the reputation" of President Trump, Justice Manual § 1-7.100, in a manner calculated to "heighten[] public condemnation," 32 C.F.R. § 776.47, while providing "no . . . adversarial opportunity for public name-clearing before an impartial adjudicator," *Mueller Report*, Vol. II at 2. Accordingly, the Department should not, under any circumstances, permit Smith to complete or submit the Draft Report in this form or otherwise disseminate it to the public.

Blanche Law PLLC
99 Wall Street, Suite 4460 | New York, NY 10005
(212) 716-1250 | www.BlancheLaw.com

The Jack Smith Report

January 6, 2025
Page 8

IV.   Preparation And Release Of A Report Would Serve No Valid Purpose

There are many practical and prudential reasons to obey the law here. Preparation and release of a report by Smith would not "be in the public interest." 28 C.F.R. § 600.9(c).

In 2023, Smith and his Office levied extremely serious, and entirely false, allegations against President Trump in two separate cases. Smith has now been forced by the rule of law to dismiss both of those cases. It would be highly improper and contrary to the public interest—as well as inconsistent with the reconciliation and public healing process that is necessary following divisive and unconstitutional actions by Smith—to allow him to create and disseminate yet another document recycling politically motived and inaccurate claims that the law has forced him to abandon. Indeed, "no legitimate governmental interest is served by an official public smear of an individual when that individual has not been provided a forum in which to vindicate his rights." *In re Smith*, 656 F.2d 1101, 1106 (5th Cir. 1981). Smith lacks the credibility that is necessary for such a report to be reliable or valuable to anyone, as his biased and unlawful approach to these cases has been widely-criticized and discredited from the outset.[5] Quite appropriately, he is the subject of an ongoing investigation by the Office of Professional Responsibility, further diminishing any value from a report.[6] Smith's unlawful plan would reinforce the "likely prospect of an Executive Branch that cannibalizes itself, with each successive President free to prosecute his predecessors, yet unable to boldly and fearlessly carry out his duties for fear that he may be next." *Trump*, 603 U.S. at 640. "The enfeebling of the Presidency and our Government that would result from such a cycle of factional strife is exactly what the Framers intended to avoid." *Id.*

At 1999 hearings relating to the Independent Counsel Act, Ted Olson argued that "the final report . . . has turned into an excuse to file long exhaustive expositions which rationalize the investigation," as well as "offer opinions regarding and/or pronounce judgments on the individuals investigated, and generally make the Independent Counsel look good."[7] Attorney General Janet Reno pointed out, more succinctly, that "the price of the final report is often too high."[8] Deputy Attorney General Eric Holder

---

[5] WSJ Editorial Board, *Jack Smith Loses in the People's Court*, WSJ (Nov. 7, 2024, 5:52 PM), https://www.wsj.com/opinion/donald-trump-prosecutions-jack-smith-fani-willis-alvin-bragg-juan-merchan-1c68f640; Jonathan Turley, *Opinion: Donald Trump just won the greatest jury verdict in American history*, The Hill (Nov. 6, 2024, 10:56 AM), https://thehill.com/opinion/campaign/4976533-trump-prosecutions-lawfare-end; Elie Honig, *So What Happens With All the Cases Against Trump Now?*, N.Y. Mag. (Nov. 8, 2024), https://nymag.com/intelligencer/article/what-will-happen-with-the-charges-against-trump.html.

[6] Letter from Chairman Jim Jordan to Jeffrey Ragsdale, DOJ OPR (Dec. 4, 2024) https://www.scribd.com/document/800789357/Judiciary-to-DOJ?secret_password=vphCtDdh3lHj7mTM5Ib8.

[7] *The Future of the Independent Counsel Act: Hearings before the S. Comm. on Governmental Affairs*, 106th Cong. 231 (1999) (prepared statement of Theodore B. Olson).

[8] *The Future of the Independent Counsel Act: Hearings before the S. Comm. on Governmental Affairs*, 106th Cong. 252 (1999) (prepared statement of Attorney General Janet Reno).

January 6, 2025
Page 9

added: "the reporting requirement goes directly against most traditions and practices of law enforcement and American ideals."[9] Based on this feedback, Congress permitted the Independent Counsel Act to expire, and DOJ promulgated a reporting regulation that was much more restrictive than its statutory predecessor.[10]

For the quarter century that DOJ has operated under these Regulations, DOJ has not released a single Special Counsel report concerning any individual who has mounted a successful defense in court, as President Trump has done with respect to Presidential immunity. For good reason: the Special Counsel Regulations state that the purpose of a report is to "explain[] the prosecution or declination decisions." 28 C.F.R. § 600.8(c). When filing and resolving a case in Court, that information, together with the defense's responses, becomes part of the public record. An additional, one-sided report, would only sow confusion and undermine the judicial process.

Here, Smith has explained himself, and sought unsuccessfully to justify his actions, *ad nauseum*. This has included routinely leaking sensitive details regarding the actions of Smith's Office to the media in violation of DOJ policy. In October 2024, it was leaked that Smith planned to "pursue his two cases against Mr. Trump for as long as he has the legal authority to do so—including during the period between Election Day and the inauguration, when Mr. Trump, if he prevails, would be president-elect."[11] A similar July 2024 report cited "a person familiar with Mr. Smith's thinking."[12] As another example, we first learned from the media, rather than Smith's Office, that they were considering dismissing the prosecutions of President Trump.[13] And we learned for the first time via private outreach from media sources, rather than Smith's Office, that Smith is working on a report.

---

[9] *Reauthorization of the Independent Counsel Statute, Part I: Hearings Before the H. Comm. on the Judiciary*, 106th Cong. 86 (1999) (prepared statement of Deputy Attorney General Eric Holder)

[10] *Compare* 28 U.S.C. § 594(h)(1)(B) (calling for a "final report . . . setting forth fully and completely a description of the work of the independent counsel, including the disposition of all cases brought"), *with* 28 C.F.R. § 600.8(c) (calling for "a confidential report explaining the prosecution or declination decisions reached by the Special Counsel").

[11] Maggie Haberman et al., *Trump Says He'll Fire Jack Smith, Special Counsel Who Indicted Him, if He Wins Again*, N.Y. Times (Oct. 24, 2024), https://www.nytimes.com/2024/10/24/us/politics/trump-jack-smith.html.

[12] Alan Feuer, *Special Counsel Is Said to Be Planning to Pursue Trump Cases Past the Election*, N.Y. Times (July 2, 2024), https://www.nytimes.com/2024/07/02/us/politics/jack-smith-trump-charges.html.

[13] Pierre Thomas et al., *Special counsel Jack Smith expected to wind down Trump prosecutions: Sources*, ABC News (Nov. 6, 2024, 3:26 PM), https://abcnews.go.com/Politics/special-counsel-jack-smith-expected-to-wind-trump-prosecutions/story?id=115571646; Devlin Barrett, *Jack Smith Assesses How to Wind Down Trump's Federal Cases, Official Says*, N.Y. Times (Nov. 6, 2024), https://www.nytimes.com/2024/11/06/us/politics/doj-trump-federal-cases.html.

January 6, 2025
Page 10

In addition to the leaks, Smith filed four gratuitous speaking indictments, held a lawless press conference before the national media, and filed hundreds of pages of briefing in two district courts, two Courts of Appeals, and the Supreme Court. Smith's inappropriate 165-page "Motion For Immunity Determinations," accompanied by a 1,885-page "Appendix," is an especially egregious example of Smith's proclivity to seize all available opportunities to issue lengthy diatribes attacking President Trump based on Smith's biased view of the law and evidence.[14] Smith insisted on the filing, which even Judge Chutkan characterized as "atypical,"[15] to further publicize his narrative in the lead-up to the Presidential election. Smith's tome was not responsive to a defense motion, had no basis in the Federal Rules of Criminal Procedure, and violated DOJ's election-interference policies and practices. *See, e.g.*, Justice Manual § 9-85.500.[16] Having previously insisted on highly restrictive protective orders that prevented dissemination of discovery, based in part on histrionic, unsupported claims about witness identities, Smith abandoned those arguments and released the contents of protected reports, grand jury material, and accounts from thinly-veiled witnesses whom the media immediately identified.

Under these circumstances, there is no legitimate need for an additional "report" to "explain [Smith's] prosecution or declination decisions." 28 C.F.R. § 600.8(c). His baseless rationales for prosecution are already fully public. So too is the selective description that his Office prepared of the legal basis for the motions to dismiss, which Smith's Office caused OLC not to further memorialize in violation of the *Brady* doctrine and DOJ policy. Moreover, the Draft Report goes far beyond merely explaining Smith's "prosecution or declination decisions," deviating instead into extensive and irrelevant discussions on purported "litigation issues," including post-indictment immunity litigation and Smith's violation of the Department's political non-interference policies. *See* Draft Report Vol. I at 107-37. Although Smith may wish to air his baseless and politically motivated grievances regarding the Constitutional importance of immunity, and otherwise provide feeble and transparent excuses for his plainly political motivations, that is not the purpose of a Special Counsel report under 28 C.F.R. § 600.8(c). A report must simply "explain[]" a Special Counsel's "prosecution or declination decisions" and nothing more. The Draft Report violates this core principle.

The issuance of such a report, in violation of the Constitution, the Transition Act, Presidential immunity, and DOJ's own regulations, would exacerbate the irreparable damage that Smith has already inflicted on DOJ's reputation for non-partisanship through his repeated violations of DOJ policies about election interference. As we noted one year ago in opposing Smith's failed attempt to obtain certiorari before judgment on Presidential immunity, which the Supreme Court rejected, Smith's actions "create[] the compelling appearance of a partisan motivation: To ensure that President Trump . . . will face a months-long criminal trial at the height of his presidential campaign." Br. in Opp. to Pet'n for Writ of

---

[14] ECF No. 252, *United States v. Trump*, No. 23 Cr. 257 (D.D.C. Oct. 2, 2024).

[15] ECF No. 243 at 2, *United States v. Trump*, No. 23 Cr. 257 (D.D.C. Sept. 24, 2024).

[16] *See also* A Review of Various Actions by the Federal Bureau of Investigation and Department of Justice in Advance of the 2016 Election, U.S. Dep't of Justice Office of Inspector General (June 2018) at 18 ("[I]n general, the practice has been not to take actions that might have an impact on an election, even if it's not an election case or something like that."), *available at* https://s3.documentcloud.org/documents/4515884/DOJ-OIG-2016-Election-Final-Report.pdf.

January 6, 2025
Page 11

Certiorari Before Judgment in *United States v. Trump*, No. 23-624, at 21 (filed Dec. 20, 2024). Smith's nakedly partisan, election-interference motivation was obvious to commentators across the political spectrum. *See id.* (citing many sources). "[T]he best traditions of the U.S. Department of Justice ... call for prosecutors to *avoid* the appearance of election interference in the prosecution of political candidates." *Id.* at 23 (emphasis in original). "[F]ederal prosecutors . . . may never make a decision regarding an investigation or prosecution, or select the timing of investigative steps or criminal charges, for the purpose of affecting any election, or for the purpose of giving an advantage or disadvantage to any candidate or political party." *Id.* (citing Justice Manual § 9-27.260). Smith's latest illegal plan to launch yet another partisan attack against President Trump, De Oliveira, and Nauta will have the same injurious effect on DOJ's reputation if not stopped in its tracks.

Further, preparing and releasing a report would be improper for the additional reason that Smith has relied on numerous legal theories that are unprecedented and incorrect as a matter of law. Many of those issues were the subject of ongoing litigation at the time Smith dismissed the cases. To name a few, these issues include the lack of statutory authority for Smith's appointment; Smith's reliance on official-acts allegations in both cases in violation of the Presidential immunity doctrine[17]; Smith's unlawful theory under 18 U.S.C. § 1512(c)(2) in violation of *Fischer v. United States*, 603 U.S. 480 (2024); equal protection violations, based on selective and vindictive prosecution theories[18]; the unprecedented and unlawful raid at Mar-a-Lago; and violations of the Presidential Records Act and NARA's longstanding practices under that Act.[19] There were also numerous discovery disputes in both cases, including unresolved motions in the Southern District of Florida regarding *Brady* obligations, the scope of the prosecution team, and Intelligence Community holdings, which further call into question the reliability of Smith's theories.[20] Smith's Draft Report presents a selective and inaccurate response to only some of these issues, and then proceeds as if his theories are well-founded and undisputed. Nothing could be further from the truth.

Finally, given the status of Smith and his team as the inauguration approaches, using additional taxpayer resources to prepare, review, and disseminate a report is not a legitimate use of taxpayer funds— even if there were a valid appropriation here, which there is not. "The Special Counsel's office has spent tens of millions of dollars since November 2022, all drawn unconstitutionally from the Indefinite Appropriation." *United States v. Trump*, 2024 WL 3404555, at *46 (S.D. Fla. July 15, 2024). For the period preceding March 31, 2024, Smith's Office had used $20 million from a permanent indefinite appropriation and an additional $16 million from other unspecified "DOJ components."[21] The costs of Smith's activities since March 2024 have not yet been released. It is clear, however, that the total figure

---

[17] ECF No. 324, *United States v. Trump*, No. 23 Cr. 80101 (S.D. Fla. Feb. 22, 2024).

[18] ECF No. 328, *United States v. Trump*, No. 23 Cr. 80101 (S.D. Fla. Feb. 22, 2024).

[19] ECF No. 327, *United States v. Trump*, No. 23 Cr. 80101 (S.D. Fla. Feb. 22, 2024).

[20] ECF No. 262, *United States v. Trump*, No. 23 Cr. 80101 (S.D. Fla. Jan. 16, 2024).

[21] Special Counsel's Office, DOJ, Statements of Expenditures, https://www.justice.gov/sco-smith.

January 6, 2025
Page 12

will greatly exceed—by an extraordinarily wide margin—what all of this lawfare was actually worth to the public, the operations of the government, and the Country as a whole.

*   *   *

Smith's proposed plan for releasing a report is unlawful, undertaken in bad faith, and contrary to the public interest. Smith's conduct also raises grave concerns under Article II because it unlawfully encroaches on the Executive authority of the incoming Administration of President Trump to resolve the issues surrounding Smith's Office in accordance with President Trump's commanding national mandate from the voters. The time has come to put an end to this weaponization of the justice system and move forward constructively. No report should be prepared or released, and Smith should be removed, including for even suggesting that course of action given his obvious political motivations and desire to lawlessly undermine the transition. If you elect to proceed with Smith's plan, we again respectfully request (1) notice of such decision prior to any publication of the Draft Report, allowing us to take appropriate legal action, and (2) that this letter and Smith's meritless responses to the legal arguments set forth herein be incorporated into the Report.

Respectfully Submitted,

/s/ Todd Blanche / Emil Bove
Todd Blanche
Emil Bove
Blanche Law PLLC

/s/ John Lauro / Gregory Singer
John Lauro
Gregory Singer
Lauro & Singer

Attorneys for President Donald J. Trump

Cc: Jack Smith, Special Counsel
       JP Cooney, Deputy Special Counsel
       (Via Email)

U.S. Department of Justice

Jack Smith
Special Counsel

January 7, 2025

The Honorable Merrick B. Garland
Attorney General of the United States
Robert F. Kennedy Department of Justice Building
950 Pennsylvania Avenue NW
Washington, D.C. 20530

Re: Letter from Counsel to Donald J. Trump of January 6, 2025

Dear Mr. Attorney General:

As you know, my Office provided counsel to Mr. Trump, Mr. Nauta, and Mr. De Oliveira an opportunity to review a draft of my confidential Report and to provide any response in writing by 2 p.m. on January 6, 2025, so that my Office could consider any issues that counsel identified in the final Report before officially transmitting it to you. Only Mr. Trump's counsel chose to provide a written response, in the form of a letter to you. That response fails to identify any specific factual objections to the draft. Instead, Mr. Trump principally objects to public release of the Report, and in service of that objection makes a variety of false, misleading, or otherwise unfounded claims. While the determination as to whether to publicly release the Report, consistent with applicable legal restrictions, is yours as Attorney General, *see* 28 C.F.R. § 600.9(c), I felt it necessary to address below certain inaccuracies set forth in Mr. Trump's letter.

As an initial matter, the Office extended Mr. Trump a special accommodation by allowing his counsel to review a draft of the Report. Such an accommodation is not required under the law or regulations. Nonetheless, the Office elected to provide Mr. Trump's counsel access to the draft Report through what it understood to be a process similar to that employed by Special Counsel Robert K. Hur: by allowing counsel to review the draft in person over the course of four days, in the Office's workspace, without contemporaneous access to personal electronics but with the ability to take notes, including the use of government laptops on which to draft a response. Specifically, on December 11, 2024, Mr. Trump's counsel requested an opportunity to review the Report before it was submitted to the Attorney General. On December 15, 2024, the Office informed Mr. Trump's counsel that it would make arrangements for counsel to review the draft Report and provided a range of dates when the review could occur. After Mr. Trump's attorneys complained that the initial review dates that the Office offered conflicted with their vacation schedules, the next day the Office changed the schedule to provide the dates they requested. It was thus surprising and disappointing to see Mr. Trump's grievances about these accommodations in his letter, *see* Trump Letter at 2-3, especially after Mr. Trump's counsel explicitly stated their "genuine" and "personal appreciation" to the Office for the new dates in a phone call on December 16, 2024.

Mr. Trump's other criticisms of the review process are similarly disingenuous. For instance, he complains that he was prevented from reviewing the underlying documents cited in the draft Report, *id.* at 1, but over the four days Mr. Trump's attorneys were given to review the Report, they never requested access to a single underlying document, despite the fact that the Office had attorneys on hand specifically assigned to respond to any questions counsel might have. Relatedly, Mr. Trump insinuates that the Office improperly "demanded" that counsel delete discovery productions prior to their review of the draft Report, when in fact that deletion was required by the protective orders that federal judges entered in both of Mr. Trump's criminal cases. *See United States v. Trump*, No. 23-cr-80101, ECF No. 27 at 3 (S.D. Fla. June 19, 2023); *United States v. Trump*, No. 23-cr-257, ECF No. 28 at 2-3 (D.D.C. Aug. 11, 2023). In sum, Mr. Trump's counsel had a full opportunity to review the draft Report, and only came to the Office to review it on the first two of the four days available. Upon completing that review, Mr. Trump has not contested a single factual representation in the Report, instead objecting only to its public release.

Other complaints by Mr. Trump are addressed and rebutted by the Report and court decisions. For instance, Mr. Trump recycles his baseless allegation that the Office's work constituted a partisan attack, a claim flatly rejected by the only court to have ruled on it. *See United States v. Trump*, No. 23-cr-257, ECF No 198 (D.D.C. Aug. 3, 2024) (denying Mr. Trump's motion to dismiss indictment based on selective and vindictive prosecution, "finding no evidence of discriminatory purpose," "no evidence demonstrating a likelihood of vindictiveness," and "no evidence that would lead the court to infer that [prosecutorial] discretion has been abused") (internal quotation omitted). The Report explains in detail the Office's steadfast adherence to neutral and evenhanded application of the law and to the Department's Election Year Sensitivities policy. Mr. Trump also persists in his challenge to the Attorney General's authority to appoint a Special Counsel, which is the subject of a pending appeal in the Eleventh Circuit. *See United States v. Nauta et al.*, No. 24-12311 (11th Cir.). As explained in my Report, the Office is confident that the Department has strong arguments to prevail on that issue.

Finally, Mr. Trump's letter claims that dismissal of his criminal cases signifies Mr. Trump's "complete exoneration." That is false. As the Office explained in its dismissal motions and in the Report, the Department's view that the Constitution prohibits Mr. Trump's indictment and prosecution while he is in office is categorical and does not turn on the gravity of the crimes charged, the strength of the Government's proof, or the merits of the prosecution—all of which the Office stands fully behind.

Sincerely yours,

JACK SMITH

JACK SMITH is from Clay, New York, and is a graduate of the State University of New York at Oneonta and Harvard Law School. Upon graduating, he joined the Manhattan District Attorney's office, where he was an assistant attorney on the sex crimes and domestic violence unit. Subsequently, he went on to serve in the United States Department of Justice as an assistant US attorney, acting US attorney, and head of the department's Public Integrity Section. He was also the chief prosecutor at the Kosovo Specialist Chambers, an international tribunal at The Hague tasked with investigating and prosecuting war crimes in the Kosovo War. On November 18, 2022, Smith was appointed by US Attorney General Merrick Garland to serve as an independent Special Counsel in charge of the DOJ's criminal investigations into Donald Trump's actions regarding the January 6th US Capitol attack, and Trump's handling and storage of government records. Smith resigned from the position on January 10, 2025 when, following Donald Trump's election to the presidency, the Justice Department had to drop the already-filed case because of its rule against prosecuting a sitting president.